The Syllabic Inscriptions from Byblos

GEORGE E. MENDENHALL

The Syllabic Inscriptions from Byblos

AMERICAN UNIVERSITY OF BEIRUT

The Syllabic Inscriptions from Byblos
by George E. Mendenhall
Published by the American University of Beirut

Printed in Beirut Lebanon

This book was composed in Roman 12 point type and seven other fonts four of which were created by the author using the software program marketed under the name *FANCY FONT* ™. The camera-ready copy was printed out on an Epson FX™ dot-matrix printer driven by the *FANCY FONT* system.

TO

EATHEL TIDRICK MENDENHALL

Table of Contents

PREFACE

Not the least of the contributions made by the infant discipline of linguistic history is the discovery of the fact that linguistic history is social history. Relatively little along these lines of thought and research has been done, however, concerning the Semitic language family. This is the more strange and regrettable since nowhere else is there such a rich lode of resources of datable inscriptions reaching back well into the Early Bronze Age. This body of evidence can in turn be combined with an ever increasing body of written and unwritten evidence for the history of ancient social entities.

The domination of nineteenth century methods and presuppositions has been almost complete. The identification of language, 'race' and culture is so taken for granted by most scholars in the field that an alternative approach to language is hardly imaginable. Added to that myopia is often enough a resistance to 'etymologizing' that actually is a contempt for linguistic history and its concomitant history of social relationships of the remote past. The fact remains that all languages are the result of changing speech habits over untold millennia of changing human social organizations, and the languages preserve the record of that past history to large extent.

The nine texts stamped on copper plates or spatulas and carved in stone were excavated at the modern site of Jebeil, ancient Byblos, by the French expedition under the direction of Prof. M. Dunand, during the years 1928 to 1932. They were published in 1945 by Professor Dunand in the monograph entitled ***Byblia Grammata***, and two years later I began to work on the texts in the hope of obtaining further information concerning the early West Semitic verbal system.

Though linguistic history was hardly the intention at the outset of this work on the Syllabic Inscriptions from Byblos, it became increasingly clear that the linguistic evidence threw enormous light upon the history of what has long been termed 'Northwest Semitic', a term that now should be abandoned in favor of more specifically historical terminology. This is particularly urgent in the light of the entire disarray of the scholarly world subsequent to the discovery of a Semitic language substratum in the Ebla texts, to say nothing of the fifty year long futile argument as to whether or not Ugaritic is to be classified as 'Canaanite'. Classification should be done, as it is in some other fields, on the basis of common processes, not merely on common forms.

Semitists and especially biblical scholars seem to have assumed a literal view of the Tower of Babel story, so that all the ancient languages are treated as though they were let down from heaven together with the verbally inspired text of Sacred Scripture. Anything earlier or cognate is therefore entirely irrelevant to the language of the Bible, and it is even perhaps faintly blasphemous to suggest that biblical Hebrew was the result of historical processes quite analogous to those readily observable in much more recent societies and languages. Actually, the story of the Tower of Babel is a quite accurate description of real historical process: a unified language as revealed in texts is the product of political power structures and their educational systems for training scribes. When those power structures destroy themselves an indefinite number of fission products result from the scattering of persons often into remote areas which are quite analogous to 'relict' areas of paleo–biology. For it is in those areas that very archaic and original traits of the various species are preserved.

In short, it seems certain that the coastal region of the eastern Mediterranean in the Early Bronze Age was the habitat of one common ancestor of both Arabic and Hebrew––and, like human beings, all languages have more than one ancestor. In spite of the nagging doubts concerning readings of signs, identification of roots, cognates in later West Semitic languages especially, interpretation of specific words, phrases, and texts, and above all, in spite of the insecurity of the all–important dating of the texts, there can be little doubt that the entire category of "South–Semitic" languages is an anachronism if applied to any stage of the history of Semitic languages prior to the Iron Age.

In the thirty seven years that this work has been going on by fits and starts, I have received stimulation, aid, assistance, and ideas from so many sources that I cannot even remember them all. I have found in my own experience and observed it frequently enough in others that insights and ideas can all too easily parade as original to ones' self, when in reality they are gifts from some one else. This is and should be understood in the community of scholars as a normal process in the pursuit of truth that should take priority over mere 'originality' and the concern for getting 'credit' for what one has received often enough from other sources.

Acknowlegement of major stimulation and assistance is called for, however, not only out of the civilized motive of gratitude, but even more in order to call attention to important contributions that have not become a part of the scholarly thinking in the fields with which this monograph is especially concerned. First, and perhaps foremost, is the enormous stimulus and insight that I have received from the personal contacts and publications of Professor Ernst Pulgram, whose descriptions of the history of language and language change have been most useful in view of the conclusions to which I was constantly being forced by the clusters of signs preserved on those nine texts on copper and stone. Similar also is the insight I have derived from the experience and wisdom of those whose work deals with modern Near Eastern dialects, the late Professor Abdel–Massih, and Professors McCarus and Windfuhr. It is this combination of stimulus and collegial support that makes possible the conviction, and I hope the demonstration that modern processes in the history and evolution of language are different only in time and detail from those that were operative in the remote past.

My particular thanks and appreciation are deeply expressed to Dr. Belinda Bicknell whose competent and patient reading and re–reading of the various print–outs of the evolving manuscript have been invaluable not only for correcting errors, but also for numerous suggestions and comments that have considerably improved the substance of the text. Her contribution has not sufficiently been noted in the body of the work, and therefore I wish expecially to emphasize it in principal at this point.

A major factor in making possible the work was the Senior Fellowship awarded by the National Endowment for the Humanities in 1971, that made it possible to spend seven months in Beirut studying and photographing the original documents. Those seven months were made the more productive through the facilities very graciously offered by The American University of Beirut, and the personal contacts and consultation by various members of its faculty, most especially Professor William A. Ward. I owe him a debt of gratitude also for a number of last–minute corrections and suggestions that have been incorporated into the monograph.

Acknowledgement is also due to the Horace H. Rackham School of Graduate Studies of the University of Michigan for research grants on several occasions during the past years which greatly facilitated the complex of activities associated with the recovery of the ancient past.

Personal thanks are also very much in order to the late Dr. Roger Saida for many personal favors, and for facilitating access to the documents in Beirut National Museum. Also I express my gratitude to Dr. and Mrs. Maurice Chehab who personally made the inscriptions available to me on a number of occasions reaching back to 1956, when I saw them for the first time.

By no means least has been the constant interest and support of Eathel Tidrick Mendenhall, to whom this work that has lasted almost as long as our marriage is dedicated. It is much too easy to forget that what we are wont to regard as civilization is made possible by those who do not write books.

The University of Michigan
Ann Arbor, Michigan

Christmas Day, 1984

LIST OF ABBREVIATIONS

Akk.	Akkadian
Aram.	Aramaic
ARMT	***Archives royales de Mari transcrits***
BG	***Byblia Grammata***
BS	Byblos syllabic
CAD	The Chicago Assyrian Dictionary
CD	Coastal dialect
CES	Common East Semitic
CS	Common Semitic
CV	Consonant + vowel sequence
CWS	Common West Semitic
DN	Deity name
DOSA	***Dictionary of Old South Arabic***
EB	Early Bronze Age
ES	East Semitic
Eg.	Egyptian
Eth.	Ethiopic
Etr.	Etruscan
FB	***Fouilles de Byblos***
GN	Geographical name
Gk.	Greek
IR	Infra–red
JD	Jezireh dialectF
LB	Late Bronze Age
LW	Loanword
Lat.	Latin
MAD	***Materials for an Akkadian Dictionary***
MB	Middle Bronze Age
NC	North Canaanite
NS	North Semitic
NWS	Northwest Semitic
OA	Old Assyrian
OAkk.	Old Akkadian
OB	Old Babylonian
OCS	Old Coastal Semitic
ONA	Old North Arabic
OSA	Old South Arabic

PN	Personal name
PPG	***Phoenizisch–punische Grammatik***
PS	Proto–Sinaitic
Ph.	Phoenician
SC	South Canaanite
Saf.	Safaitic
Syr.	Syriac
Ug.	Ugaritic
WS	West Semitic

1

INTRODUCTION

The Syllabic Texts from Byblos have been a challenge and an exasperation to me now for thirty–seven years. Not long after I finished a dissertation on the verbal system of Bronze Age Semitic dialects, I began work on these texts in the hope that unsolved problems raised in the dissertation might find a solution. As is usual in such situations it soon became clear that it was not solutions that were needed, but more adequate questions. The process of deciphering this pitifully meager corpus has been painfully slow, but at the same time it has been progressively productive in many ways that often enough had little to do with the attempt to understand what the texts were saying. Decipherers have frequently in the past been regarded as 'wild' for very good reason: if the unknown texts conformed to the grammatical regularities of well known languages, they would not require decipherment. The deciphering process is therefore inevitably one that involves the disregard of old grammatical 'laws' and at the same time the discovery of new ones that can be observed to be operational in the corpus of texts being studied.

This tiny corpus of nine texts on copper plates and stone would have been read, studied, and translated decades ago if their language had been in reasonable conformity to known archaic Semitic dialects. Though the syllabic system of writing is considerably more complex than an alphabetic one with only a third as many signs, nevertheless the problem of decipherment would still have entailed only a simple substitution cipher. That this has not been the case, that the problem was far more complex than a subsitution cipher type is clear from the following discussions of the various texts.

It has long been known that decipherment problems fall into several categories:

1. Inscriptions in which the language is known, but the writing system is strange: previous attempts to deal with the BS texts seem to have proceeded upon this assumption, which is now completely untenable.

2. Inscriptions in which the writing system is known, but the language is unknown.

3. Inscriptions in which both the writing system and the language are unknown. It seems clear that the syllabic texts fall into this category.

4. Inscriptions in which both the writing system and the language are unknown, but the language is cognate to known languages. This description also fits these syllabic texts, and the elaboration of that relationship to the Semitic language family has been a most important part of the method, as well as resulting in a highly significant body of observations that are revolutionary not only for comparative Semitic studies, but also for the discipline of historical linguistics that has very recently (1968) emerged as a sub–field of linguistics––in my opinion, long overdue.

The nagging question concerning the date of these texts cannot be answered with certainty on the basis of data now available. I have little doubt that there will be considerable scholarly debate on this subject, and most of it will be futile simply because the factual evidence is not at hand, and the arguments will therefore be based upon pet theories concerning what is and what is not possible in ancient cultural and linguistic history. The thesis held here, which is a conclusion I have been forced to accept during the past three decades, is that this language is a 'primitive' one. The term 'primitive' is used in the same sense that it is in historical zoology: it does not mean an undeveloped or crude, uncivilized type. Quite the contrary, it is 'primitive' in the sense of ***primus*** 'first, original': one source from which subsequent dialects evolved and specialized.

In absolute terms, this means that the language and the writing system derive from the coastal region of the Early Bronze Age, and they antedate the enormous social and linguistic changes that attended the demise of that Early Bronze Age culture and society, and the Amorite migrations that certainly attended that process. Over the years I have been forced to a progressively earlier dating. The working assumption at first was that the texts have to be pre–Hyksos in date, then twenty years ago the conclusion was necessary that they had to be prior to the Egyptian Middle Empire and the Execration Texts that constituted our only usable corpus of material for the coastal cultural area. The reason for that conclusion was the fact that there is absolutely no evidence for Egyptian cultural or linguistic influence, plus the fact that Text D illustrates a process of kingship formation in sharpest contrast to the social context portrayed in those Egyptian sources.

The kingship at Byblos is then to be regarded as a continuity of the Early Bronze Age social organization, perhaps being reestablished after some previous disruption. The primary evidence is of course the language itself, which is enormously more 'primitive' in the above sense than is Ugaritic. The numerous isoglosses that made the decipherment possible constitute also primary evidence that this language by far antedated the later development of regional dialects of North Canaanite (Ugaritic) and South Canaanite known primarily from Iron Age sources such as biblical Hebrew, Phoenician, Moabite, and Ammonite, but also very rudimentarily from the Amarna glosses and a few inscriptions of the LB Age.

An entirely unexpected development was the progressive demonstration that there was no such thing as a separate 'South Semitic' language group until well into the Iron Age, and that this concept is highly deleterious to the understanding of linguistic and cultural processes, as well as cultural history itself. This will be discussed at length in Chapter X, and needs no further elaboration here.

Parallel to the evidence for the 'primitive' nature of this language is the evidence for a similarly 'primitive' nature of the writing system. It is beyond question that almost all of the later alphabetic signs had their origin in this syllabic writing system, together with some of the names of those signs——which in several cases, interestingly enough, were confused. The long–held thesis that the Canaanite alphabet was somehow derived from the Egyptian hieroglyphic writing system has been demonstrated to be too simplistic: the connection was indubitably through this syllabic system, and it was only in this indirect mode that Egyptian writing underlay the much later alphabets. The process was much more complex than most modern theories about the alphabet allow. The idea that there was an invention of **The Alphabet** ***ex nihilo*** by some unknown genius of the Middle Bronze Age is naive, based merely upon the fact that virtually all Bronze Age inscriptions so far known come from Palestine and culturally related areas (notably the Proto–Sinaitic inscriptions), which have been most intensively explored and excavated. Regional writing systems are demonstrated for the Biqa' of Lebanon and the Euphrates Valley in Syria in the Bronze Age, and further exploration and excavation will in the future demonstrate that writing systems in the Late Bronze Age were characterized by the same sort of regional diversity that is well known from early systems in Greece, Italy, and the Arabian peninsula, and have the same sort of chaotic history as dialects themselves.

My earlier work ***The Tenth Generation*** was largely a study of the historical processes involved in the social, political and consequent cultural discontinuities that frequently took place during the first half of human history. Many aspects of that work were made possible (even if not so far plausible) by the continuing involvement with this corpus of archaic texts. It should be clear now that the rise and fall of empires and the discontinuities of social organization have in turn an enormous impact upon language itself. This work is a monument to the grass roots people who are the actual foundation of any worthwhile cultural continuity, and whose anonymity in carrying out the daily tasks of producing food, of rearing children and paying for the ephemeral superstructures of politics and war that bring about discontinuity and suffering, is illuminated by the continuities of language that preserve the oral, social past long after it had been forgotten by everyone.

In this exceedingly complex body of material every attempt has been made to keep the presentation as simple as possible while at the same time citing the linguistic evidence upon which the conclusions are based. Since that evidence is almost entirely actual usages known from later texts and literary sources, it is usually well summarized in the various lexica. For Arabic the eight volume work of Lane (1863) has been the primary source, and for pre–Islamic Arabic inscriptions, the monumental work of Harding (1971) on personal names, and the dictionary of Biella (1982). For Ugaritic the cited items can be found in Aistleitner (1974), and Groendahl (1967). Primary sources for South Canaanite are Koehler–Baumgartner (1951), as well as the work of Jean–Hoftijzer (1960). The latter was also useful for Old Aramaic evidence.

It should be noted that the text on the stone fragments H and J is so greatly at variance from the other texts of the corpus that it is either a different language or such a radically different stage of the Byblos language that no sense could be derived from the readings of the signs. It is therefore not treated in this monograph.

2

THE TEXTS AND THEIR HISTORY

1. The Archaeological Contexts

The archaeological method in use at the time the texts were discovered did not yield conclusive proof of their date. However, it is useful to summarize here the data from the excavation reports and from *BG*, for the little evidence available seems incompatible with the general tendency to date these texts to the Late Bronze Age.

Text a: Found in the foundations of a cistern belonging to a house of the post–Crusader period. In *FB*, 30, this text is attributed to the Eg. Middle Empire period.

Text b: Derived from a nonhomogeneous archaeological stratum. Objects found at the level were dated to the Middle Empire period. The foundations of a Hellenistic period edifice intruded into architectural remains of the Middle Empire, and thus the text could hardly be later than the MB I period. *BG*, 74.

Texts C & D: These were found together in a location where there was construction activity during the Twelfth and Thirteenth Dynasties, then abandoned until the Hellenistic period.

Text e: This spatula was reported to have come from a level of the Hyksos period. It was found on the floor of the fore–court connected to the southern entrance of the 'obelisk temple'. There also the area was abandoned from the Middle Bronze age until the second century A.D.

Text f: This was recovered from the dump, and thus has no archaeological context.

Texts g & h: These fragments were found reused in walls of the hellenistic period.

Text i: This text was found near the great cistern. Just below there was a deposit of pottery that had been scorched by the burning of the 23rd century B.C., and Dunand believed the text to have come from the level immediately following which he assigned to the Twelfth Dynasty.

Text j: Reused in a wall no earlier than the Persian period. The texts h and j are parts of the same monumental inscription.

Two points are clear, so far as the archaeological evidence is concerned: first is the fact that throughout the subsequent history of the site those levels from which the inscriptions came were accessible to the later inhabitants, and stone materials from those levels were reused in later constructions, even as late as the post–Crusader period. Second, the available evidence for some of the inscriptions would appear to make a post–Hyksos date impossible, but how much earlier they are is a question that the archaeological data cannot settle. It is the evidence from internal context of the texts that must be evaluated and placed into an appropriate social, cultural, and historical context. For an attempt in this direction, see Chapter X.

Though the dating of the texts is extremely uncertain the usual assignment to the Late Bronze Age appears to be entirely outside the range of possibility. That dating itself was based upon the completely mistaken idea that one of the later alphabetic spatulas had an archaic alphabetic inscription on one face, and a Byblos Syllabic inscription on the other. The extremely close connection between the syllabic signary and the subsequent alphabetic one, plus the fact that there are several inscriptions from Byblos that seem to belong to neither system is sufficient guarantee that no conclusions concerning dating can be drawn from some superficial similarities between signs on the reverse of the spatula.

The extreme paucity of evidence for the second millennium West Semitic writing traditions, plus the inevitable tendency on the part of scholars to ignore inscriptions that seem to lie outside the range of relevant materials has led to just that sort of unilinear evolutionary scheme concerning the history of the alphabet that has proven to be illusory in many other aspects of cultural history. In addition, it is understandable that scholars would read into the Bronze Age those well–known systems of Iron Age language and writing systems without realizing that the transition to the Iron Age was accompanied by an almost total disruption of the earlier linguistic as well as social and cultural structures.

The conclusions drawn from the materials we now have in this corpus are argued later, but here it will be useful to summarize the results. The language is so archaic that it is impossible to place it into the Amarna period. The little archaeological evidence available associates the texts with the Egyptian Middle Empire period, i.e. pre–Hyksos, and that is of course entirely possible. However, that would seem to be the latest possible date, and the complete absence of any connection with Egyptian culture other than the hieroglyphic writing system that largely inspired the syllabic signary strongly suggests that the writing and the language itself belonged to the period of prosperity and stability that Byblos enjoyed in the Early Bronze Age. It is not at all impossible that the extremely chaotic period between the destruction in the 23rd century and the rise of the Egyptian Middle Kingdom was the time of creation of some of the texts, but this period is so poorly attested everywhere that it amounts to an ***obscurus per obscurius.*** My own preference is for the 24th century B.C. for the origin of the language and writing system, though arguing that the internal lack of homogeneity of the readable texts strongly suggests that the texts stem from a range of dates that may cover several centuries. The writing and language alike are systems that contrasted most sharply to those known from the Middle and Late Bronze Ages, and it is this fact that made decipherment impossible in the past.

2. Materials and Techniques

This topic has been covered very well by M. Dunand in the original publication, and needs no further elaboration here. Inspection of the documents with a six power comparator entirely confirms his description of the process by which the copper plates were inscribed. The tedium involved in writing these documents may well be imagined.

3. Collation and Establishment of the Readings.

My first view of the original inscriptions was kindly made possible by M. Chehab in early 1956. By that time a considerable amount of progress had already been made in the identification of the more frequent signs, and visual inspection confirmed a number of readings that then seemed necessary. At the same time it confirmed the very high degree of accuracy of M. Dunand's readings of the signs. This was the more important because a considerable part of Text C had disappeared in the course of attempts to clean the reverse, and the hand copy as well as photographs of this text are the only evidence left for the signs that had been on the now missing parts.

There is, fortunately, very little doubt concerning the readings of the lost portions of the text.

However, the most important breakthrough took place in November of 1968, when the late Dr. Roger Saidah and Mrs. Chehab made it possible to study the originals at leisure, and even more important, to photograph them with the Infra–Red Ektachrome film that had been released for public use just four years earlier. As I had hoped, the proper filtration and a polarizing filter with very flat lighting from electronic flash yielded superb results. Not only did the inherent high contrast of this film clearly delineate the characters, but also in quite a few locations the film showed the outline of characters where the original surface had entirely eroded away. I counted 18 items on the obverse and 19 on the reverse of Text D alone where the film yielded information that supplied missing characters, modified earlier readings, or confirmed very doubtful ones. These improved readings were greatly responsible for the successful decipherment of the texts, for they often removed anomalies that made reading of the words in question impossible.

The results with the very badly eroded stone inscription *A* were not nearly so dramatic, but even in this case the high contrast and lighting without shadows did yield further information that made possible progress on the text that had seemed hopeless.

The improved readings will be dealt with in the discussion at the respective locations, and need no further elaboration here. The study of the slides was done at 24 power and 36 power magnification using a microfiche reader.

3

DECIPHERMENT PROCEDURES

1. The Operating Presuppositions

Any approach to a body of unknown texts in an unknown writing system will inevitably be guided either by consciously chosen hypotheses concerning their nature or by working assumptions that are not critically examined. In the present case, when work on the texts began thirty–seven years ago, the following presuppositions seemed both reasonable and justified in the light of what could be known concerning the geographical and chronological context within which those texts were produced.

A. There seemed to be no reasonable alternative to the proposition that the texts are written in some dialect recognizable as West Semitic, and more specifically archaic Canaanite. It seemed also to be reasonable to expect that the language would be fairly similar to that of the more archaic texts of Ugarit. This assumption proved to be false, and for some years it was a handicap to further progress. However, there were enough common West Semitic features in both languages to form the basis for further progress.

B. The texts are much earlier than those of Ugarit. Though the archaeological evidence for context was far from satisfactory, information that was available pointed to a date before the Hyksos period. In addition, the writing system itself which was later simplified to produce the subsequent Canaanite alphabet strongly suggested a date prior to the earliest known alphabetic inscriptions, thus before the seventeenth century B.C. As it has been argued above, this proved to be in error on the conservative side. Though there is no conclusive proof for date even yet, nevertheless there is no reasonable means for placing the language and writing system into the context of the Late or even Middle Bronze Ages.

C. The writing system is some kind of syllabary that includes the vowel indicators. The signs were too few to include very many logograms, if any, and too few to justify the conclusion that it was an extensive and complex system like those of Egypt or Mesopotamia. Each sign should designate a single syllable, and since West Semitic contains virtually no syllables that have initial vowels, the CV syllabic pattern could be assumed to be dominant, though the possibility was recognized that CVC syllables might exist, and also purely consonantal vowelless characters might also be used, as in Egyptian. Though in the decipherment there are two characters interpreted in this way, the problem of writing closed syllables was solved merely by the reading device of 'dead vowels': i.e. the reader simply ignored the vowel embedded in the sign's phonetic value.

D. The writing system ought to be related in some way to the later alphabet complex, since there were so many signs that were very close in form to the latter, and several that were identical. Ironically enough, some of those identical forms are now proven to be the result of sheer coincidence. The evidence now is massive, but the decipherment proceeded upon the basis that there is no necessary connection between form and function, and for the first thirty years those graphic similarities were almost entirely ignored in the process of identifying the phonetic values of the various signs. Not until after most of those phonetic values had been assigned and meaningful words and morphs resulted, did the attention turn to the formal comparisons between the syllabic and the various alphabetic signaries. There were two exceptions to this procedure: the ⚭ *ʿayin* and the ∓ *samek* characters were inescapably identical to the later alphabetic signs——the only question that was not solved for a couple of decades was which vowel the sibilant sign denoted.

E. The number of signs was compatible with the assumption that the number of consonants was analogous to that of Ugarit, and that there was a three vowel notation system, with *a, i* and *u*. This would yield a syllabary of approximately 90 characters if only CV type syllables were represented. The initial publication by M. Dunand distinguished a substantially larger number than this, and therefore the probability that other types of syllables were represented was constantly kept in mind as a possible source for readings. With possibly two exceptions, this proved to be unnecessary, for there are a considerable number of graphic variants as should be expected in texts of such early date, that reduce the total number of signs to only 63, since a number of syllables do not occur in the texts.

So far as I can now recall, it did not enter my mind at all that the texts would yield a language that was a common ancestor to what was then universally accepted as two distinct Semitic subgroups, i.e. NW Semitic and South Semitic. This was a conclusion forced by the evidence that began to accumulate about 1960, and has progressively grown ever since.

2. The Reduction of Variables

The problem of matching some 90 CV syllables with a similar number of signs is not a process that must assume that any sign can represent any syllable. The most elementary principle in substitution ciphers is applicable here also, for in the Semitic languages all the consonants do not occur with equal frequency. Granted, we cannot assume that this unknown dialect will exhibit the same distribution frequency as cognate dialects, and above all we cannot assume that the distribution frequency of this tiny corpus will even be truly representative of this particular dialect. This is underlined by the fact that one sign cluster appears 18 times in the corpus. With these caveats a rough comparative frequency count was done, and it was useful, for there is no other way to proceed.

A consonant frequency count was carried out for Ugaritic, utilizing a segment of the myth of Anat and Baal under the assumption that this text is archaic, and therefore would be more likely to reflect older phonetic structure as well as vocabulary. The section chosen was a sample roughly similar in length to the total number of lines in the Byblos Syllabic corpus. The results are given in Table 1, where the first column gives the total number of occurrences, while the second and third columns give the numbers of times the consonant occurs in medial and final position respectively.

Table 1 Consonant Frequency

Cons.	Total	Med.	Fin.	Cons.	Total	Med.	Fin.
m	111	29	44	*w*	30	27	0
t	87	11	51	*ḥ*	25	11	5
b	78	20	9	*p*	21	4	4
r	78	9	19	*q*	16	2	3
l	76	20	23	*g*	16	1	2
ʾ	64	33	7	*ḫ*	15	5	5
k	59	19	19	*ṣ*	14	3	3
n	52	7	31	*s*	10	5	0
d	51	9	8	*z*	5	2	0
y	46	28	6	*ś*	5	2	0
ṯ	46	19	12	*ṭ*	3	0	0
š	45	12	7	*z*	3	0	1
h	38	3	25	*ẓ*	3	0	0
ʿ	32	6	7				

A comparison of the order of frequency with early biblical Hebrew prose yields the results shown in Table 2. For this count, a segment of a roughly similar length was chosen from a part of Genesis generally recognized to be from the 'J' document.

Table 2 Consonant Relative Frequency

	Ug.	SC		Ug.	SC
m	1	1	ʿ	14	10
t	2	11	*w*	15	5
b	3	8	*ḥ*	16	15 (=*ḥ* + *ḫ*)
r	4	3	*p*	17	16
l	5	4	*q*	18	17
ʾ	6	2	*g*	19	20
k	7	9	*ḫ*	20	—
n	8	12	*ṣ*	21	19
d	9	14	*s*	22	18
y	10	7	*z*	23	21
ṯ	11	—	*ġ*	24	—
š	12	6 (=*ṯ* + *š*)	*ṭ*	25	22
h	13	13	*ẓ*	26	—

It is immediately apparent that the frequencies are remarkably analogous, though there are great discrepancies in particular consonants that are readily accounted for by the enormous linguistic changes that took place at the transition from the Late Bronze to the Early Iron Age. The *t* no longer was written at the end of fem. nouns and verbs, and its frequency dropped from second to eleventh place. The enormous use of the *waw* consecutive verb form raised its frequency from fifteenth to fifth—and so on. The least frequent consonant in this sample of SC was the *ṭ*, which has not been identified at all in the BS corpus, and is the third least frequent in Ugaritic. In nearly every case where there is a sharp contrast in frequency, there is a known linguistic change that accounts for it. It is not the purpose here to point out further interesting implications in this remarkable consistency of phoneme frequency, once known historical changes are allowed for. Rather, it is the conclusion that such a frequency count can be assumed to be broadly reliable as a base for eliminating from consideration certain less frequent consonants as possible syllabic values for the more frequent signs.

A further yield from the table was the fact that in Ugaritic, many consonants show marked tendencies for preferred positions:

In initial position: *ʾ, y, w, ṯ.*
In final position: *m, t, n, h, s.*
In medial position: *d, ʿ, p, q, ǵ, ṣ, ṭ.*

3. The Identification of Afformatives

A glance at the frequency table shows that all but *r* among the ten most frequent consonants are used as grammatical affixes, either as personal or number endings, gender markers, prepositives and postpositives to the verb, or as prepositions and demonstratives. The significance of this fact is not limited to its importance for identifying such morphemes, but in addition it is of considerable value in the extremely crucial problem of locating word boundaries. It is a matter of simple common sense that recurrent strings of signs cannot be assumed to coincide with word–division, and this was of especial importance for the very frequent cluster read as *kawana* = , for in nearly every case the verb has a preformative personal marker.

The next step was to construct concordances of every occurrence of the most frequent signs to determine their relationships to the recurrent sign strings. Immediately, the identification of several signs as personal preformatives to verb forms was suggested. The initial syllables involving *ʾ, t, y* prefixes to the imperfect verb form, and the final syllables *–ma, –ni, –ta, –ti, –tu* were identified with relatively little difficulty, and at the same time they introduced word divisions which in turn made much easier the identification of still other syllabic values for the preceding and following words. It is particularly the most frequent sign *–ma*, that occurs in final position in a very high percentage of uses that helped enormously in the identification of word boundaries.

The identification of the vowels was more difficult than that of the consonants, and there are still a number of cases in which the vowel reading is not certain. Most useful, however, were the case endings, once the function of the noun in the sentence could be reasonably ascertained.

4. The Reduction of the Number of Signs

As the process of decipherment proceeded, it became increasingly clear that many signs listed in *BG* as distinct signs, and which were treated as such in the initial stages of decipherment, were in fact merely graphic variants. The result of this grouping of variants into their various categories was to reduce radically the total number of characters in the signary from over a hundred, to just over seventy, and eventually to the present 63 signs. This in turn meant that the range of variety of syllables was severely limited. With three vowels and an assumed 28 to 30 consonants, it was clear that not all of the CV syllables were represented, and there was almost no possibility that other types of syllable could be signalled at all.

The types of graphic variants were also interesting. Since the texts on copper plates were produced by blows from a blunt chisel shaped tool, the width of the chisel blade used seems to have determined the shape of the sign, and this is particularly true of overlapping right–angle strokes. Curves were made by a series of successive impressions from a very narrow chisel blade: e.g., the *pu* ○ sign, in one instance was made with eight separate chisel strokes. Variations of form were virtually inevitable and also recognizable once it was clear that varying lengths of chisel blade were used. The kinds of blades used were determined by examining the originals with a six–power comparator with collimator grid capable of measuring to one tenth of a millimeter.

Other variations are entirely familiar to those acquainted with pictographic types of writing. The number of strokes necessary to produce a picture of the object represented by the sign is frequently reduced to a few diagnostic essentials. The bee sign  for example is written as an elegant picture on the stone stele *g*, but elsewhere it is reduced to a simple four–stroke sign. Similarly the sign depicting a man with upraised arms  familiar from Egyptian hieroglyphs is reduced to the loop used for the *ʾalif* sign with a wave stroke below representing the legs. It is thus clear that the distinction between monumental and cursive scripts already existed.

Other variations include rotation of signs, especially frequent for the *mu* and the *tu* characters, and attested probably for the *ša* and the *di*. The rotation has nothing to do with direction of writing whether horizontal or columnar, but may be in some cases the result of a desire to avoid running into other characters or approaching too near the edge of the tablet. In the case of the *mu* sign only, it appears that the rotation signals a phonetic contrast: *mi* instead of *mu*, but only in Text D.

5. The Process of Elimination

As the number of signs identified with syllabic values increased in number, beginning with the frequent ones used in afformatives, the number of unidentified consonants as well as signs decreased dramatically. In other words there were fewer and fewer unread characters and also fewer consonants as candidates for their readings. It is at this stage that the criterion of semantic relevance became operative, for by this time a considerable number of words could be recognized with some degree of probability, and syntactic relationships also were emerging. In view of the fact that even Ugaritic after more than 50 years is still about 50% obscure, it is only to be expected that these texts which are considerably older will include many words or meanings that are unparalleled and therefore cannot be readily explained except on an *ad hoc* basis, if at all, depending on the completeness of the context.

The semantic criteria became increasingly important and also useful, for identified roots and verb forms gave strong indication concerning the subject matter of the text, and the general nature of the document. By the time this stage of decipherment was reached, the primary problem was no longer the readings of the signs, nor often even the grammatical structure of the language. It is rather a semantic problem: the root may look very familiar from later cognates, but it is used in a context that is quite unfamiliar and puzzling. On the other hand, there are numerous examples of words in which the meaning found in Arabic lexica and sometimes SC fits perfectly.

The idea that words retain their meanings unchanged over millennia may be true of the simplest label terms that refer to constants in human experience, such as 'house, father, mother, water', etc., but even these obviously have transferred meanings, connotations, usages, and even value associations that are not constant, but are culturally bound. In Arabic, for example, the vast range of word usages that have to do with the camel must be innovations, transferred meanings that could hardly have existed before the large scale utilization of the domesticated camel in comparatively recent times. It would be the height of academic naivete to take such a meaning as the 'primitive' base meaning from which other usages were transferred, though it is entirely probable that many such terms were already in use with reference to other domesticated animals prior to the widespread use of the camel.

A comparative semantic method may be much too pretentious a term to apply to the experience of the past decades in trying to determine the semantic range of words read in these texts. Nevertheless, the comparison of roots together with the range of meanings found in the various interrelated Semitic languages, has gradually forced me to the conclusion that we are very naive about the systematic interrelationships of meaning and the historical processes of semantic change in comparative Semitic. At the same time, an exaggerated reverence for the 'linguistic laws' drawn up largely by scholars in the nineteenth century when extremely meager historical evidence was available, has led to a rejection of semantic relationships even when they are obvious. The recognition of the fact that 'linguistic laws' are "mighty useful hyperboles" as Kenneth Pike once put it, is long overdue in comparative and historical linguistic studies. Perhaps even more important would be the recognition of the fact that even those 'laws' are culturally conditioned and therefore often enough chronologically limited.

Though this topic deserves much more extended treatment, this is hardly the appropriate place, and it will be abundantly illustrated in the treatment of the various texts. Here it needs to be pointed out that only those lexical items that have similar form and similar meaning across the Semitic family range in time and space are likely candidates for the term 'proto-Semitic', and this lexical inventory probably does not exceed much more than 35% of the vocabulary of any given Semitic language. On the other hand, the vocabulary items of SC that are specific to that language--in other words have no known cognates in other Semitic languages, does not exceed 5%. It follows that in any of the West Semitic languages particularly, the meaning of any root is a function of historical linguistic processes that can now be traced back a thousand years perhaps before its first appearance in a specific language/culture situation.

It is apparent that we are dealing willy-nilly with the much despised "etymological method" in determining--or rather, discovering, meanings that fit the emergent context and in turn become part of the linguistic context and then the linguistic history. Apart from the fact that there is no other way to proceed other than to declare the task "impossible," it is valuable to point out that etymology is after all merely the history of the language. To neglect or even to despise it is merely to engage in a specialized form of obscurantism--a chronological or academic snobbery that arbitrarily refuses to deal with the possibility of observing social or linguistic history beyond the limits of that with which the scholar in question customarily deals. It is particularly an occupational hazard of Assyriologists who customarily have the luxury of using the simplistic 'combinatory' method to deal with tens of thousands of documents. It will simply not do to dismiss etymology loftily as 'unscientific' or 'imprecise': of course it is, like all human history, and of course it has been engaged in with grossly inadequate information and working assumptions, if not even vicious ideological axes to grind. But the neglect and even contempt for etymology is merely the process of grinding a different axe, and results in an inability to learn something new especially in that all–important and most difficult arena of radical cultural and linguistic change that always takes place at "juncture periods" of human cultural history.

If after fifty years the decipherment and understanding of Ugaritic is far from complete, it goes without saying that this first attempt to find meaning and social and historical context for these enigmatic texts from long ago Byblos is not likely to be the last word on the subject. Perhaps Horace had the appropriate comment: ***nec possum tecum vivere, nec sine te.*** "I am neither able to live with you, nor without you."

4

THE SYLLABARY AND ITS RELATIONSHIPS

For many decades scholars have posited an ultimately Egyptian origin for the Phoenician alphabet, but the details of this hypothesis have never been satisfactorily documented. The similarities between archaic forms of the alphabet and Egyptian hieroglyphs have always been vague and not very convincing. It now seems quite clear that the hypothesis was correct in essence but wrong in its particulars. In *BG* Dunand documented in detail the very close connection between Egyptian and Byblos Syllabic signs, even labelling the latter 'pseudo—hieroglyphic'. Though that discussion may now need correction in minor details, the point has been thoroughly made and need not be further elaborated upon nor reiterated here.

The evidence is now massive that the Phoenician alphabet was only **indirectly** derived from Egyptian, through the syllabic system. Having made this observation, however, it is necessary to emphasize that it is a generalization that holds true only for the idea of a syllabic writing system, and for the specific forms of a considerable number of characters. As it is generally true in cultural history, so also in respect to writing it is extremely rare that an entire **system** is borrowed. It is the general idea and often specific forms that are usually borrowed but it is a valid law of cultural history that forms transferred from one culture to another always undergo a 'functional shift'. This is simply a truism too often ignored, that a borrowed form whether across cultural space or time cannot have the identical relationship to other forms or to the culture itself in the recipient culture that it had in the culture of origin.

To cite merely one example from the syllabary, the form of a snake is readily recognized everywhere no matter how it is drawn. There can be no doubt that the pictorial representation in the Byblos syllabary is a copy of the Egyptian hieroglyph, but the functional shift took place simply by giving it the native name in what may now be termed Old Coastal Semitic (OCS) which is of course *naḥas*. The phonetic value was the first syllable of that name, and its epigraphic function was then to signal the syllable *na* instead of the Egyptian word and syllable *ʾiʿrt* 'uraeus'.

BYBLOS SYLLABIC CHARACTERS

Table 3

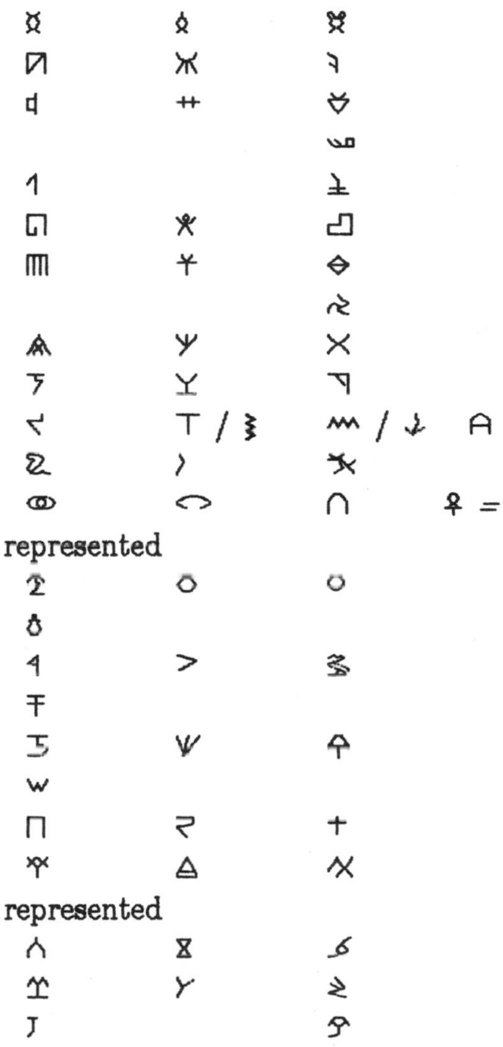

Consonant +		Vowel *a*	Vowel *i*	Vowel *u*	
ʾalif	*ʾ*				
bēt	*b*				
dal	*d*				
d̲al	*d̲*				
gimel	*g*				
hē	*h*				
ḥēt	*ḥ*				
ḫet	*ḫ*				
kaf	*k*				
lamed	*l*				
mim	*m*				= m
nun	*n*				
ʿayin	*ʿ*				= *maʿ*
ǵayin	*ǵ*	Not represented			
pe	*p*				
qof	*q*				
rēš	*r*				
samek	*s*				
ṣade	*ṣ*				
šin	*š*				
tau	*t*				
t̲a	*t̲*				
ṭet	*ṭ*	Not represented			
waw	*w*				
yod	*y*				
zayin	*z*				

Table 4: Acrophonic Syllables

Sign	Name	Syllable	Meaning
	*ʾa–la–pu*	*ʾa*	Ox
	*ʾi–ḥi–du*	*ʾi*	Ox + Numeral 1
	*ʾu–ḏu–nu*	*ʾu*	Ox + Ear
	*ba–yi–tu*	*ba*	House
	*ga–ma–lu*	*ga*	Throwstick ?
	*da–la–tu*	*da*	Door
	*du(g)–gu*	*du*	Fish
	ḏu–ru–ʿu	*ḏu*	Arm
	*hu–du–mu*	*hu*	Footstool ?
	*ḥa–yi–tu*	*ḥa*	Fence
	*ḥi–tu ?*	*ḥi*	Yarn
	*yu–du*	*yu*	Hand ?
	*ka(p)–pu*	*ka*	Palm & Fingers
	*ma–ga–lu*	*ma*	Sickle
	mu–u	*mu*	Water
	*mu–ru–ḥa*	*mu*	Lance
	*na–ḥa–su*	*na*	Serpent
	*nu–bu–tu*	*nu*	Bee
	*sa–ma–ku*	*sa*	Pillar
	*ʿa–yi–nu*	*ʿa*	Eye
	*ʿu–ši–ru*	*ʿu*	Ten
	*pu–u*	*pu*	Mouth (saying 'pu')
	*ṣi–ṣu*	*ṣi*	Sprout
	*qa–ba–ʿu*	*qa*	Jar
	*ra–ʾi–su*	*ra*	Head
	*ru–ḥa–mu*	*ru*	Vulture
	*ša(n)–nu*	*ša*	Tooth
	*tu–u*	*tu*	Cross/Mark

1. The Acrophonic Principle

The relationship between picture, word–label, and phonetic value is an extremely useful one, for it occasionally offers some suggestions for the identification of syllabic readings, and helps to confirm those readings especially when the same or a derived sign shows up later in alphabetic writing. As Table 4 above shows, a considerable number of signs can be correlated with their OCS names. Not all of these names actually occur, of course, in this tiny corpus of texts, but they can easily be inferred or even reconstructed on the basis of now available evidence for the phonetic structure of this primal language. The forms are derived where possible from the monumental stone inscriptions that are characterized by an elegant pictorial representation.

It seems clear that some of the signs are artificial constructions to which the acrophonic principle could not apply. Though there are meaningful words associated with all three forms of the *ʾalif*, in which the vowels are differentiated by what may be termed 'diacritical marks', there are two other cases of signs that are modified from the base sign in one way or another. The clearest example is the *pi* syllable that is written with the base *pu* character, but differentiated from it by a horizontal mark: Ꝺ̄. It is possible that the *ʿayin* sign <> *ʿi* is also an artificial differentiation from the 'eye' sign.

2. Pictorial and Linear Forms

Much has been made of the contrast between representational or pictographic signs and abstract or linear signs as a basis for drawing up an evolutionary scheme for the history of writing, and even for the relative dating of specific inscriptions. As it has been pointed out above, this syllabary already contains both types, and often enough both realizations of the **same** sign. The *ʾalif* signs never appear in pictographic form, but are in a form that derives from an Egyptian hieroglyph. Similarly the 'head' is never representational, but has the form that appears in later alphabets. The contrast is not one of evolutionary development in any absolute fashion. Even if it were, the evolution had already taken place in a markedly uneven manner centuries before these texts were written, and as the Proto–Sinaitic inscriptions prove, what was characteristic in the continuity of one particular cultural tradition has no necessary correlation with what was happening or happened later in another culture.

Most cultures have, after all, specialized types of writing systems. The BS texts prove beyond reasonable doubt that pictorial signs were in use especially for monumental inscriptions, and a much more cursive form in less formal inscriptions. It is inherently very probable that still more cursive types of characters were also in use, utilizing less adamant writing materials. The contrasts between these two 'ideal types' will be discussed at the passages where the signs involved actually occur.

3. Orientation

In most typologically early writing systems the direction of writing is not a rigidly fixed social convention. The same is true of the BS syllabic writing. Though there is certainly a preference for the right to left direction, examples in this tiny corpus include the left to right direction on the final line of Spatula b, and the entire reverse of Spatula f. There is also the columnar writing from top to bottom on one stone monumental inscription.

A few of the characters appear in a rotated stance. This is especially characteristic of long, narrow signs such as the *tu, di* and *ša*. The only explanation for this fact that seems to make sense is simply the constriction of space in particular contexts. Sometimes the line is too near the top of the copper plate to give room for a vertical shaft, as in D 1; perhaps the writer felt that a vertical shaft might on occasion impinge upon a sign in the line above, as in D 16, 19. These are not very strong arguments, and all that is necessary is to observe that rigid conventions of stance were not operative. Furthermore, these variations as well as the lack of variations in the columnar inscription prove that changes in the direction of writing in later inscriptions had no necessary connection at all with the rotation of characters, and are merely specifically cultural conventions that are random in origin.

The ⦚ *mi* sign was at first taken to be a similarly rotated ᴧᴧᴧ *mu*, but it now seems quite clearly to be a deliberate constrastive form to represent the syllable *mi* in Text D only.

It is tempting but unjustified to rely upon models derived from the rigidities of form and stance that characterized Greek paleography and that constitute reliable criteria for dating manuscripts. Those inscriptions are the product of a professional scribal elite who had undergone no doubt a highly competitive educational training system that was already centuries old and cross culturally uniform. To transfer such criteria into the highly diverse ancient Near Eastern cultures is merely to engage in an exercise of systematic anachronism, and to impose modern concepts of precision and formal conformity upon ancient inscriptions where such practices were not a part of the ancient cultural pattern. (They still are not, as any professor who has had to decipher the variety of handwritings in a collection of examination papers can abundantly testify.)

4. From Syllabary to Alphabet

An unexpected side effect of the decipherment process was the accumulation of new evidence concerning the origin of the alphabet. From the outset it was evident that a number of the signs in the syllabary were very similar if not identical to those of the standard tenth–century Phoenician alphabet, but those similarities were at first disregarded simply on the grounds that a similarity of form furnished no basis for concluding a similarity of linguistic function. The fact that an entirely different writing system was involved furnished good reason to accept the hypothesis that the Phoenician phonetic values were no more a basis for readings than were the Egyptian. This was further reinforced by the fact that it rapidly became necessary to conclude that the syllabic system was many centuries older than the standard tenth century alphabet. As time passed, however, and more words began to emerge, it became increasingly clear that there was some sort of systemic connection between the syllabic and alphabetic signs, if only because of the connection between name and phonetic value discussed above which is a constant in both systems. Dunand had already argued this in *BG*, but until the signs could be read such conclusions drawn only from formal similarities were perhaps rightly distrusted, but wrongly ignored.

The relationships between the syllabic and alphabetic forms consist of two main types: the obvious, and the not so immediately obvious. The latter are naturally more difficult to prove, and consequently in many cases remain uncertain. Furthermore, even the 'obvious' similarities of form may be highly misleading, and one case of this sort is certainly the 𐤊 sign that is virtually identical to the Iron Age Phoenician sign, but this is purely accidental.

Two processes in particular can be observed to be functioning in the evolution from syllabary to alphabet: first, and most obvious is the very frequent change in stance. Rotation of many characters took place either 90 or 180 degrees. Second, and this is not so obvious, is the fact that the later forms were often simplifications of the syllabic characters by the mere

Table 5: Comparative Forms

BS Sign	Eg.	Object	Phoen.	East. Alph.
¤	V–7	Cord Loop	Ƙ	Ӎ
◸	O–1	House	𐤁	⊓
ꟼ	O–31	Door	––	ꟼ
♉	K–2	Fish	Δ	––
※	A–28	Rejoice	––	Ɣ
⏋	Q–1	Seat	ẞ	
⋏	?	?	Y	
Ʒ	?	?	I	⧖ ?
⩋	O–43?	Fence	Ħ	Ψ
≳	?	?	Ꝋ	––
⩓	?	Hand	Ѵ	––
7	?	?	Ꞁ	1
ʍ	N–35	Water	𐤌	∃
Ƨ	I–12	Cobra	ל	٦
₸	R–11	Djed–pillar	₸	––
⦶	D–4	Eye	O	O
Σ	?	?	ʖ	––
○	?	Mouth	––	0
Ꞅ	T–16?	Scimitar??	ⱨ	––
Ѱ	M–22	Sprout	––	¥
ꝺ	W–22	Jug	φ	ɸ
𐤓	D–1	Head	𐤓	⟩
w	?	Tooth?	w	Ȝ
+	Z–11	Cross	+	+

Note: Some of the Old South Arabic characters in this font are taken from the more archaic forms cited in Figure 1 of ***The Proto–Sinaitic Inscriptions and Their Decipherment***, by W. F. Albright (Cambridge, 1966).

omission of strokes that were not necessary for maintaining the contrast between characters. The fact that this was not a **systematic** process is illustrated by the Proto–Sinaitic retention of even more complex pictographic forms, particularly striking in the case of the *ʾalif, dalet*, and *reš*. It is extremely probable that this return to pictographic forms or their retention is the result of direct influence from the Egyptian hieroglyphic system with which the sculptors of the Proto–Sinaitic inscriptions were in intimate contact.

5. Comments on Specific Signs

In this section the development from Egyptian hieroglyphs to the later alphabets will be traced for each specific sign for which there is evidence. For convenience' sake, the Eg. hieroglyphs are cited following the standard notation of Gardiner's ***Egyptian Grammar.***

ʾalif: ¤ ⚲ ¤: This series posed enormous difficulties for many years, and still there is no good explanation for this form of the ox–head sign. I suggest that for some unknown reason, it was assimilated to the hieroglyphic sign V–7, that had no connection with the ox. It is entirely clear that the ancient Byblos scribes were perfectly capable of pictographic forms, as the 'bee' sign shows, but this highly stylized abstract form comes as a surprise, especially in comparison with the pictographic form always used in the Proto–Sinaitic corpus.

Though the *pu* and *pi* signs were also distinguished by the addition of a diacritical mark, this is the only consonant in the signary in which all three vowels are indicated by diacritics. The *ʾa* sign is of course the stylized ox–head with the horns indicated––in fact the horns are all that is left of the ox–head. The form with the vowel *i* represents the pronunciation of the numeral that actually occurs as *ʾiḫid*, and the vertical stroke is the universal graphic representation of the numeral 'one'. The form with *u* depicts a pair of ears certainly reflecting the mnemonic word *ʾuḏun*. In some of the Proto–Sinaitic inscriptions the *ʾalif* is actually drawn with one ear showing, as it is also in Eg. F–1. The continuity with the later Canaanite *ʾalif* K is obvious and need not be argued here. It does not seem to have been observed, however, that the later Safaitic and sometimes Thamudic form of the *ʾalif* can only have been derived from the tenth century Canaanite form. This character that is very similar to the Phoenician *alif* occurs already in the 7th– 6th century caravansarai at Umm er–Rujam, just North of Amman.

What the latter two signs of the series represent is an "overlay" of a second mnemonic word superimposed upon the basic ‘ox–head’ sign, and thus taking the form of a diacritical mark. It should be considered as a very sophisticated device, that unfortunately was not continued in use until the revival of a similar systematic usage in the Ethiopic syllabic system.

It may be coincidence, but the fact that the Ug. alphabet also treated the *ʾalif* differently from the other consonants by using three distinct signs for the different vowels may dimly reflect the peculiar special status of the consonant in this system. The Ug. syllabic rendering with *ʾa* presupposes the name *ʾa–la–pu* and the corresponding picture that universally underlay the various alphabetic forms of later times. The other two members of the series had no posterity.

bēt: The normal form of the ◸ *ba* sign is virtually identical to that which became the alphabetic *bēt* centuries later. It is possibly the local adaptation of the Eg. *pr* O–1 ‘house’. Very significant, however, is the fact that the closed square occurs also as a variant form in this corpus, for it is also used in some inscriptions of the Proto–Sinaitic corpus, and probably underlies the form used in pre–Islamic Arabic. The stance of the sign actually occurs much later, but rotation 90 degrees became the norm in the Iron Age Phoenician alphabet 𐤁. Such rotation in later derived writing systems is very frequent, but there is no apparent pattern. Many are rotated 180 degrees, while others exhibit this 90 degree shift. The rotation has nothing to do with horizontal vs. vertical writing, for it is not present in the vertically written monumental text G.

No convincing explanation for the other two forms of the *bēt* has been found. Dunand suggested for the ⋊ *bi* sign an origin in the tripod bowls or mortars that he attributed to the Twelfth Dynasty and the Hyksos period, and this is quite possible though tripod bowls are commonplace in the Early Bronze Age as well.

dalet: ᑫ=*da* ⧺=*di* ᗐ=*du*: The first two of the series are clearly to be equated with Eg. O–31 ‘door’, and O–34 ‘bolt’, respectively. In the case of the ᑫ sign it is clear that the Egyptian sign has been rotated, no doubt for calligraphic reasons, while the Sem. writing systems, to my knowledge, never rotated it. It is equally clear, however, that only the Eastern alphabets perpetuated the use of this sign that continued to represent the consonant until their demise in the early Islamic period.

Less clear, however, is the ♉= *du* sign. It is here taken to be a highly stylized representation of a fish, and therefore connected with Eg. K–2. The Proto–Sinaitic system is again far more 'pictographic', and probably directly influenced by the Eg. system that we know was in common use at the mining site from which those inscriptions came. At any rate, they prove that the consonant *d* was associated with the word for 'fish', which could only have been the OCS form of later Canaanite *dag*. This is reconstructed as having been pronounced *dugg–*, and the Ugaritic syllabic representation as *di* strongly supports this interpretation. The *u/i* interchange is so strikingly frequent in this OCS dialect that it can be taken for granted. Bronze Age *dig* would have to become *dag* in Iron Age Canaanite by Philippi's Law.

Even more support for this position is furnished by the actual Canaanite alphabetic form of the *dalet* Δ. The triangular character is **not** the 'door' sign, but is actually the 'fish' sign minus the tail fins. As usual, it is rotated in various stances throughout the early history of the alphabet. The sign itself, however, became associated with the **name** of the ꟼ character to the present day. These facts are quite convincing evidence for the position that the Eastern Alphabets are not derived from the standard Canaanite alphabet, but are in fact independent and parallel developments from the same reservoir of graphic signs, though certainly until the close of the Bronze Age they were in contact with the conventions that later became the 'standard' alphabet.

he. ⊔=Phoen. ᖷ? This is clearly Eg. Q–1 'seat', here taken to be a *hudum*, in Ug. at least and later, 'footstool'. The later Phoenician character is one of the very few that do not have immediately clear prototypes in the Syllabic system. It is diffidently suggested that the BS *hu* ⊔ became the alphabetic form by the process again of omitting unnecessary strokes, in this case the two vertical strokes on the left side of the character, and attaching the central horizontal line to the main vertical on the right side of the character. It is highly significant that the Proto–Sinaitic alphabet continued the use of the BS ᛯ *hi* sign, and this in turn became the still further simplified OSA *he*.

The signs *ha, hi* ⊓ ᛯ are clearly Eg. O–4 and A–28 respectively.

waw: It seems quite clear that the much later Phoenician *waw* Y is the BS ∧ *wa* sign turned upside down and with the shaft much elongated.

What it originally represented is a complete mystery, for the monumental inscriptions render it in a way that is not symmetrical. It therefore cannot be the Eg. F–13 'horns' sign that it otherwise resembles superficially. The Eastern Alphabet *waw* seems to be an innovation, for there is not any sign in the BS repertory that is a reasonable candidate for its origin.

zain J=*za*: The hook at the bottom of BS J has become a cross–bar in the Phoen. I. The Eastern Alphabet again went its own way. Its *zain* is identical to the BS X sign that is read as *ṯu*, but since there is no phonetic correspondence, it is likely that the similarity is accidental.

ḥet Ⅲ *ḥa*: This sign quite clearly represents a fence or wall, though there is not a good Eg. equivalent. (The archaic O–43 is a possible analogue, simplified and turned upside down.) It is the source for Phoen. H as well as the Proto–Sinaitic and the much later Eastern Alphabet character. Professor Ward has suggested O–27 *ḥ*ʾ or W–17 *ḫnt* as other possible prototypes for this sign.

ḫet ϒ=*ḫi*: There can be little doubt concerning the identity of this sign with the OSA *ḫ* character. The Eg. prototype may have been the 'spindle' hieroglyph U–34. The Proto–Sinaitic substituted the 'result' for the 'cause' in using the 'hank' of yarn, Eg. V–28, sign. Incidentally, it has the phonetic value *ḥ* in Egyptian itself.

ṭet: Neither the prototype for the Alphabetic ⊕ or the phoneme itself is attested in the corpus. It is surprising, but there is not one identified word that requires a cognate with this consonant anywhere in later Semitic. Relatively speaking, it is rare in later WS and it is of course possible that its absence is accidental. On the other hand, the high infrequency of the velarized consonants in this dialect raises the distinct possibility that the velarized *ṭ* did not yet exist at this time and place.

yod ≧=*yu*: This sign is again virtually identical to the later Phoenician Ꙇ, though the vowel is somewhat surprising. The Eastern alphabets went a different way, for the Proto–Sinaitic used an abbreviated form of the ♈ *ya* sign, and this in turn then died out of use. The later OSA *ya* sign is evidently an innovation from an unknown source.

kaf ⩕=*ka*: This sign furnishes another illustration of the extent to which the syllabary departed from pictographic representation. It is clearly cognate to the PS *k* sign, but the middle 'fingers' are crossed and the entire sign is inverted from the perspective of the later figures. The *ki* Y figure is an excellent example of what apparently is a purely accidental coincidence in form with the later Iron Age Phoenician character. It made considerable difficulties in the decipherment and dating of the texts, but serves as a warning against too far-reaching conclusions on the basis of merely **formal** similarities.

lamed 7=*la*: This offers a classic case of the simplification of form that accompanied the reduction of the writing system to consonantal signalling only. The top two strokes were dispensed with as unnecessary to the maintenance of contrast to other characters. It was then rotated and the acute angle rounded to a curve in most scripts. It is not at all impossible that the curve was present also in BS cursive writing on other materials, for curves were much more difficult to incise than straight-line angles on the copper plates.

mim ʌʌʌ=*mu*: This sign remained remarkably stable through the centuries, from its Egyptian origin to the tenth century Phoenician alphabet. It is an indication of the fluidity of this syllabic system that there were two signs for both *mu* and *mi* in different texts. Only Text D uses this sign, and seemingly its rotated form to indicate the syllable *mi*.

nun ᘔ=*na*: Still pictographic in Proto-Sinaitic, by the Late Bronze Age this sign had evidently become everywhere an abstract geometric form that was levelled through the Semitic alphabetic systems. It is curious that the name as it survived has preserved no phonetic or mnemonic connection with the original object represented.

samek ǂ=*sa*: This is another case where the syllabic sign is virtually identical to the later alphabetic one. Fortunately, the monumental inscription G makes possible its identification with the ***Djed*** column of pre-historic Egypt, and therefore the name has preserved the original meaning, '(support-)column'.

ʿayin ⦶=*ʿa*: This character as well as its name was levelled through West Semitic writing systems. By the LB age the nonessential extra strokes had been discarded, and as a result the circle with the dot coincided with the Eastern *pe* sign after the dot in turn was omitted.

pe ꝛ=*pa*: What this sign originally represented is far from clear.

There is no Egyptian hieroglyph that seems to be a probable candidate as its prototype, and it is sheer speculation to suggest that it might have been a depiction of some kind of plant. In later times, the entire right side of the character was dropped, and only the left side of the top and the curving vertical column was retained. It is possible that the Proto–Sinaitic character illustrates another form of simplification, by discarding the top portion altogether and retaining the horizontal base with the vertical line.

The Eastern alphabets ignored the sign altogether, continuing to use the BS ○=*pu* character, that was highly mnemonic in its representation of the mouth pronouncing the word 'pu'. It fell together with the simplified *ʿayin*, and differentiation had to be made by making this sign larger, oval in shape, or in some traditions even diamond–shaped.

ṣad Ͻ=*ṣa*: This sign changed relatively little other than in stance, but like the *pe* was preserved only in the Central Alphabet. The suggestion in the chart that it may have derived from Eg. 'scimitar' is not highly convincing, but there seems to be no more probable candidate. No suggestion for the origin of the later name of the character has presented itself.

The Eastern alphabets chose and perpetuated the BS *ṣi*=Ѵ character, which clearly represents a growing sprout with basal leaves. The name is actually preserved in SC *ṣiṣ* which has that meaning. The Eastern alphabets on occasion even furnished the (underground) bulb from which the sprout arose, and this became normative in the later OSA alphabets. It was then turned upside down, all connection with its original meaning having been lost.

qof ठ=*qa*: This is clearly the representation of a jug that may be identified with Sem. *qubaʿat*, and the form from the common Eg. hieroglyph. The Ug. rendering with *qu* coincides with the vocalization of the SC word as well as the traditional pronunciation of the name of the sign. The reading *qa* here is uncertain, since the sign is rare, and the other two members of the series either do not occur or have not been identified. The form of the sign certainly does not resemble a 'cup' that is the fairly secure meaning of the word from the Ug. on. Another possibility is SC *qaśwah*, the archaic nature of which is guaranteed by the fact that it is mentioned only in connection with the libation rituals of the Jerusalem temple (projected back of course into the Mosaic period by the post–Exilic priestly tradition). I would further suggest that its very archaic source is indicated also by the unassimilated sibilant following the *qof*, and the fact that the other word *qbʿt* may be cognate to the Eg. *qbḥt* that also was used in connection with libation rituals (*K–B*).

reš 𐤓=*ra*: Identical to the Iron Age Central Alphabet sign. Like others in the signary it is very highly stylized over against the pictographic form preserved in Proto–Sinaitic.

šin w=*ša*: Identical to the Iron Age alphabetic signs. Other than occasional rotation, there are no variants that throw light on the origin or meaning of the sign. Association with 'tooth' is not very probable in light of the sibilant shift, for this word normally would have been pronounced with *s* not *š* in this dialect.

tau +=*tu*: Identical to the Iron Age alphabets. It is most gratifying to find that the Ug. syllabic equivalent to this consonant was *tu*, not *ta*, for the sign actually signals the syllable *tu*, contrary to my original expectations.

ṯa ᛉ=*ṯa*: It is astonishing to find that this sign was divested of the vertical base stroke, and rotated 90 degrees to become the controversial OSA *ś* character.

5

BYBLOS SYLLABIC TEXT D

LINE	Transliteration	TEXT
1.	*ha-wa-tu ḫu-ru+ba-ʿi-lu ʾi-ʾi-tu-ʾu-*	
2.	*-ni ma-ta-ti la+ki-ti ya-tu-ha-ʿi- -[hi-du] ha-ki-*	
3.	*-ʿa bi+ha-ʿi-la-li-ni pa+ti-sa-ta-ru+ni*	
4.	*ta-ḫi-ma mu-la-ki+hi-ya ma-mu*	
5.	*ba-ʾi ba+nu+ma pu-tu-ya ba+nu+ma*	
6.	*la+ʾi-ḫi-di ya-ha-tu ṯa-wa-ra-ti ta-*	
7.	*-[ka]-wa-na+ma ba-ʾu-ni+ni-ta pa+ka-wa-*	
8.	*[na] bi-tu ṯa-wa-ra ḫu-ḫa-ša+ma ta-*	
9.	*[li]-ti ta-ka-wa-na+ma la+hu ya-ha-*	
10.	*[tu] ḫu-ru+ba-ʿi-lu li+tu-ha-li-du gu-*	
11.	*-ḫi-[ti] ta-li pu-li-ta-ti+ya ʾi-li-la ha-ki-*	
12.	*-mi-ʾu pa+ti-sa-ki-ru li-ʾi-mu+hu lu-ḫi-*	
13.	*sa+ma mu-ra-ʿa mu-ru-ʿi pu-li-ta-ti+*	
14.	*ya ʾi-li-la ti-ʿa-ṯu ya-la-nu lu-mi ya-*	
15.	*-da-ša-na ma-ʾi-hu-di ʾu-ba-ru ka-wa-*	
16.	*-na tu-ʿi tu-ṯa-wa-ʾi yu-ḫu-bu-ba-ta ta-*	
17.	*-tu-sa-ta-ru ʾi-ya ʿu-bu-du-tu+ni-ya*	
18.	*ta-ti ya-tu yi-ba-mi mu-na tu-ʿi*	
19.	*[ṯa-wa]-ʾu-tu ḫu-ru+ba-ʿi-lu ʾi-ʾu*	
20.	*-ta-ti ya-ru-ni ʾu-ḫa ʿa-ni+ya ha-*	
21.	*-ki ha-ʿi-mu-ru bi-ʿu+ma ʾa-*	
22.	*-[ka]-wa-na+ma ʿu-bu-di ṯi bi+pu-li*	
23.	*[ ] ki-ti ṯu ya-tu-ha-ʿi-hi-du pa+ti-*	
24.	*sa-ta-ru+ni ʾu-ya-ta-ta la+ki-ti+ma*	
25.	*[li]-ta-li ti-ḫa-ta tu-ʿi la+ki-ti+ma*	
26.	*ha-ki-ʿa+ma ba-yu-ti pa+ti-sa-ta-ru-*	
27.	*[-ni] ʿu-ma ʾa-ka-wa-na+ma ʿu-bu-di*	
28.	*zu-ku-ta la+ki-ti+ma zu-ku-ta d̲u ya-*	
29.	*-ru-ni la+ki-ti ma-na-ma ṯi-ʿu-ʾu+ni*	
30.	*yu-du-ḫu tu-ʾu ʿu-bu-du-tu-ni ka-wa-[ta]*	
31.	*bi-ra-ki ḫu-wu+ma du-ga-la ha+bu-ʾa*	

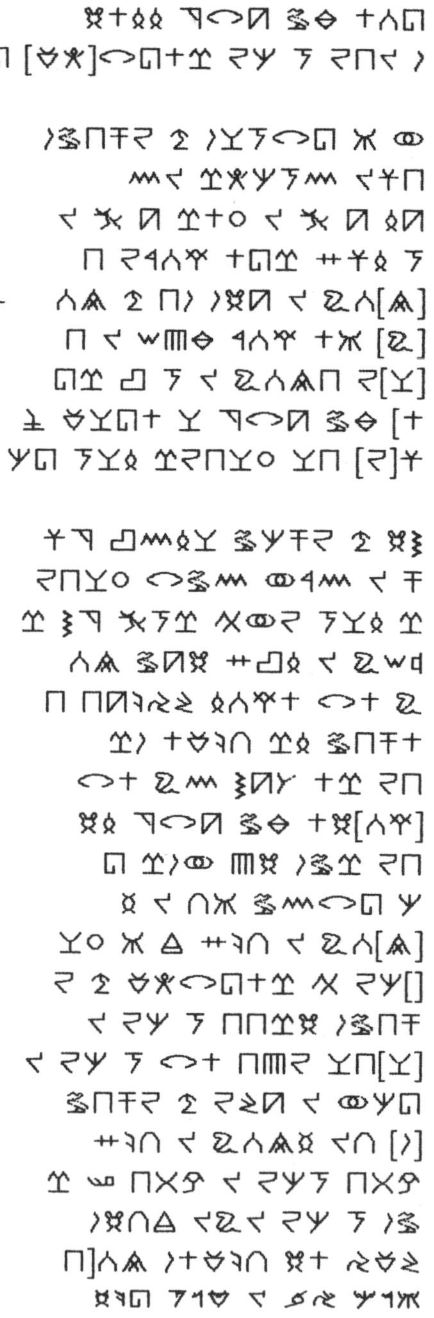

32. *bi+maʿ-bu-du sa-nu-bi tu-ni-bi ma-nu-*
33. *-ya+ma ša-du-da bi+ʾa-ḥu-sa-pa-yi*
34. *[ʾi]-ba-ʿa-ti+hu d̲u ma-la-ki ṣi-*
35. *[ru]-ra pu-la ʾu+ma ha-ḥi-tu-yi*
36. *[? ?] ha li pi ma-ti-ma ra-ha-ʿa*
37. *[ma]-ʾa-la du-ʾa-ʾi+ma yi-yi-ʾi-la ʾu+*
38. *ma la yi-ki-ni-wu+ma+hu pi-ta+ni-ta*
39. *ḥa-wu-bu+ma ta-ḥu-ba+m ba-wa-ʾi+ni*
40. *ta-di-m ʾi-ma la+ki-ti+ya+ma ha-*
41. *[? ?] ḥu-mu-pu[? ?*

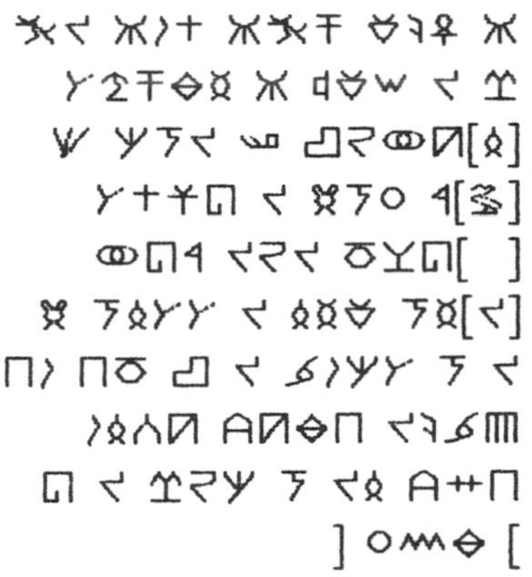

Text D: A free translation.

"The words of Huru–Baʿil. I brought the lands into the covenant to which they have bound themselves submissively because of my mighty deeds. Therefore you shall guard the ordinance of my kingship. Whoever enters honorably among us becomes one with the multitude. Thus the house has become the tribe of Huhash, and they shall be the loyal followers of Huru–Baʿil. Verily you shall beget offspring loyal followers of my dominion. They have made the covenant binding, and therefore may his ancestral deities curse anyone who whispers or does evil against my dominion, harms the covenant, or murmurs, or destroys my power. Those who were deviant have been received and purified as a mighty force; those who take refuge in me are my servitors. (Lines 18–20a not translatable.) Thus they seek length of life. I make them my servants who are in the dominion of the covenant to which they bound themselves by oath. And so, you shall observe the obligations faithfully, to be loyal instead of straying from the covenant, devoted to my household. Furthermore, you shall protect the people whom I have made my servants, who are pure with respect to the covenant, and pure in abiding by the covenant. Those who follow me are submissive, they are marked (and) serving me is great blessing of life. He who enters into the work of making flourish the fruit (of the land). Whoever has done violence to the Ahusapay I will punish. Whoever of my reign becomes hostile and alienated, whether instigating destruction or strife, he shall be cursed with sickness; or whether he fails to be upright in fulfilling our obligations you are guilty. Joining us is (? ?). . . if you act ruthlessly against my covenant."

TEXT D

L.1a: ***ha-wa-tu ḫu-ru+ba-ʿi-lu*** 

"The words of Huru–Baʿilu."

hawatu: is here assumed to be the nom. pl. constr. of Ug. ***hwt*** = Akk. ***awatu***. Unfortunately, the syllabic writing system as deciphered does not enable us to determine whether or not case endings were lost on words standing as the first unit in a construct chain, but since the long final vowel is essential as a marker of plural nouns, it would seem to be a necessary conclusion that the final vowel must have been pronounced in a plural form, and by analogy probably also in the singular form.

ḫuru-baʿilu: is a PN that occurs again in exactly this form at D 10 and 19; both elements of the PN seem to be indeclinable, and it is quite possible that both final vowels are "dead vowels," i.e. not pronounced at all. The word *baʿilu* is evidently a very archaic verbal noun of the same *qatil* form as that better known from such words as *malik* 'king' and *ʿapir* 'transgressor'.

The word *ḫu-ru* occurs so frequently in WS onomastics that it is very difficult to interpret here. Ug. has no attested theophoric names with *ḫr* or *ḫr* in initial position. The root stands alone, however, in the Keret epic name *mṯt ḫry*, which is certainly a hypocoristicon. A very tentative suggestion would link it to the CS *ḫur* 'noble', 'freeborn', derived from an old root *ḫwr* that is preserved in Arab. *ḫawar* 'whiteness', and Syr. *ḫwr* 'garments became white like light'.

From these uses preserved in late sources it is easy to reconstruct a semantic history of a root that originally meant something like 'pure', 'shining', whence then the meaning 'free of vice or legal claims' and thus 'noble' or 'freeman'. Compare Ug. 1005:2 *km.špš dbrt*: 'as the sun is pure' and thus 'free' so is *ṣṯq-šlm*. Cf. Arab. *ḫurru*, almost certainly a LW from Aram. where the loss of the medial *w* caused compensatory lengthening of the final root consonant. Finally, note the *ḫurīs* 'white ones' of Paradise in Islamic tradition.

Consequently, it is most probable that BS *ḫuru-* can be

normalized as *ḫūru<ḫuwru* in keeping with the rule that *w* after the vowel *u* is represented as zero. The name may be regarded as a construct chain of a type well known from Ugarit as well as later Phoenician: *mdd-bʿl* 'beloved of Baal', and *mtn-bʿl* 'gift of Baal'. In the light of the above analogies I would suggest 'Pure One of Baal'.

Ugaritic names such as *ʿbd-ḫr* might suggest the interpretation 'Horus is Lord', but this is improbable for the following reasons: (1) There is no assurance that Ug. *ḫr* designates Horus. (2) As noted above Ug. does not attest names with *ḫr* in initial position. Furthermore names of the type ***DN+ba'al*** do not occur at all. This type consisting of DN + appellative is probably Amorite. (3) Eg. Horus, as W. A. Ward comments, could hardly have been written as *ḫūru* at this time. Further, other than the hieroglyphic forms of the signs, there is no evidence of Egyptian cultural influence in these texts as deciphered. This is further reason for placing them into the period before the powerful Egyptian Twelfth Dynasty.

The introduction to the text immediately is reminiscent of the introductory formula of Hittite suzerainty treaties, e.g.: "These are the words of the Sun, Mursilis. . . ." Particularly after the three forms of the *ʾalif* had been identified, it was unavoidable to identify the following word as a verb in the first person. Royal proclamations in the first person are of course commonplace.

Not until much further progress had been made in the identification of individual words and the recovery of difficult passages did it become increasingly clear that Text D is closely connected with the very long history of covenants in the WS world, and yields evidence for an important and hitherto unsuspected source for the LB Hittite suzerainty form. After all, it was the West Semitic population area that was immediately contiguous to the Hittite Empire.

It is unfortunate that the name of the king is not one attested in our existing sources. It is, however, of good Canaanite form and vocabulary that would further suggest a date prior to the Amoritization of the Byblian dynasty in the nineteenth century at least (cf. OB Sumu–abum, and MB Byblian Yapa–shemu–abi). The theophoric element proves that Baal names are not a relatively late innovation as Albright once suggested.

In view of the fact that Byblos at the time of the Execration Texts had no king or chieftain, Huru–Ba'ilu must be placed a considerable time before the reestablishment of kingship in Byblos, and thus most probably in the closing phases of the Early Bronze Age. We know from an Ur III source that Byblos had an *ensi*, Ib–Dadi, at that time. This name is difficult, but the frequency of names in Ugaritic with the initial element *ib*, plus the fact that it seems entirely foreign to the Syllabic corpus, strongly suggests that the disorders and destruction between 2300 and 2100 B.C. had already been accompanied by the introduction of a new socio–linguistic population element. Finally, the very archaic features of the language would support a very early date, and in addition the fact that there is no sign of the typically Amorite linguistic or onomastic influence makes it fairly certain that the texts stem from EB III cultural horizons.

L.1b–2a: *ʾi–ʾi–tu–ʾu+ni ma–ta–ti la+ki–ti* 

"I brought the lands into covenant."

ʾiʾtuʾu+ni: This is the normalization of the 1 sg. impf. verb + enclitic *–ni* from a root *ʾtʾ* that has survived nowhere else, except in dissimilated form for very understandable reasons. It is the CS root *ʾty* 'come' though there are difficulties of formal, grammatical and semantic nature.

The formal difficulties are the easiest to dispose of. A root *ʾtʾ* is impossible in later West Semitic, and therefore it became dissimilated to *ʾtw* or *ʾty*. As for the grammatical problem of a seemingly intransitive verb followed by a direct object, there is a remarkable parallel in OSA: *wʾtw bslm sbʾ wqtbn* 'and he brought S. and Q. in peace'. With this compare now Deut 33:21, *wytʾ rʾšy ʿm* 'and he brought the chiefs of the people'. Here, curiously enough, the final *alif* has been preserved and the initial one assimilated after the impf. preformative. (The curious spelling *ʾtʾ* in Isa 21:12 is a sixth century Aramaism that is graphic only. There is no reason to think it is actually a phonetic survival of an EB Coastal dialect phenomenon.)

In all three passages we have a transitive use of the verb that is anomalous in the light of later WS usage, but with a radical semantic shift the transitive function of the verb is preserved as normal usage in Akk. *atū* 'to find' < 'come (upon)'. Note the strange semantic parallelism with Ug. *mǵy* and Aram. *mṭʾ* 'to arrive', and SC *mṣʾ* 'find'. A still later development of this root and its usage may be seen in two other SC passages, Gen 34:15, *ʾk bzʾt nʾwt lkm* 'only on this condition will we come in to you' where either later language usage or the much later textual tradition has treated the verb as a medial *waw* root, as it has probably also in II Kgs 12:9, *wy'tw* 'and they entered (i.e. a solemn engagement) not to take money from the people'. Both of these latter passages are perhaps best explained as deriving from a popular etymology of an extremely archaic and rare usage by connecting it with *'wt* 'sign--of a binding promise'. It is not inconceivable that this latter word is itself an archaic dialect variant of the root under discussion.

The remarkable persistence of the idiomatic usage of this verb to mark covenant relationships is illustrated in the Qur'an ii.143: *ya'ti bi-kum jami'an* '(God) will bring you all back to Himself', where the grammarians explain that the verb is transitive by means of the preposition *bi-*. Note also the classical Arabic usage, *'ty 'l-qwm* 'he came to the people', i.e. asserted his relationship while not being of them (Lane, s.v.). Cf. also, *'atiyyun*: 'a man who asserts his relation to a people of whom he is not', and *'ataha*: 'he lay with her'.

The ending *-ni* is just as inexplicable here as it is in Ug.: *aṯbn. ank. wanḫn* 2 Aqhat II 12. In view of this documentation from Ugaritic alone, Friedrich's statement that the *nun paragogicum* is not an old form but comes into Phoenician under Aramaic influence is not easily comprehensible (*PPG* 135b). In this particular passage it seems that the verb form with *-ni* is followed by a main verb with no copula (i.e. *-ma* or *pa-*), and could conceivably be construed as a subjunctive as in OAkk. (Gelb, 170), but the distribution of *-ni* and its occasional duplication *-ni-ni* in BS texts does not encourage such an interpretation.

matati: There are two possible explanations for this word: (1) Preferred here is Akk. *matu* 'land'. (2) Ug. & SC *mut* 'man'. In either case it must be a collective plural form that is the logical subject of the following verb, as well as the object of the preceding verb. If *matu* 'land' is correct, then it must mean the inhabitants of territorial units, not merely geographical phenomena. For this cf. the semantic shift between *'ahl* 'people' and *alu* 'city'.

There is a remote possibility of still a third explanation that is intriguing. In view of the strong tendency in these texts for a weak consonant to be elided at syllable-closing position it is conceivable that there is here another example of the cognate accusative construction that is remarkably frequent in this tiny corpus of texts. Thus the cognate noun *maʾtaʾtu* > *matatu*, and the rendering would be, 'I brought in those brought in'. Again it is curious that Classical Arabic has two words that are remarkably relevant particularly since they seem to be isolated phenomena: *matatun* 'that by which one seeks to bring himself near, an approach', and *matatun* 'anything sacred or inviolable--bond, tie, near relationship' (Lane, s.v.). However the word may finally be explained, it certainly must be the fem. pl. acc. referring to a collectivity of persons who are the subject of the following verb or verbs.

la+ki-ti: for *la+kiynti>kitti*. Cf. Amarna *ki-ti* 'truth, faithfulness, covenant'. Note also the parallel with OSA: *ʾtw bslm = ʾtʾ lkt*. The preposition *l-* has the vowel *a* before the *i* vowel of the following syllable in accordance with the general rule, and as in CS it governs the genitive case.

As a partial parallel to this phrase compare the reports in the Mari archives referring to the establishment of a *salimum* between various social groups. After all a 'covenant' is historically and etymologically a 'coming together', an instrument for social bonding, not merely a 'loyalty oath' that covenants certainly became in the course of the Iron Age and most emphatically not a mere 'theological concept' as it seems to be regarded in most contemporary biblical scholarship.

L.2b–3a: *ya-tu-ha-ʿi-{hi-du} ha-ki-*
(*3*) *-ʿa bi+ha-ʿi-la-li-ni*

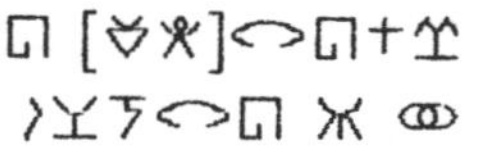

"They have bound themselves by covenant submissively because of my deeds."

yatuhaʿ{hidu}: Though emending the text is hardly a procedure to be recommended in dealing with such an obscure and difficult language, it seems necessary to supply two signs here from line 23 of this text where the six-character verb is clearly a unit, and the following word *ha-ki-ʿa* also occurs as an equally demarked word in line 26 written with enclitic *-ma*. On the other hand, the four-sign group as it stands is impossible to analyze. The scribe or artisan should have written the ✱ *hi* sign but wrote the ◻ *ha* sign instead, which was the initial sign of the following word. Since the two signs have no formal similarity at all, the haplography indicates that the actual inscribing of the text was probably done by a person who was aware of the consonantal values of the signs. The emendation yields unchallengeable grammatical and semantic sense.

Normalized as *yatuhaʿhidu*, the form is analyzed as impf. + reflexive infix *-tu-* + causative infix *-ha-* + 3 masc. pl. suffix *-u* from the root *ʿhd*. The absence of the final *-ni* indicates that this suffix does not function as a plural marker. Classical Arabic uses the same root in the VIth form with the meaning 'make a treaty', *taʿāhada*. In the light of the form attested here and in line 23, it is most tempting to see the Arabic form VI as the result of a metathesis and compensatory lengthening resulting from the loss of the *-ha-* causative infix: *ta-ha-ʿ-hada* > *ta-ʿā-hada*.

On the other hand, SC *hʿyd* exhibits the shift from *h* > *w* >*y* that took place during the second millennium B.C. at varying speeds in various WS dialects, which must have been a very complex and uneven process. We know that the causative impf. in the LB age preferred a thematic vowel *i*. As these texts prove, in the presence of this vowel there is a strong tendency for an original *h/w* to become *y*. SC *ʿedut* is therefore a neologism, while *teʿuda* may well go back to a time when the *w* was still pronounced. Aramaic *ʿade* on the other hand can be explained only on the basis of the BS, Arabic, and OSA *ʿhd* where the *h* had not shifted to *w*, but was represented by zero at the end of a syllable after the vowel *a*.

hakiʿa: This is again a root that is incompatible with later WS phonology. Neither in Ug. nor in SC is an initial *h* root consonant followed by a *k* except in the Sumerian LW *hekal*. The root was barely preserved in Arabic (it is not mentioned in Lane or Dozy), but it does occur in the pre-Islamic *qasida*, and it is regarded by the grammarians as a synonym of *ḫašaʿ*: 'religious submission, fear' (*ṭaj al-ʿarus*, s.v.). Meanings given for it range from 'rest, be quiet, stop, abide' to 'be humble, submissive' and also 'be impatient, grieved, afraid, worried'. All of these meanings except the transferred 'stop, abide' designate internal emotional states that presuppose an external stimulus. In this passage it is identified deliberately as external, political authority.

In view of the observation that this verbal root is impossible in later West Semitic, we need only apply the observed regularities of phonetic change to project a shift from *h,w* to *y*, and from the voiceless to the voiced back consonant to identify here the archaic root that became SC *yagaʿ* 'toil, be weary' and Akk. *egū* 'be negligent'. With this new context of historical semantics, it is possible to see that the traditional translation of this word in SC is a purely formal rendering taken out of its larger context. This is beautifully illustrated in the late but marvelously illuminating passage in Isa

43:22–4, where twice the causative *hʿbd* is placed in parallelism with *hwgʿ* 'place under obligation', or perhaps better 'to cause to submit to'. Cf. also the very concrete passage in Jos 7:3, *ʾl tygʿ šmh ʾt kl hʿm* 'do not draft thither all the people'. In good universal human fashion, the reaction to externally imposed obligation is reflected in Babylonian *egū* 'be negligent'.

The form is here taken to be the adverbial accusative with case ending in *a*, of a *qatil* type of verbal noun. This usage is familiar from Mari *re-qa+mi* and SC *ḥinnam, reqam*.

bi+haʿlali+ni. The preposition *b* takes the vowel *i* before the vowel *a* of the following syllable according to the common rule in these texts. The translation is based upon the assumption that the root is SC *ʿll*, which is used in the Bible almost exclusively with pejorative meaning: 'ruthless, arbitrary deeds' except in a few cases in the Psalms where it refers to the 'mighty acts of God' in parallelism usually to *nplʾwt*: 'wondrous deeds'. The semantic development in biblical Hebrew can easily be traced to the social rejection of the ***LU.GAL*** 'big man' ideology of ancient paganism by which military success constituted grounds for political authority. Though this original and unique religious ideology was later given up in favor of the 'big man' Saul and his successors, the language retained the older polarization.

Though the semantic development in this case is transparent, the grammatical analysis defies solution on the basis of known patterns. First, is the *ha-* prefix a demonstrative or is it a causative preformative? In view of the fact that this root is not attested in Ug., Ph. or Aram., and in view of the fact that SC uses the root as a verb only in the highly irregular forms *ʿolel, ʿolal, hitʿolel, hitʿalel*, most of which are very late (esp. Lamentations), it is very probable that the *ha-* preformative is indeed a causative prefix that has been lost but in the process induced compensatory lengthening of the following vowel. Cf. OSA *whʿlln ʿbdhw . . . mhrgt* 'continue (to grant) slaughters' (*DOSA*, 368). It is exactly the same phenomenon suggested above as the historical connection between BS *yatuhaʿhidu* and Arab. *taʿāhada*, for the *o* of SC *ʿolel* can derive only from an original long *ā*, and this in turn has no grammatical explanation or parallel apart from the Arab. VI form that has already been shown to derive from an assimilated and transposed *h* prefix form.

The function of the enclitic *-ni* is again perplexing. If the sense of the phrase has been correctly grasped, there should be a 1 sg. possessive suffix involved. Possibly the *n* is merely a bridge between the *i* of the genitive case ending and the *i* of the possessive suffix? One would expect *-ya*.

L.3b–4a *pa+ti-sa-ta-ru+ni(4)ta-ḫi-ma* 
mu-la-ki+hi-ya

"And you shall guard the ordinance of my kingship."

pa+: This conjunction that is so well known from Ug., Ya'udi, OSA and Arab. is surprisingly frequent in these texts, in view of the fact that it was evidently replaced in both later Phoenician and Hebrew by the prefixed conjunction *wa-*, which does not occur at all in BS. (It is a curious fact that *pa-* is the most frequent conjunction in Hittite and Luwian––the result of a linguistic "areal phenomenon?") As in the other Semitic languages it has a definite consequential significance in BS: 'and therefore', introducing a clause that is regarded as a necessary sequel to that which precedes.

ti-sa-ta-ru+ni: Two normalizations are possible, depending on the meaning appropriate. First, *tissataruni*, analyzed as a *nifʿal* form with the *n* assimilated to the following *s*, or *tisattaruni* that can only be a D-stem with transitive meaning. This would require that the following phrase be the direct object. The interpretation of *taḫima* is then the main problem, and here also two solutions are possible (see below). If this verb be construed as the N conjugation, then the following word would be the preposition governing the genitive case. Identification with CS *tḥt* is, however, difficult, and the specifically biblical concept of 'taking refuge' under the kingship does not commend itself as a means for interpreting such an archaic text.

On the other hand, the obligation to 'protect' the ordinance of the kingship can hardly be a more archaic and universal concept. For the linguistic usage, Gen 31:49 is very relevant to this passage, even though the N passive is used. The *nissater* of the Jacob–Laban covenant thoroughly presupposes Bronze Age covenant patterns of thought as well as Bronze Age WS linguistic usage, for the 'seeing' (*ṣph*) of God is the means by which the protection (*str*) of each is secured. Cf. also the identical usage in OSA: *bḏ hstr ʾlmqh* "in (the territory) which the god ILMQH protects" (*DOSA*, 347).

There is a very interesting and important contrast between these two verbs, *yatuhaʿhidu* and *tisattaruni*, involving the thematic vowel between the second and third root consonants. As the text has been interpreted, the first verb is a preterite with thematic vowel in *i*, while the second is interpreted as a present–future and it has the thematic vowel in *a*. There is so far too little material in this tiny corpus of texts to justify the conclusion that there is a systematic contrast here analogous to that of Akkadian, but the possibility certainly suggests itself in this particular context, especially since the consequential conjunction *pa*– connects the **past** actions of the king with the **future** obligations of the citizenry. We thus have further indication that the basic structure of biblical covenant thought, as well as that of the Hittites, was already current in political ideology in the Early Bronze Age.

taḫima: *qatil* type noun in acc. case, the direct object of the preceding verb. I identify it with Ug. *tḫm*, which also designates a 'decree' that established kingship: *tḫmk mlkn ʾalʾiyn bʿl ṯpṭn*. Probably the same word survives in Akk., Aram. & Arab. with the meaning 'boundary'. The word developed a semantic history similar to that exhibited in *medīna*: from 'jurisdiction' to 'province': here, from 'decree (of royal legitimacy)' to 'boundary'. This is the ideological and linguistic semantic structure that furnished the base for the concept of the *ʿapiru* as 'one who **crosses** the boundary of legitimate political authority'.

mulaki+hiya: Noun in gen. case + inexplicable *-hi-* + 1 sg. poss. pronoun. The word is of course the *mulk* familiar in much later times: 'dominion, kingship', and cf. also SC *melūkā*. It is a verbal noun of *qutal* type that is exceedingly common in Bronze Age WS. It perhaps could be regarded (as here) as a form that designates states or abstractions, over against the *qatil=malik* type that designates an action. There is probably, therefore, no independent *qutl/qatl* noun form, since these almost certainly resulted merely from the elision of the second vowel, and thus became 'segolates' in the much later SC language.

The infixed *-hi-* is inexplicable from the grammatical inventory of later WS. To speculate concerning various possibilities serves no useful purpose. All that can be said is that the *-ya* is certainly a 1 sg. poss. suffix attached to a noun that is in the genitive case. Perhaps the *-h-* is merely a glide sound inserted between noun and suffix.

L.4b–5: *ma-mu(5)ba-ʾi ba+nu+ma*
pu-tu-ya ba+nu+ma

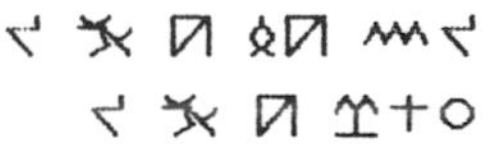

"Whoever enters among us, honorably among us . . ."

mammu. <*man+ma+hu*. Cf. OSA *mnm/mnmw*. The OSA form is evidently the original form that occurs regularly also in Ug. But cf. also *mm* 54:9 'anyone' just as here. In these texts *ma-na-ma* also occurs (D 29) as well as *ma-nu-ya-ma* (D 32–3) and *ma-nu-ma* (C 12). In view of the analysis of the following word, the possibility must be raised that this is a plural form of the indefinite pronoun.

baʾi: for *bā-hi-ʾi*, a gen. pl. participle from the root *bhʾ*>*bwʾ* 'enter'. Again the most archaic form has been preserved in OSA where *bhʾ* means both 'to go in (to a woman)', =SC *bwʾ ʾl*, and 'to become friendly', as also in Arab. and SC: *bsdm ʾl-tbʾ npšy* (Gen 49:6). Cf. also *lblty-bwʾ bgwym hʾlh* (Jos 23:7) 'not to enter (into covenant) with these political entities'. Further, the idiom *bwʾ bbryt* 'enter into covenant', is definitely a neologism (II Chr and Ezr only) based upon a misunderstanding of an old idiom that required a social or personal designation after the preposition.

banu+ma. The preposition has *a* before the *u* of the following syllable in accordance with the general rule. Cf. *bwʾ b-* in the SC passage cited above. Note also the semantic similarity to Lat. ***con+venire***, whence 'covenant'. Possibly 'come in **with** us' would be a closer approximation to the semantic range of the idiom. The enclitic *-ma* seems here to function as a weak conjunction introducing the adverbial qualifying phrase that follows.

putuya banu+ma. This phrase is strange, but not at all inexplicable. If it be taken to be an epexegetic phrase there is no formal or semantic problem. The first word is an adverbial accusative form of a verbal noun that actually occurs in Classical Arabic: *futuwwa(n)*, 'honorableness, generosity'. The root itself has a difficult and peculiar history, and it seems nowhere to have survived except in isolated or secondary usages. Aram. *pty* 'breadth' is likely an isolated survival; SC wisdom literature yields a unique, certainly archaic, proverbial, usage in *wlpth śptyw* 'open wide the lips' Prv 20:19, and the same root is made the base for a popular etymology of the PN *ypt* in Gen 9:27 'make wide'. From 'wide, open', then to the transferred figurative meaning here, it is an easy step to 'simple, foolish' as in English 'simpleton', and 'fool' regularly in the SC wisdom literature. Arabic shows semantic elaboration based on the identification of the simple or open with youth, and thus our word *futuwwa* means not only 'honorableness', but also 'silly, foolish youthful behavior'. Corresponding nouns refer simply to 'youths', but this is the semantic end of the history, like SC 'fool', not its starting point. Cf. also Gk. *haplous*.

The semantic history of the WS root *pty/w* (both are used in Classical Arabic) can be reconstructed as follows: from an archaic, simple word that was more or less the semantic equivalent of *rḥb* on the one hand and used already in the EB period in a figurative, ethical sense, it fell largely out of use except in archaic survivals involving proverbs and fixed idiomatic expressions. Some of these became the base for reelaboration such as 'seduce' in SC, and 'youth(fulness' etc.) in Arabic. Ug. has yielded one possible usage: *ʾil ʾaṯṯm kypt* usually translated as 'when El seduced the two wives', but under the circumstances 'seduce' is hardly the right word (transferred, of course, from much later SC usage). It probably reflects archaic survival of original usage: 'When El **opened** (i.e. sexually) the two wives'. Akk. has a number of idiomatic expressions that are semantically similar, involving the root *petū*.

banu+ma: Form identical to the previous one, but the preposition has a different nuance if the analysis is correct. *pty b-* would mean something like: 'to act toward us in such as a way as to obtain the response' that is introduced with the enclitic *-ma*. The following clause describes the expected or guaranteed consequence.

L.6–7a: *la+ʾi-ḥi-di ya-ha-tu ṯa-wa-ra-ti ta-*
(7) [ka]-wa-na+ma ba-ʾu-ni+ni-ta

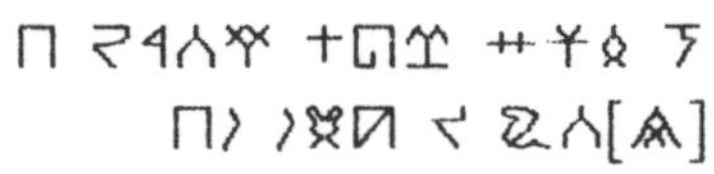

"To a unity of the multitude shall become those who enter among us."

la+ʾiḥidi: Prep. *l-* with the vowel *a* according to rule before a syllable with *i*, + noun *ʾi-ḥi-di* in genitive case following the preposition. The starting point for the interpretation is the stich parallel to the one from Gen 49:6 cited above. After *bsdm ʾl-tbʾ npšy* comes the parallel: *bqhlm ʾl-tḥd kbdy*, thus there is not only a parallel pair, there is also an explanation for the otherwise enigmatic *teḥad*, which has simply lost the initial consonant, doubtless due to the shift from *alif* to *yod*. The root *yḥd* is well attested in SC, and the adverb *yḥdw* presupposes an original verbal noun such as this.

Just as striking a parallel is Deut 33:5:

wyhy byšrwn mlk
bhtʾsp rʾšy ʿm
yḥd šbṭy yśrʾl

And He became king in Jeshurun
when the chiefs of the people came together,
became one the tribes of Israel.

The parallelism of *ʾsp* and *yḥd* makes it clear that the former root is used in the sense found elsewhere as 'take into, receive into' e.g. a house, Jud 19:15,18, or into the community as was Miriam after her temporary ostracism, Num 12:14. Finally the very archaic idiom *nʾsp ʾl ʾbwtyw* implies clearly the archaic pagan concept of 'reunification' with the assembly of deceased ancestors to which Bronze Age burial customs bear most eloquent witness.

The vocalization *ʾiḥid-* is strange, from the perspective of later Semitic usage. It is probably not an accident that the syllabic sign ♁ *ʾi* represents the ox–head with the vertical stroke signifying the numeral 'one' above––and therefore the sign represents the first syllable of the word *ʾiḥid*.

OSA has the prep. phrase *kʾḥd/kwḥd* = SC *kʾḥd* 'as one', but there does not seem to be a parallel to this 'to (become) one' over against 'as one', perhaps because the social phenomenon was too rare to receive a conventional linguistic label. At any rate, the OSA dialects show the process of shift from *ʾalif* to *waw* still in process, but only in SC did the shift go further to *yod*, while the numeral preserved the original *alif*. Cf. also OAkk. *a-na a-ḫa-meš iḫ-ḫi-du+ma* 'unanimously they came to an agreement' (so Gelb ***MAD*** II. cf. ***CAD*** *s.v. ḫadu*). It may be that Karatepe ii, 5f is also relevant here: *lḥdy*. Aram. of course lost the first root consonant entirely: *ḥdy* and added a final weak *y*.

yahatu: This word that occurs also in D 9 is evidently a particle of uncertain function. It is most probable that we have here the archaic source of SC *ʾ(w)t* and Aram. *yt* by a very simple process of eliding the *h* at the end of a syllable after dropping the vowel: *yah(a)tu>yahtu>yat*. The variety of the spellings of the word in various dialect regions reflects well the instability (even in SC!) that is entirely predictable with a word such as this. The medial *ʾalif* was everywhere lost or subjected to the normal shift from *h* to *w/y*. For the shift from *y>ʾ* note the well–attested *yantin*>*ʾentin* of Bronze Age WS. It is conceivable that Ugaritic has preserved one example of this intermediate form in a very difficult mythological text: *ʿbr ʾiht npš mm* where *yahatu*>*ʾehatu*. Aistleitner (1974) takes it to be a mythical DN.

The grammatical and semantic function of the word is obscure. It is not clear whether the following word is gen. sg. or oblique pl. In the other occurrence in D 9 it is followed by the PN which is probably indeclinable since it ends in the nominative case that is incompatible with the grammar, and therefore it must be concluded that the case ending is actually a "dead vowel" not pronounced at all. The word is not really translatable, as in later SC, but it seems to function as an appositional marker such as ***viz*** 'namely'.

ṯawrāti: Probably gen. fem. sg. form of *ṯwr* 'bull' used as an abstraction to designate a social group. It is in apposition to the preceding noun *ʾiḫidi*, and therefore has the same case ending. The word is paradoxical from the point of view of later grammar——what can a female 'bull' be?——but it illustrates the thesis, if not fact, that the contrast between 'feminine' and 'masculine' in archaic WS has little or nothing to do with gender or sex contrasts, rather with perhaps concrete vs. abstract usages, or some such concept.

For the semantic development, note the parallelism in Semitic:
Akk. *luʾu* (WS LW) 'bull' > *līmu* 'eponym' > *līmu* '1000'.
WS *lʾm* *'bull' > '(deified?) ancestor' > 'people'.
WS *ʾalpu* 'ox' >*ʾaluf* 'chief', *ʾelef* 'social unit' >'1000'.
WS *ṯwr* 'bull' > Arab. 'lord, master, chief' (OSA: designation of the deity *Ilmqh*)> Arab. *ṯawratun*: 'a great number'.

The word here certainly designates the social unit that Huru–Baʿil claims to have brought into existence. This constant transference from the 'bull'='head of the herd' to the herd itself must be an extremely old linguistic convention. Cf. Ug. where *ṯwr* is also used to designate social authority figures, and by transference from social designation, *ṯwr*/*ʾlp* is a constant appellative of deity in virtually all ancient societies in one context or another. As an interesting aside, note that the SC *rʾm* and its Ug. and Akk. cognates almost certainly derive from a very archaic dialect variant of *lʾm*, in view of the frequent interchange of *l*/*r*/*n* in Semitic. It is also an interesting commentary on early Israelite religious ideology, that *rʾm* became a symbol of utter evil——the wild bull, which ended up as the 'unicorn' in medieval European ideas about the biblical words.

ta/ka/wana+ma. Pres.–fut. of root *kwn* with enclitic *+ma* for which no function is discernible. The construction *kwn l–* is an exact semantic parallel to SC *hyh l–*, but here there is the reversed word order no doubt for the sake of emphasis familiar from later SC texts. The preformative can be either the 3 pl. already abundantly attested in other sources, or a continuation of the 2 pl. direct address: 'you who enter to us'.

baʾuni+nita: Pl. participle, nom. case + *–ni* and very probably an oblique 1 pl. suffixed pronoun. It is evidently the subject of the preceding verb, and recapitulates the indefinite pronoun *ma–mù ba–ʾi* at the beginning of the sentence.

The background of what is described here is exactly what is given us in the Execration Texts: *wḥyt kbn* 'the tribes of Byblos'. What is happening is the formation of a large social unit under the leadership of the author of the text who evidently claims the title 'king'. The large social unit is evidently comprised of a number of smaller units that had 'entered', and as we see now, such terminology is scattered all across the Semitic languages, though sometimes usages are almost entirely separated from the original primary semantic base. The process is analogous, but far from identical of course, to that involved in the formation of a *ben ʿameh* among Bedouin, which has been described by Jaussen (*Coutumes*, p. 149ff). As in so many other traits, Bedouin have preserved customs and cultural traits that originated in very ancient urban and village cultures, e.g. swearing an oath of alliance on a sword: cf. swearing oaths *maḫar patrim ša aššur* in the Old Assyrian tablets.

Part of the point of the *ben ʿameh* is the fact that they become by definition blood relatives, and real kinship has nothing to do with the alliance. It is a device for transfering the loyalties of the kin group to a larger society, and when this was done in ancient society as in many modern simple cultures, the new 'brotherhood' was given a common ancestor by constructing a new 'genealogy'. The common ancestor often gives his name to the 'tribe' (or vice versa!), and soon is given historical 'reality' by all sorts of narratives that are derived from traditional motifs and themes, exactly like the 'lives of the saints' in medieval Christianity and Buddhism.

The extremely close linguistic and semantic ties to early Hebrew poetry in this text is astounding, entirely unexpected, and as a matter of fact undiscovered until a decade after the decipherment began to show results. The parallelism of *bwʾ* and *y/ʾḥd* can now be added to the many 'parallel pairs' that biblical poetry inherited from the Bronze Age language. It is very tempting to conclude that the terminology actually derives from marriage customs and terminology, and conversely biblical concepts of marriage derive also from the linguistic parallelism: a man 'comes in' to a woman and they 'become one' flesh. Similarly, marriage has been long before the dawn of history a principal means by which relationships were established between non–kinbound social units or groups.

7b–8a: *pa+ka-wa-(8)[na] bi-tu ṯa-wa-ra ḥu-ḥa-ša+ma* 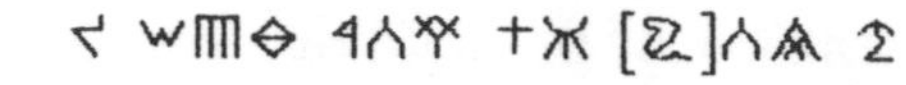

"And the house has become the tribe of *ḥuḥaša*, and . . ."

pa+kawa[na]: Again the translation reflects the word analysis. The loss of the final syllable of the verb at the beginning of D 8 leaves however, no conceivable restoration other than the usual final *-na* of the copula–verb, for there is room only for one sign. The verb form is the 3 masc. sg. perf. form of the common later WS root, but it might be better to regard it as a sort of 'stative' that acts nevertheless as a copula, equating *bitu* in the nominative case with the noun *ṯawara* in the accusative: identical to the treatment in classical Arabic. This analysis implies, however, that the following noun *bitu* is construed as masc. gender––unless the 3 sg. as well as probably 3 pl. in this dialect had a 'common' gender, which is not at all impossible.

bitu: The only possibility that presents itself without inventing a new word is *bay(i)tu>betu*, though *bi-(iy)-tu*, actually occurs in Arabic, but is certainly a specialized derived word. I have no explanation for the word, and for the fact that it is evidently construed as a masculine noun (for which one parallel exists in SC Prv 2:18, usually regarded as a textual error). On the other hand, the curious fact that the word takes a masculine plural, may just have some correlation with other very archaic linguistic traits. The ***editio princeps*** read the sign ♈=*ya* here, but the Infra–Red Ektachrome and autopsy make the reading ⋊= *bi* virtually certain.

ṯawra: Sg. form of the noun discussed above, D 6, and in the accusative case after verb ***kawana*** in accordance with the rule in classical Arabic, to indicate the predicate.

ḥuḥaša+ma: Here taken to be a tribal name——the designation of the new socio–political unit that had come into existence. It is in the accusative case, evidently in apposition to the preceding common noun. It is again an impossible form in later WS, but curiously enough, it actually occurs in Ug. One cannot help but speculate that it is a very archaic form metathesized from the root *ḥšḥ* 'desire'. For the semantic content cf. the common name *Maḥmud*; for the form cf. *no‘am*.

This line deals with a particular 'house' that must designate some kind of socio–political unit. The line confers upon it the status of the *ṯawar* of *ḥuḥaš*, under the king as the following lines abundantly indicate. It is suggested that it is precisely social phenomena such as this that gave rise to such place names as *bt–šmš*, and many others characterized by the word *byt* followed by a PN, usually a divine name. Could *ḥuḥaš* possibly be a divine name or appellative? At this time and place the possibility that the name was that of a deified or even fictitious ancestor deserves consideration.

L.8b–10a: *ta–(9)[li]–ti ta–ka–wa–na+ma la+hu*
ya–ha–(10)[tu] ḥu–ru+ba–‘i–lu

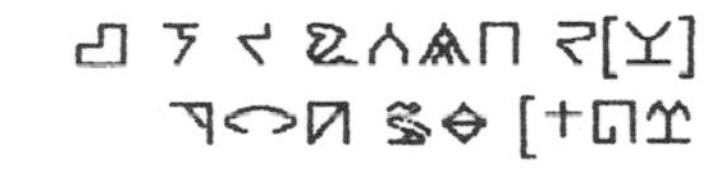

"they shall be for him dependents, namely, for Huru–Ba‘ilu."

ta[li]ti takawana+ma la+hu: One sign is missing at the beginning of D 9, and there are few reasonable possibilities for the missing consonant + vowel. The form is probably the acc. pl. predicate of the copula verb *kwn*, so that the subject is understood to be the *bitu* of the preceding sentence as a collectivity of persons. In view of the verbal noun *ta–li* of D 11, it is possible to read *ta<li>ti* in the sense of Eth. 'be devoted to', or perhaps here 'be dependent upon', and even OSA *tlw* 'follow', > 'be tributary to', > 'follower, servant, officer'.

yahatu ḥuru+ba‘ilu: The phrase seems to be included to specify the referent of preceding *la+hu*. If so, then the deictic function of the curious particle *yahatu* is further supported, and the construction is also compatible with the grammar illustrated at D 6.

The clause is probably a definition of the status of the group vis–a–vis Huru–Ba‘ilu, particularly in view of the stipulations that follow in succeeding statements. For the concept involved in *taliti*, compare the famous Mari letter (*Syria* 19 [1938]: 117) where 10 or 15 kings 'walk after'

Hammurapi, 15 kings after Rim–Sin of Larsa, . . . and 20 kings after the king of Yamkhad. Thus this word that continues in use with very similar meaning is the semantic equivalent of the Amorite/Inland dialect *hlk ʾḫry*. It is interesting that SC used the root only in the primitive meaning 'to hang', while the Inland Dialect idiom *hlk ʾḫry* continued to be used in SC to designate political dependency, particularly with reference to deity in Deuteronomy.

L.10b–lla: *li+tu-ha-li-du gu-*
(11)-ḫi-[ti] ta-li pu-li-ta-ti+ya

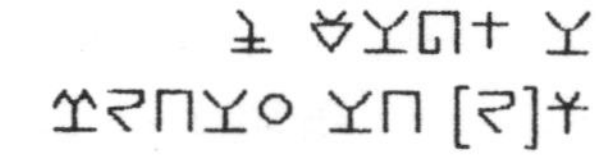

"Verily you shall beget offspring, dependents of my dominion."

li+[tu]halidu: Only a portion of the top horizontal bar of the second character is preserved, but this reading is the most probable, even though it produces unknown grammar. The *li+* prefix can hardly be the preposition before a finite impf. verb form. It is most probably the precative *lu+* dissimilated to *li+* before the following syllable with the *u* vowel. At any rate, there is hardly an alternative reading and interpretation possible to the verb *tuhalidu*, the 2 pl. collective causative of the root *w/yld*. The problem is that the initial consonant has disappeared without a trace. Either *waw* or *yod* would have to be written after the *a* vowel––but *he* would not! Do we have here another extremely archaic original *h* that later shifted in all dialects to *w>y*? The spelling then would be consistent with other cases of these weak consonants being represented by zero after a homologous vowel: *tuhahlidu>tuhālidu*, which normally would result in the lengthening of the vowel, and therefore in Iron Age SC would become *holid*.

guḫi[ti]: This word is unparallelled, but the root is well known though rare and clearly obsolescent in Iron Age Semitic. The first sign read here and several other passages as *gu-* is an illustration of the results of comparing unknown signs with unassigned syllabic values in the context. Since the context is determined by the preceding verb, 'beget' or 'give birth' the following word should have something to do with the results. The root *gwḥ* in SC has to do almost exclusively with wombs and springs. It has not been attested in OSA or Ug., though there are five PNs that could have the root.

In the first place, there is no doubt that the very ancient name of the spring at Jerusalem *giḥon* derives from this root, and the name of the river of primordial paradise in Gen 2:13 is probably derived from the same name, particularly since it is associated with the land of *kš*, and this in turn is associated with Jerusalem where already in the Amarna period the king had *kaša* enemies (and Moses had a *kšyt* wife, later identified as Ethiopian.)

Secondly, this passage may throw light on the difficult verse of Ps 22:10, where two participles refer to the functions of deity with reference to the king. The first stichos *ky ʾth gwḥy mbṭn* has to do with divine action in the birth of the king, while the second refers to the giving of security at the mother's breast. It would be normal to translate this stichos 'for Thou art my begetter from the womb'—and there is no reason to think this ideologically impossible in view of Ps 2:7b. In any case, it is entirely unnecessary to emend the text as virtually all commentators have done in order to force the meaning into a preconceived tradition.

The supplied final syllable *-ti* is one of the very few in the syllabary that is compatible both with the low diagonal trace sloping to the right that is visible on the copper plate, and with the grammar necessary in the context: an oblique plural ending that marks the direct object of the preceding verb. Note the parallelism to *ta/li/ti* of D 8–9. In both cases the fem. pl. ending designates collectivities as abstract entities, and it is such usages that seem very frequent in these texts that probably account for the 3 masc. pl. impf. verb preformative with *t-*.

tali: A verbal noun from the root *tly* used above, but here in the masc. pl. oblique case describing the characteristics of the preceding noun: 'dependent, devoted'. The form also illustrates the fact that 'gender' agreement is not necessary formally, for the two verbal nouns have different functions, and the second is not a mere 'adjective' modifying the first.

pulitati+ya: This word recurs in exactly the same form at D 13, and perhaps without the 1 sg. pron. suffix at D 22–3. It is translated from contexts that leave no reasonable alternative. At the same time, no clear etymon or even later descendant has been found. From the form, it should be a fem. verbal noun from a root *plt*, which does not exist. Even the vocalization of *qutilat-* is strange, since it falls together with the Qal passive of later WS. It is very attractive to see in this word the (unstable—and therefore not preserved in this form) root *ply/ʾ*, that in Iron Age WS becomes differentiated into OSA *fly>flytn* 'oracular response; ordinance (established by oracle?)' which fits perfectly here in the sense that it refers to the 'divine charter' political theology whereby the political head derives his authority from the decision of a god. On the other hand, the SC root *plʾ>nplʾwt* 'wonder, miracle' became separated from political functions in order to refer directly to divine acts and functions. But cf. classical Arabic *flt>faltatun* 'sudden or unexpected event'.

The word can therefore be construed as *puli(y/ʾ)* +-*t*- designating an abstraction (later -*ut*) + fem. ending in gen. sg. or pl., more likely the latter. The coincidence with the vocalization of the later passive form is accidental: it could well be the very common *qutal* noun form with the second vowel shifted to *i* under the influence of the root consonant *y* represented as zero after the *i* vowel.

It is quite clear that we have here an extremely archaic linguistic usage that gives expression to the "mandate from heaven" political theology. It is also most significant that in the same sentence there is reference to the "be fruitful and multiply" theme that crops up in the Creation story: another example of the transference and radical transformation of very ancient cultural traits from political to religious and transcendent contexts. For the lowest common denominator of political power structures is the determination to have the largest population base possible in order to maintain and extend the area of political and economic control, and the most natural (and usually peaceful) means is of course by increasing the birth rate. The symbol for the process is of course the "mother goddess" the symbol of productivity--of population (cf. Ug. *ybmt lʾmm*), as well as wealth in the form primarily of agricultural products.

L.11b–12a: *ʾi-li-la ha-ki-(12)mi-ʾu*
pa+ti-sa-ki-ru li-ʾi-mu+hu

"They have made binding the compact. So may his ancestral gods curse . . ."

ʾi-li-la: For *ʾilla*?--the second *i* vowel is then a 'dead vowel' as observed so frequently in these texts. For form and meaning cf. Arab. *ʾill*- 'compact, covenant, relationship', and by sequential semantic development, > 'lordship'. This word seems to be an isolated lexical item in classical Arabic: there is no verbal root associated with it and no cognate words. It thus gives every indication of being a very archaic and isolated survival. Cf. also OB *ʾilu* 'written agreement' that *CAD* derives from *eʾelu* 'hang up, bind'.

There are a number of variants of this root in Semitic as the examples cited above show. If the starting point were the doubly weak verb of Akk., then it is not difficult to see its modification to a doubled root *ʾll* in BS, and further development to CWS *ʾlh* 'curse'.

hakimiʾu: Probably there is a 'dead vowel' after the first root consonant. Thus we have a classic causative 3 pl. perf. verb *hakmiʾu* following the dir. obj. Thus the *haqtil* form of WS is an extremely archaic form that survived from the EB period in local dialects from Palestine to South Arabia where also the /h/ causative is attested.

The semantic content and later history of the verb is difficult. Since the root *kmʾ* survived nowhere else in WS (everywhere it designates 'truffles'), and since also later WS had very few words with the initial consonants *k+m*, there is a strong suspicion that there was a phonetic shift involved, particularly in view of Akk. *kamū* 'bind'. The later WS languages preserved the root in the form *klʾ/y* 'restrain' and the like. The semantic content of the phrase is then entirely appropriate: 'they caused the oath/compact to be binding'.

pa+tisakkiru: This is a beautiful example of the sequential significance of the prefixed conjunction *pa+*: 'and therefore (as a consequence)'.

The following verb can only be construed as a D–stem preterite (with thematic vowel in *i* not *a*), functioning here as an 'optative', an expression of both a wish and a consequence. Again the *ti–* prefix is associated with a plural/collective subject, though the defective nature of the writing system makes proof impossible. If the subject *liʾimu* were actually sg., it would have to be feminine gender, which seems inherently very improbable.

The semantic substance and history of the verb is especially interesting and equally complex. It illustrates both a form and a meaning that is so archaic that it probably goes back to the time before the separation of the Semitic and Indo–European language families. Like the word for 'bull' (*ṯwr*), this word has equally good Semitic and IE etymons: cf. Etr.>Lat. ***sacri/sacni>sacer*** and Gk. ***hagios/hagnos***.

Common Semitic *skr* 'to close (up or in)' is the basis for the development to the meaning 'cursed'––i.e. **delivered** over to the power of the deity for punishment. Cf. the parallel meaning of Lat. ***sacer*** and WS *ḥaram*. Later WS underwent a semantic specialization, for 'to close' became *sgr* already by the LB Age, as in Ugaritic. Most curiously, the OSA and

Classical Arabic seem to have lost the verb entirely, except in modern colloquial where *sakkar al-bab* still means 'shut the door'. An entire dissertation could easily be written on the semantic history of this and cognate roots, ending up with the 'binding and loosing' of the NT texts and the ***sacramentum*** of the early Christian church.

liʾimu+hu: The ***editio princeps*** read the sign ꕤ *ʾi* before this word. The reading is understandable, but wrong. The copper plate and the infra-red color photograph show only a part of the upper left curve of the sign--which was deliberately left incomplete. What probably happened was that the scribe started to write *ʾi-li-* 'god' but what the text required was *li-ʾi-mu*. Since there was no way to erase the false start, the sign was simply left incomplete and the proper sign written in the next space.

The word is of course to be identified as Ug. *lʾim*, SC *lʾum*, and Akk. and Mari *līmu*. Like CS *ʾalp-* the word means both some kind of social unit, and 'thousand'. The semantic process almost certainly stems from uses attested from Ug. to Palmyran and survives in recent Bedouin usage by which the head of a social group is designated as 'bull' or 'ram'. The usage is of course transferred from herds dominated by the most powerful male to organized societies. From the designation of the leader the term was expanded to signify the entire unit over which he presided. Exactly the same semantic process is involved in the SC transference from the *šbṭ* as the 'marshal's baton' of authority (Jud 5:14) to the 'tribe' over which the *sōfēr* presided.

The parallelism of usage between *ʾalp-* and *lʾim* points to an earlier meaning 'ox' for the latter word that occurs only in Akk. from OB on, and presumably, therefore, derives from a local Amorite dialect of the EB period. However, cf. the CS *lʾtu* '(wild) cow'. It is most probable that the words *rʾim* and *lʾim* eventually go back to a common origin in some very remote dialect, and the two words became differentiated semantically perhaps already in prehistoric times. There are few phonetic changes more frequent than the *l/r* interchange. Curiously, where we have evidence, WS languages kept them carefully distinguished: e.g. where Ug. has *lʾim* and *rʾum*, SC has *lʾum* and *rʾim*.

Though we have evidence for the designation of social heads as 'bulls' in both Ug. and SC it is highly likely that under a sophisticated political organization with a corresponding elaboration of titles, such old grass-roots terms stemming from village agricultural life were regarded as undignified and rustic. Both *ṯwr* and *rʾum* are used as titles only in the mythical and legendary texts of Ugarit. In SC the same process may be observed. The old premonarchic poem of Deut 33, vs 17 has a cluster of words that derive from these extremely archaic language and thought patterns:

bkwr šwrw 'firstborn of his bull' correlates with BS *ṯawra. . .tuhalidu guḫi*;

qrny rʾm qrnyw correlates with Ug. *bhm qrnm km ṯrm*;
yḥdw with *laʾiḫidi*;
ʾlpy mnšh with *ṯawra ḫuḫaša*.

Later uses of *rʾm* in SC are almost exclusively pejorative as symbols of ruthless power uncontrolled by ethical principle. One of the most interesting such usages is in the exilic passage of Isa 34:7 where the 'wild bulls' of the sacrifice of Edom cannot be separated from the *ʾlwpy* of Gen 36:15 that designates the tribal chiefs of Edom. In Exod 15:15 also *ʾlwpy ʾdwm* is parallelled by *ʾyly mwʾb* 'rams of Moab'.

Since there can be no doubt that the various terms for 'bull' designated also persons in positions of social authority all over the ancient world, it remains to justify the translation 'ancestral gods', or better, 'deified ancestors'. First, it is certain that the *liʾimu* here must designate some sort of supernatural power capable of imposing punishment as indicated in the curse. Except for Mari and now Ebla royal names, there is virtually no other evidence for a deity 'Lim'. However, in the context of this BS passage, the *ti-* preformative of the verb virtually proves that the noun is a collective, if not an actual plural, and the collectivity of deceased ancestors is by far the most reasonable interpretation of the word. It is they——those supernatural powers most intimately connected with the persons bound by the covenant!——that are thought to be observing and capable of bringing reward and punishment to their living descendants.

In the Bronze Age there is abundant direct and indirect evidence for this concept, including Byblos itself. First the fact that the *kispu* funerary banquet for the deified (?) ancestors seems to have been a powerful compulsion in the royal house of Mari, and one wonders whether this cult of the ancestors was not already an obsolescent survival in the royal court ritual——for which there are innumerable parallels throughout the history of politics. The Obelisk Temple at Byblos itself with its steles including the 'naos' type so familiar from Egypt, can hardly represent anything other than the collective cult of ancestors in which the obelisks represented the permanent petrification of the 'souls' of the deceased. This concept still lives on in some central African tribes, but it is illustrated in the pyramid capstone of Amenophis III with its inscription that specifically identifies that stone with the person of the deceased king, and represents his eyes in relief. Underlying much later linguistic idiom is doubtless the same concept such as in some Aramaic inscriptions where *nbš* 'soul' actually means 'tombstone'.

Probably archaic idiomatic expressions such as SC 'be gathered to his *ʿm*' or 'fathers', discussed above, stems from the same complex of funerary rituals and concepts. It would seem very probable that the phrase 'god of my father' (singular!) originally designated the actual deceased father, and only later with the demise of the old mortuary customs was the phrase reinterpreted to the now familiar 'God of your fathers'. It is very probable that the connection between the bull and the deceased in ritual is illustrated already in the curious Anatolian pre–pottery Neolithic cultic installations that include the bull, the fertility goddess giving birth and the vultures' skulls. The identification of the 'souls' of the deceased with birds is also a quite frequent phenomenon.

The constant epithet 'bull' applied to El in Ug. myth as well as similar terms in virtually every other ANE culture probably derives, therefore, from very remote and archaic concepts of the continuing power of a deceased social leader, which concept was then transferred to transcendent deities with the development of less kin–bound political societies and states. As anthropologists have pointed out, even in modern primitive societies the death–cult is no mere 'superstition'. On the contrary, it is a ritual means by which societies maintain or attempt to maintain the existing fabric of social and political structures, and to confer political legitimacy on those existing structures.

As one final note, there is good reason to believe that a parallel conceptualization of the function of the deceased was also preserved in linguistic idiom, long after its original meaning was forgotten. The strange references to the *rpʾm* in SC, and in Ug. myth stems from a more sophisticated political conceptualization of the function of the deceased. The *rapiʾu* (as in *ʿmrpʾi = ḫammu-rapiʾ*) or *rubaʾu* (frequent in Old Assyrian texts) are certainly archaic local dialect variants of the CS *rb* 'great one, lord'. But the deification of the king after his death is also known from Anatolia, Ugarit, and Egypt, and therefore he becomes one of the Rephaim, a term for 'ghosts' that survived long after the actual term had fallen out of usage as the designation of a living ruler. Old Assyrian regularly used *rubaʾum* as the term for 'prince' in Anatolian societies, and it is very probable that the Philistines continued that usage in early Iron Age Palestine. Note the repeated *hrph* in 2 Sam 16:16–22. In spite of all the romantic speculation about 'giants' or 'shades', the term is nothing more or less than a local dialect variant of *rb* that was used as a semantic equivalent for *baʿal* 'lord' who continued use of his title after his demise, no doubt especially in the funerary rituals.

L.12b–14a: *lu-ḫi-(13)-sa+ma mu-ra-ʿa mu-ru-ʿi*
pu-li-ta-ti(14)+ya

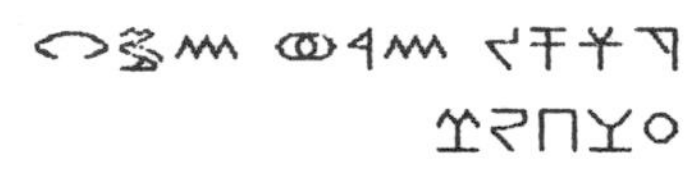

"the whisperer and the evildoer of evil–doing of my dominion."

luḫisa: The meaning is well attested in CS 'whisper' esp. in connection with incantations and the cult of the dead. It is the direct object (together with the following phrase) of the preceding verb, but the vocalization of the form is enigmatic. There can hardly be any doubt that it as well as the following word is an active participle, but the *qutil* form is attested in later WS only as a passive. One would expect *lāḫis-*, and though spellings with *u* for original long *ā* are found already in Amarna, e.g. ʼ*zu-ki-ni* for *sōken*, it is difficult to believe that the shift *ā*>*ō* had taken place this early in the Coastal Dialect of WS. There is no alternative explanation, however, and the sign readings, the grammatical construction, and semantic context converge to demand either this conclusion or some other explanation still unknown. It is entirely possible that the long *ā* was pronounced with a vowel darkening that made plausible its representation with the *u* vowel.

The implications of the 'whispering' are quite interesting, for it illustrates the constant insecurities of politicians who already in the Early Bronze Age cannot tolerate opposition. It is reasonably certain that the 'whispering' here refers not merely to private 'murmuring' but to appeals to supernatural forces (perhaps family deified ancestors?) to act against the political powers, in other words, a curse. Note also the oldest SC lawcode of Ex 22:28, which prohibits cursing the highest social authorities of the time: deity, and the *nasiʾ*. As late as Thucydides (Bk.v, 103) it was a well recognized pattern of behavior that "when visible grounds of confidence forsake them, (men) have recourse to the invisible, to prophecies and oracles and the like, which ruin men by the hopes which they inspire in them." At this early stage, however, there was still sensitivity to the possible deleterious consequences of appeals to the "invisible," and therefore the selfsame "invisible" forces are called upon to punish any appeal to them against the legitimate king.

muraʿa muruʿi: Lit. 'evil–doer of evil–doing'. The ***figura etymologica*** here involves two verbal nouns, the first the agentive "participle" indicating the actor, and the second the action. The first is in the accusative case since it is the object of the verb *tisakiru*, and it is followed by an oblique case verbal noun in a "construct chain." The forms are also interesting particularly in view of the perfect tense form in D 36: *ra–ha–ʿa*. This proves that the verbal root was of the same class as the "hollow verbs" (*ʿayin–waw*) of later WS, and presumably there was at this time an alternation between *h/w* and even *y*, depending upon vowel and syllable position. The agentive verbal noun has to be a derived stem, since the Qal would presumably be stative, not taking a direct object, and further the prefix *mu–* was not used for the Qal participle until very late times. There is no alternative to the interpretation of the form as a causative, for the D–stem would have protected the medial consonant. Assuming an elision or absence of the *–ha–* causative prefix after the participle prefix *mu–* the normal form would have been *murhaʿ =muqtal*. With the elision of the medial consonant, the form becomes exactly that written: *mu–ra–ʿa*. SC *meraʿ* could be accounted for in many ways including the well attested shift from *u* to *i* in the prefix, but it is evidently a neologism. Of the original *ʿayin–he/waw* root nothing is left in SC except the poorly attested derived noun *roʿ*. The alleged root *rʿʿ* is purely a figment of the grammarians' system–building.

The cognate genitive noun *muruʿi* is more difficult. One would expect a noun with the *m–* prefix to be vocalized with the vowel *a*, but the same sign is used and therefore the same vocalization as on the participle form. Since it is a **transitive** verbal noun, i.e. 'evil doing' not 'evil being', presumably for this reason it takes the preformative used in cognate stem forms. The case ending can be construed in two different ways: first, used in the translation here, is to regard it as in the (later) 'construct chain' syntactical relationship to the first––and therefore in the genitive case. This is perhaps most natural to our thinking, especially because of an extremely similar locution esp. in the Psalms: *pʿly ʾwn* 'workers of iniquity'. It could just as easily be regarded however as the verbal agent transitive noun followed by its direct object in the oblique plural case.

pulitati+ya: See the discussion above at line D 11.

In Ps 41:8 there is a parallelism of *ytlḥšw* and *yḥšbw rʿh*, and so another 'parallel pair' of biblical religious poetry finds its origins in the political conceptualizations of the Early Bronze Age. In addition, there is also the utilization of participles in a context of proscribed patterns of behavior that is continued in what has over–hastily been termed the 'apodictic' participial form, familiar from the more archaic sources of the early biblical tradition.

It is further of significance that these EB concepts are continued in modified form elsewhere as well. If the interpretation of this text is correct, then the 'gods of the *ʿapiru*' of the Hittite suzerainty treaties are a conceptual parallel, nearly a thousand years later. Instead of the kin–group or clan deities, the nonestablished deities that outlaw groups would have to rely upon are invoked also to sanction the treaty. In both cases, it is the subjects' own supernatural patrons who oversee the adherence to obligations. The two actions stipulated here as subject to curse and also in the above cited Psalm 41, are two stages actually of a unitary process. First, there is the (ritual?) invoking ('whispering') of supernatural powers against the political regime combined no doubt with an appeal for divine protection. Second, is the actual engaging in acts of violence which are thus thought to have divine approval and protection. The development of both political and religious thought in the ancient world is thus illustrated in first the enlargement of the social unit from the kin group of the *leʾum* to the territorial state, and secondly the appeal to the gods to control the behavior of their own devotees vis–a–vis outside groups or authorities. It is in this respect that ancient religious and political development shows considerable sophistication, over against the usual tendency to regard nothing but 'national self–interest' as an adequate ground for the establishment and implementation of national foreign policy. What we have here is the beginning of the ability to see that certain types of behavior are intrinsically wrong––just as the deity is a factor that has an existence apart from the social group and its ephemeral 'interests' and desires.

This problem is very much involved in the contrast between the biblical and extra–biblical ancient near eastern concepts of the historical process, but it cannot be further explored in this context. The whole problem of the nature of the "gods" is intimately associated with the problem of understanding how to make predictable––or reciprocally, how to feel secure in the predicament of arbitrary unpredictability––the manifold phenomena of violent nature and more violent humanity. It is this, and not some abstract metaphysical speculation about divine 'essences' that constituted——and constitutes——the foundation of religious life and thought.

L.14b: *ʾi-li-la ti-ʿa-ṯu ya-la-nu* 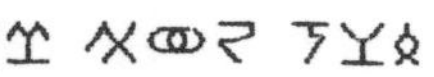

"The compact they injure, they grumble . . ."

ʾilla tiʿaṯu: The construction is identical to the phrase at D 11, 12, but with the verb in the pres–fut. instead of the preterite. The verb is cognate to Arabic *ʿaṯa* 'act corruptly', and probably Mari and OB *ešū* 'tangled, confused, troublesome'. The latter is probably closer to Arab. *ʿaṯaw/ya* 'act corruptly, do mischief, injury' but in any case the two Arabic roots are certainly doublets——dialect variants of the same original root. At any rate, the verb is transitive, if the interpretation of *ʾilla* is correct, and it would be perhaps better to construe it therefore as a D–stem: *tiʿaṯṯuwu>tiʿaṯṯu*, since the Qal seems elsewhere to be a stative/intransitive. The root, preserved in Amorite>OB and Arabic seems to have become obsolete elsewhere in WS.

The syntax of this clause is also very difficult, since there is no conjunction or other sign of a connection or a juncture separating or tying it to the preceding phrase. It seems to indicate a complete stop after the preceding word, for there is a change of subject and a change of person and number. There would seem to be a deliberate parallelism between the *ʾilla hakmiʾu* above, and the *ʾilla tiʿaṯu* here. There is also a hiatus between this phrase and the finite verb following; one would expect at least the weak *-ma*. It was tempting to interpret the *ʾilla* here as the Arab. *ʾilla* 'if', but this is even more difficult especially in the earlier occurrence of the word, and the Arab. itself seems definitely to be a new formation from *ʾin + la*.

yalānu: Probably for *yalhanu* where the medial *h* has dropped without visible compensation. It is certainly SC *lwn* which is a very archaic survival, since it occurs only in connection with the events of the Sinai Desert wanderings, and in the narrative of the covenant with the Gibeonites. It seems that the word was embedded in the original narrative or tradition of those events at the very beginnings of ancient Israel, and therefore was preserved in those two contexts only without becoming incorporated into the lexical inventory of the later language of actual usage. Though no CS cognates have been pointed out, the occurrence in this text indicates an extremely ancient origin both in form and meaning. As in the biblical tradition also, 'grumbling' or complaining against established authority is a violation of covenant only if there has already been acceptance of the suzerainty of the overlord. It seems certain that there is a cognate in Arab. *lama*, inf. *lawm* 'blame, censure, reprehend'. A shift from *n* to *m* has taken place, and the meaning 'blame, censure' is certainly much more appropriate than the traditional biblical rendering 'murmur'.

It is another indication of the complexity of the grammar of this archaic dialect that the first verb has a *ti-* preformative for what seems to be a 3 pl. impf., while the second verb has a *ya-* preformative. Could there be a deliberate distinction between the corporate, collective breach of covenant and the specific act of any individual——the distributive plural? It is not beyond the realm of possibility, particularly since the *ti-* preformative is fairly frequent elsewhere.

L.14c–15a: *lu-mi ya-da-ša-na ma-(15)ʾi-hu-di* 

". . . or one destroy my strength."

lu+mi: Certainly the CS particle *lu* 'verily, or'. Cf. Panamuwa 11: *lw. . . lw* 'either. . . or'. It seems definitely to tie the two verbs together, one plural and the second singular. These two verbs in turn describe actions that are stipulated to be those which are injurious to the compact/covenant at the beginning of the sentence. It is quite plausible here to interpret the sentence as an implied relative clause with the main verb at the beginning after the logical subject which is the main concern of the entire text: the covenant: "They injure the covenant, they (who) grumble, he (who) destroys . . ." and therefore the difference in the preformative, the first generalized, the second specific.

yadaššana: There is no entirely satisfactory answer for the problems of both form and meaning. The simplest suggestion for the root is CS *dāšu* 'thresh, tread upon' > 'destroy', a semantic transference common to Akk. SC and Arab., and therefore extremely old——as here. Conceivably, it could be the root reflected in Akk. *dašnu* which is equated with the normal Akk. *dannu* 'powerful', but known only from vocabulary lists where it is labelled as 'Amorite'. Cf. Ug. *dṯ, dṯn*, but Arab. *dāsa*——the sibilants simply do not match in accord with the usual systems, but this is frequently the case in this corpus. Unfortunately, the word does not seem to be attested in OSA. As usual, the sibilants seem to be antinomian.

Whether or not the final *-na* is a root consonant, or an enclitic particle suffixed to the impf. form of a hollow root it is difficult to say. Both of the final syllables end in the 'optative' *–a* vowel instead of the expected plural *–ū*. Since the final *–a* in later WS can indicate either a wish or a consequence––or both––it is possible that the form signifies the progression from subjective attitude 'grumbling' to the objective intent or attempt at violent destruction of authority, and therefore the 'optative' or 'conative' form of the verb: 'attempt to tread down'. In any case it seems most probable that the form is a D–Stem.

ma–ʾi–hu–di for *maʾhud+i*: 'my strength'. It is here taken to be the familiar *meʾod*, but again with the archaic medial *h* instead of the medial *w*. The vowel after the *ʾalif* is again a 'dead' vowel, and as so frequently the case it is the consonant sign bearing the *i* vowel that is written when the vowel is not pronounced (though this is by no means a 'law'). Cf. also Akk. *maʾadu*, and Ug. *mʾad* 'much, many'. Since a root *ʾhd* is inherently unstable in later WS (only the roots *ʾhb, ʾhl* have a *h* after an *ʾalif*), either the first or second consonant shifted, and thus we have the archaic PN *ʾohad* and *ʾehud*, <*yaʾhud* in accordance with the well known MB shift of *ya– > ʾe. yantin > ʾentin.* Thus also from an original *yaʾhud* by elision of the first weak consonant we have the well known *yahud*, and by elision of the second weak consonant we have the second dialect form *yaʾud*. It would seem that both are shortened forms of an original theophoric name such as *yaʾhud–ēl* 'El is great'.

L.15b–16a: *ʾu–ba–ru ka–wa–(16)na tu–ʿi*
tu–ṯa–wa–ʾi yu–ḫu–bu–ba–ta

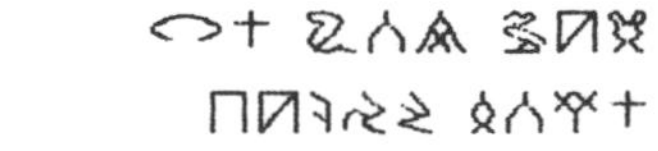

"A mighty force have become those straying, received, purified."

This translation is a measure of desperation, an attempt to render at least the semantic content of the words as they are known from later WS. The grammar is very difficult.

ʾubaru: The CS root *ʾbr* is usually associated with the meaning 'strength, power', but in Ug. the possible primitive meaning may be preserved: 'young bull'. By the LB age the meaning had long been shifted to designate a collectivity of the powerful. Cf. *EA* 20:73 where Tushratta speaks of being 'honored(?)' before his *u–pa–ru–ti–ia* in contrast to his 'land'. Similarly, in a roughly contemporary Ug. text a *mrʾu ʾbrn* designates some kind of social stratum, probably upper class. In view of these usages and this text under discussion, it seems most probable that the Hurrian word *ʾwr* 'lord' is actually a loanword from WS involving a shift from *b>w*. Note also in SC the very early Ps 68:31 where *ʿdt ʾbyrym* contrasts to the *ʿgly ʿmym*: the 'congregation of bulls' over against the 'calves of the peoples'.

The surprising frequency of the *qutal* verbal noun form should also be commented upon here, if only because it does not seem to have been recognized in earlier grammars as a standard word–formation category. Cf. Gelb's compendium of 'Amorite' where there are several pages of *qutal* forms occurring in proper names alone. From Mari note the title *suqaqum*.

kawana tuʿi: The copula–verb seems to indicate the identity of subject and predicate, and at the same time to indicate that the subject is a new entity: not 'a'='b', but 'a' has come into being from 'b'. From our point of view the subject and predicate are reversed, but no matter: the grammatical requirements are met in that the subject is in the nominative case and the predicate in the accusative/oblique plural, and so the verb is 3 masc. sg. preterite.

The predicate *tuʿi* can hardly be equated with anything other than CS *tʿ* 'wander, stray', again a term transferred from flocks in the pasturelands to populations in the social wastelands of political life. The form is again the Qal active participle with initial vowel /u/ as in the form *luḫisa* discussed above. In view of the occurrence of the word later in the text (lines 18, 25), and the close association with the root *ṯwʾ* there can be little doubt that it designates some social group identifiable by some common trait that they share. It is extremely probable that the term is an EB semantic equivalent of the later *ʿapiru* 'outlaw'. Cf. Ps 58:4 where *zr*, the SC Iron Age term for one who is estranged from society is paralleled by *tʿ*——and both words are used as (denominative?) verbs. If the concept should seem too "sophisticated" for the Early Bronze Age, note the evidence for social upheaval in the "Admonitions of Ipu–Wer" which are probably nearly contemporary, and for the 'straying' compare the Hittite text that speaks of the ox that 'has chosen his stable' (i.e. the Hittite sphere of influence), and the parallel proverbial adaptation in Isa 1:3.

tuṯawaʾi: This word is difficult, for the + *tu* sign doesn't fit comfortably either here or as a suffix to the preceding word which would make it a nominative fem. case ending. The root must be identified with Ug. *ṯwy* where the shift from *ʾalif* to *yod* has taken place. In the Krt epic the hero is rebuked for engaging in an action designated as *ṯwy* with reference to the *ǵrm*. The Ug. epic passage is eloquent commentary on this text under discussion, for the Ug. *ǵrm* can hardly be any other than the CS *ṣr* 'enemy' or at least 'alien'. The root has a cognate in the Arab. *ṯawa* 'receive as a guest' which is probably a specialized usage derived from the much more ancient usage attested here and in Ug., and which is too restricted a meaning to fit well in either of these Bronze Age contexts. It is possible that these contexts represent a development from the Amorite and SC *šwh* 'to be or make like', or in the D–stem: 'establish, make equal'.

In the present passage, the word can only be in apposition to *tuʿi*. It is far from certain that the prefixed *tu*– is a nominal preformative to the noun such as SC *tpʾrt, twrh*, but this analysis is certainly the easier way out grammatically. The word would indicate, then, an abstraction or collectivity meaning something like 'those who have been received'——or even 'made like/equal'. In other words, it designates the establishment of some sort of status in the socio–political organization that is coming into existence with this royal proclamation. It is not at all unlikely that it designates specifically those who have become the recipients of the king's largesse and therefore have become also his clients and dependable allies. The client–patron relationship of ancient Roman society immediately comes to mind. For years I have argued simply on the grounds of linguistic phenomena that something analogous must have been characteristic of the ancient Near East, for this is so constant a feature of religious terminology in which deity is spoken of as benefactor, protector, and patron——all of which terms have to be social realities **before** they can be transferred to transcendent concepts.

yuḫububata: The root is certainly the same as that underlying the Mari *tebibtum* and the SC *ḥobeb* of Deut 33:3, but the form as it has been read here is full of linguistic impossibilities from the point of view of the received comparative Semitic philology. In the first place, the reading ⇜ *ḫu* instead of ⟐ *ḥu* is inconsistent with every other attestation of the root from OB *ebbu, ebēbu* to OSA *ḥbb*. To reverse the readings, however, creates more difficulties than it solves. It simply has to be admitted that this EB dialect cannot be forced into the bed of Procrustes of linguistic 'laws' of a millennium later, especially in view of the unimaginable social chaos and disorder that had happened twice in the meantime. It goes without saying that we do not know how any of these phonemes were actually pronounced; all that can be done is to establish historical, i.e. etymological, relationships and continuities.

The second problem is how to construe the form: is it a verb or a noun? The preformative *yu–*, if it is that, would point to a pres–fut. form of a derived stem such as the D–stem form known particularly from Mari *ubbubu*, but the suffix *–ta* indicates rather a fem. sg. noun. To be sure, there are rare examples of verb forms with both personal preformatives and afformatives such as *EA ibašati*, but these are probably hybrids and not true linguistic regularities that can be utilized for the interpretation of a passage such as this. It is possible that the *yu–* is a pronominal suffix attached to the preceding noun: *tuṯawaʾi+hu > tuṯawaʾi+yu*. This solution to the problem is the more attractive because in the specifically Byblian dialect of Phoenician this sound shift became regular, so that the *–y* suffix regularly designates the 3 masc. sg. possessive pronoun. But then the question arises concerning the suffix *–ta*: if it is 3 fem. sg. what relation does it have as a designation of something in the preceding phrase? It has already been suggested that *ubaru* is a collectivity, so that this word is a further description of that social designation, in the accusative case because it is the predicate of the verb *kawana*, and fem. because collective/abstract nouns are construed as feminines though formally masculine.

The third problem is semantic. Tracing back into this earliest usage of the root from later attestations in a wide variety of geographical and social contexts is not simple, but neither is it an impossible undertaking. In the first place, two very early occurrences prove that *ḫbb* is the semantic equivalent of words meaning 'pure, holy'. In Akk. *ebbu=ellu*, while in SC (Deut 33:3) *ḫbb* occurs in parallelism with *qdš*, a fact that has been ignored by all translators of that very difficult passage. The word is also a ***hapax leg.*** in SC, and its distribution in Semitic justifies the conclusion that it is an archaic word common to the coastal and inland dialects in EB period, but survived into the Iron Age only in Arabic and Aramaic in addition to its integration into East Semitic (Akk.) from the Amorite period on. In the meantime, it underwent considerable semantic shift, which accounts for the fact that the Mari *tebibtum* has been regarded as linguistically inexplicable.

Starting from the undeniable equivalence of *ḫbb* and Akk. *ellu* 'pure, holy' on the one hand, and with WS *qdš* on the other, the conditions in which the word is used evidently include, if not stipulate, a freedom from guilt (like *naqi*), the absence of outstanding obligations and at the same time the consequent harmonious relationship with social authority. In fact, at least in SC the only satisfactory definition of *qdš* is 'property of deity', and therefore a condition that is compatible with the nature of deity. The same is true elsewhere in WS: in this particular context under discussion, the term evidently indicates the status with reference to the king that is described in the preceding words, and also stipulates that there are no unfulfilled obligations that create a situation of hostility between those persons and the highest social authority. This also, then, is the usage underlying the Mari *tebibtum*. It is entirely possible that some ritual form accompanied the process——in fact, given the obsessions with ritual forms that seem to characterize all important human organizations, it would seem inevitable. However, what is important about the process was its social, political, and economic function: the *tebibtum* was the 'census taking' whereby the population was placed under obligation to answer the call to arms, and having made a commitment to do so in the ritual form, they are considered 'pure' with reference to the king.

This combination of status and function implied in the term is most beautifully illustrated in two meanings of the root in OSA: (1) 'Clients, dependents', and (2) 'Love'. From this to all later survivals of the root in WS notably Aramaic, the meaning 'love' was the only one to survive——and therefore was read into Deut 33:3 by all subsequent translations. The fact is that nowhere before the OSA can the word be translated this way. It is a semantic development arising out of the social relationship, and already in the Bronze Age other words for 'love' were also used to designate political loyalties. This is specifically spelled out in Deut 6:5.

L.16b–17: *ta-(17)tu-sa-ta-ru ʾi-ya*
ʿu-bu-du-tu+ni-ya

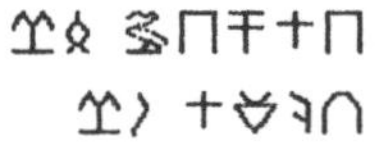

"Those who place themselves under my protection——they are my servitors."

The phrase seems to be a continuation of this complex sentence that began back on L. 15 with *ʾubaru kawana*. The translation is an attempt to render the rough meaning in a context where both forms and grammatical relationships are far from clear.

tatusataru: The root is the same as that occurring at D 3 and D 24, but with a very interesting nuance of meaning deriving from the fact that here there is a reflexive infix *-tu-* which as usual makes the subject equivalent to the object: 'they protect themselves'. Again, the verb has the 3 masc. pl. personal prefix in *ta-*, but this time evidently reflecting the fact that the logical subject is the following noun which is evidently a feminine collective.

ʾiya: This particle that separates the reflexive verb and what appears to be the grammatical subject was particularly troublesome. It turns out to be a most dramatic illustration of the linguistic continuity between these inscriptions and early Arabic. For the word, see the discussion in Lane, s.v.: "*ʾiy* is a particle denoting a reply, meaning *naʿam* (Yes, or yea); imparting acknowledgment of the truth of an enunciation. . . ." Cf. also *ʾay* "Also an explicative particle" like *yaʿniy* 'I mean, that is'.

ʿubudutu+niya. For an analogy perhaps cf. the much later SC *ʿedut* 'congregation', as an illustration of the *-ut* suffix, but perhaps even closer is Arab. *ʿubuwdatun* in the religious sense meaning 'approving what God does', and therefore *ʿubuwdiyyatun* 'humility, and submissiveness'. The Arabic has made an abstraction out of what is here a clear description of a group of persons. The noun has an infixed *-ni-* before the possessive again with no observable function; its interpretation as a 1 pl. suffix does not commend itself.

L.18a: *ta-ti ya-tu yi-ba-mi* 

(No translation attempted.)

The word divisions, grammar and lexicon are all too obscure to attempt a translation, which is particularly unfortunate in view of the probable word *yibami* that can hardly be separated from Ug. and SC *ybm*. In both dialects both masc. and fem. forms occur, and the root would seem to be simply a very archaic word having to do with procreation. This is the more probable in view of the very rare *-bm-* sequence of consonants that was usually avoided through dissimilation in later Semitic dialects. Cf. already in Ug. where the goddess ʿAnat is termed *ybmt, ybnt,* and *ymmt*.

Even this equation is very dubious, however, in view of the rotated *mu* sign that is taken here and elsewhere in Text D to be read as *mi* in view of the fact that the normal *mi* sign: T is not used at all in this text. The same rotation occurs also at lines 12 and 14, where also the reading *mi* is necessary. Rotation of the + *tu* sign also occurs, but seemingly only because of spacial considerations.

L.18b–19a: *mu-na tu-ʿi (19)[ṯa-wa]-ʾu-tu*
ḥu-ru+ba-ʿi-lu 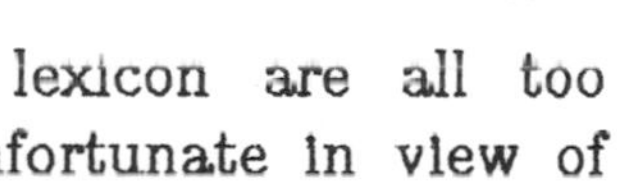

Again translation is impossible, though a probable identification of most of the words can be suggested:

muna: Possibly cognate to the later *min* 'who', but this is not satisfactory in view of the indef. *man-* that occurs repeatedly. If it is correct, then there would be still another example of the *u/i* shift that is so well attested.

tuʿi: This has already been discussed at D 16.

[ṯa-wa]-ʾu-tu: The supplied signs seem to be reasonably certain from the traces seen on the IR Ektachrome photograph, and this is reinforced by the occurrence of the root in association with the preceding word at D 16. It is most interesting to find the same root with the abstract fem. ending *-utu*, evidently again a collective designator which is followed immediately by the royal name——a relationship that looks very much like a 'construct chain'. Why the word is in the nominative case is a problem that cannot be solved in this obscure context to which the key is so far missing.

L.19b–20a: *ʾi-ʾu(20)-ta-ti ya-ru-ni ʾu-ḥa ʿa-ni+ya* 

(Translation is not yet possible.)

ʾiʾutati: Possibly from the same root with which the text begins? If so, then we have again a verb form with both personal preformative and afformative like *EA ʾibašati*, plus the elision of the second ***'alif***. This solution does not commend itself.

yaru+ni: Perhaps from *wry* 'lead, guide'. Cf. the possible reading at D 28–9: *ya-ru+ni la+ki-ti*.

ʾuḥa: Perhaps cf. Ug. *ʾuḫ*: 'brother(hood)'. The sign 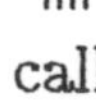 more frequently corresponds to the unpointed *ḥ* than to the *ḫ* which is called for in the word *ʾaḫ* CS 'brother'; perhaps the values should be reversed, but this procedure raises as many new problems as it solves.

ʿaniya: 'respond, answer'? Or 'humble, submissive'? In view of the acc. case ending, it would seem to be verbal noun in apposition to or describing the previous *ʾuḥa*, which is itself the dir. obj. of the verb *yaruni*.

L.20b–21a: *ha-(21)ki ha-ʿi-mu-ru bi-ʿu+ma*

"Thus they seek prolongation of life."

haki: The traces of the first character of line 21 seem to be compatible only with the reading *-ki*, thus yielding the particle to be identified with WS *ʾk, hk*, and again esp. Arab *hek* 'thus, so'.

haʿmuru: This seems to be a hendiadys with the following verb also in the 3 pl. preterite: 'they live (long), they seek'. For the meaning, again cf. Arab. *ʿamara* 'live long, inhabit', and also OSA, where it designates 'to settle, dwell'. This furnishes the background for the stipulation of the Decalog, which ties respect for parents with continued long life in the land——but note the contrast: here, as everywhere else in pagan antiquity, long life and security of property is a function of proper respect for ambitious politicians. In all probability this was not mere rhetoric.

biʿu+ma: If the interpretation is correct, then there is evidence for a major modification of traditional views of Semitic historical linguistics. The root meaning 'seek' is attested in Aram., Ug., SC, and as no doubt a LW in Neo—Babylonian. It is to be equated with Arab. *baǵiya* and it is spelled with the *ǵayin* also in Ugaritic. It is a curious fact that there has occurred so far no identifiable occurrence in this dialect of the later Sem. *ǵayin*, and the same is true of Amorite, as Gelb has already observed. The possibility must be considered that the consonant was **not** a part of the phonetic inventory of early Semitic, at least not Common Semitic in the Early Bronze Age.

Note again the weak suffixed conjunction (?) *-ma* that separates this hendiadys from the main verb that follows.

L.21b—23a: *ʾa-(22)[ka]-wa-na+ma* 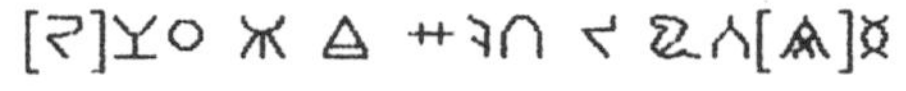
ʿu-bu-di ṯi bi+pu-li-(23)[ti]

"I make them my servants who (are) in the dominion of . . ."

The phrase is similar to the one at D 27, and the grammar is classical: the copula verb takes the predicate in the acc. It is very difficult to interpret *ʿubudi* as anything other than a collective plural and therefore a remote ancestor of one very common type of 'broken plural' of classical Arabic. Contrast the *ʿubudutu* of line 17.

ṯi=△: This sign cannot be connected either to the preceding word or to what follows, and consequently it almost inevitably must be a free–standing particle functioning as a relative between the preceding phrase and the following. Candidates for the identification are few: CS *ṯ*– and CWS *d̲/z/d*. Since the reading *d̲u* is already preempted by the ꟷ *d̲u* sign, it is most probable that this is a relative pronoun in the oblique plural, and thus to be read as *ṯi* in agreement with the case/number of the preceding noun.

bi+puli[ti]: This reading is the only conceivable one, even though there are some difficulties involved. In the first place, one would expect the reading *ba+* before the *u* vowel: elsewhere, *bi+* occurs only before the *a* vowel. For the following noun note the *pulitati* of lines 11 and 13, where it is followed by the 1 sg. personal possessive suffix. That is excluded as a possible reading here––there is room for only one sign at the beginning of line 23, and therefore there is a semantic contrast between the earlier forms and the present one. This contrast is also demanded by the present context. Whatever the form may be, there is a distinction between the reified 'dominion' of the king, and the state of being ruled that is stipulated here as a function of covenant. In the previous cases we have the fem. pl. designating the sovereignty––a sort of plural of totality (?), but here there seems to be a concrete sg. indicating the binding nature of the specific *kittum* to which they had bound themselves.

L.23b: *ki–ti ṯu ya–tu–ha–ʿi–hi–du* 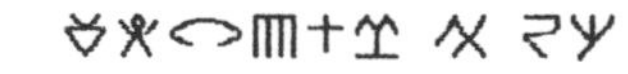

". . . of the covenant to which they bound themselves by oath."

kitti: Gen. sg. possessive case after the preceding **nomen regens**. At first it seems strange to find this word in so early a context, particularly since it is so crucially important a term in Mesopotamian political ideology. It is not so strange, however, since the word is probably common WS in the first place, brought into Mesopotamia with the Amorite migrations and dynasties, and surviving in WS usage (Ug. and Amarna) into the LB period, but becoming extinct there with the collapse of 'civilization' at the transition to the Early Iron Age. However, note the continuity of the political function of the root from OSA to the present day: *kwnhmw* 'their allies'.

ṯu=ᐱX: Again there is a single–sign particle that can hardly be anything other than a conjunction or relative pronoun. In the previous case the particle refers to persons, here it refers to an abstraction, and it would seem therefore to belong to a different order. It is for this reason (in part) that it is not read as the *ḏ/z* demonstrative/relative, but as the conjunction *š*- here taken to be the ancestor of later *ša/še* but read *ṯu*. It could be the ordinary *šin* with *u* (or possibly *i*) vowel, since neither of those syllables has as yet been identified in the corpus. In any case, regardless of the phonetics and the later history of the particle, its function here seems to be entirely clear grammatically.

yatuhaʿhidu: The form has been discussed above at line 2. Together with the reference to the *kittu* preceding, there can be no doubt that the document deals with the process of creating a social organization by covenant. It is difficult to understand why this should be so surprising in view of the hundreds of thousands of "constitutions" created every year by corporation lawyers, and even the semantic parallelism of *kittu* < *kwn* with 'constitute'.

L.23c–24 *pa+ti-(24)sa-ta-ru+ni*
ʾu-ya-ta-ta la+ki-ti+ma

"And so, you shall observe the obligations faithfully . . ."

pa+tisattaru+ni: The consequential conjunction *pa+* is followed by a finite verb probably in the D–stem transitive that has the thematic vowel *a* perhaps indicating the present–future, and again contrasting to the thematic vowel *i* of the preceding verb which in the context must indicate the past. The suffixed *-ni* again has no observable function, but to judge from later usages, it would seem very improbable that this verb form is a command, i.e. jussive. It is not entirely certain that it is 2 pl., in view of the frequent *t*- 3 pl. preformatives that occur in this and other WS texts, but the direct address is most likely in view of the 1 sg. verb *akawana* of line 21–2.

As for the meaning of the verb here, compare the later usages of OSA *hstr* 'protect' and the later SC semantic equivalents, *šmr* 'observe', *nṣr* 'protect (obligations)'.

ʾuyutata: This word and its root is one of the most difficult in the document. Note the following unexplained forms that may be related:

D 17–18: *ya-ʾ?-ta-ti*
D 19–20: *ʾi-ʾu-ta-ti*

D 24: *ʾu-ya-ta-ta*

The first two forms should be impf. verb forms, but there is no such form known later that ends in *-ti*. As for the root, it seems beyond reasonable doubt that it is ancestral to later SC *ʾwt* and Arab. *ʾayat-* (cf. Ayatollah), 'sign, mark'. The noun form is evidently of the frequently observed *qutal* form, and this could account for the later SC form *ʾot*, by the regular sound shift from *u* > *o*, and the subsequent lengthening due to the elision of the medial consonant. The duplication of the final *t* proves that the root is *ʾyt*, and the noun form is a feminine singular, possibly again a collective or even a 'broken plural' of the type *qutalatu* that actually occurs in classical Arabic in a particularly restricted type of noun.

Again the major problem is semantic, for the later meaning 'sign' does not fit well into this context. The word designates that which is to be 'guarded, protected' and under the circumstances the generalized translation 'obligations' seems warranted. From this to 'sign' is an easy semantic shift--for the law of increasing ritualization of social norms would almost guarantee it. It is interesting that both the main verb and the object of the verb continue in use in classical Arabic with especially religious semantic content. Most interesting is one meaning given for *ʾayat-* "a portion of the Kur'an denoting any statute, or ordinance of God".

la+kitti: The vocalization of the preposition is according to the general rule: *a* before *i*. It is taken to be an adverbial expression 'faithfully' though it could just as well be taken literally: 'in accordance with the covenant'.

L.25 *[li]-ta-li ti-ḫa-ta tu-ʿi la+ki-ti+ma* 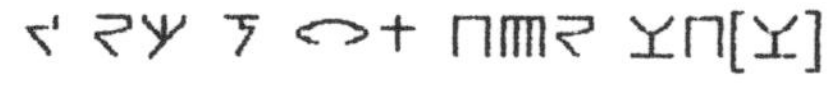

"to be dependent instead of straying from the covenant . . ."

The rhetorical device here is unmistakable. The assonance of the antonyms *tala/taʿa* is exactly the sort of device much beloved in much later times. Just as interesting, however, is the fate of the two words. In Arabic, the positive, political meaning of *tlw* as '(faithful) follower' has entirely driven out the meaning 'hang upon>be dependent', while in SC the meaning 'hang' is applied predominantly to the barbaric custom of hanging the corpse of a political opponent from a tree or stake--a beautiful irony that certainly was not lost upon the EI population of Palestine who eschewed such dependency upon political demagogues. It is curious that the English usage of the antonyms 'dependent' and 'independent' have also undergone semantic specialization to large degree—–the first primarily indicates economic status, while the second is largely political in connotation.

Curiously, the meaning 'stray' for *ta'a* seems to have been preserved only in SC where it is used both in the grassroots literal meaning of a straying domesticated animal, and figuratively as here of human beings straying from the paths of rectitude, Isa 53:6. The possibly related root of Aram. and Arab. *ṭ'h/ṭġy* is definitely derived or dialectic, and nowhere does it preserve the primitive meaning 'to stray'. Furthermore, this EB dialect of the coastal region is far more sparing of velarizations than is true of the Iron Age semitic languages.

The preposition *ti-ḥa-ta* is used here already in its classical meaning attested in Ug. and SC: 'instead of'.

L.26a: *ha-ki-'a+ma ba-yu-ti* 

"devotedly with respect to my houses."

Cf. D 2–3 for the first word, which is used here also as an adverbial accusative but with the enclitic *-ma* that is taken to be a weak connective to the word following.

bayuti: This is again difficult, and it seems impossible to find any word or meaning other than CS *bayt-* 'house'. As the translation indicates, it is here taken to be a plural, for which compare classical Arabic plurals *buyut-* which is also pronounced *biyut-* according to Lane's sources. Again, it is difficult to avoid the conclusion that we have another example of an ancestral 'broken plural'. Note also the unusual plural in Ug. *bhtm*, and SC *bottim* which reflects the original *u* vowel of the plural form.

Why the noun is plural is a question that is probably answered in the following lines. The king in question must certainly have had an important support group if not power structure based upon a complex of 'houses' in a lineage or consanguinuity. As the head of this structure, he could well speak of 'my houses'. In classical Arabic, the plural form is still used to designate the 'nobility' of a large tribal group. Cf. also in SC Ex 8:17 and 10:6 where the 'houses' of the Egyptian king are referred to, probably designating 'crown property'. The 'houses' of the Jerusalem temple are also mentioned in I Chr 28:11.

L.26b–27: *pa+ti-sa-ta-ru-(27)[ni]* *ʿu-ma* 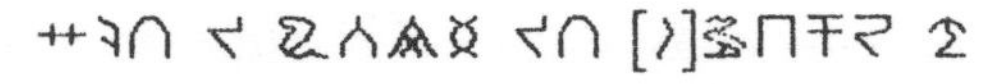
ʾa-ka-wa-na+ma *ʿu-bu-di*

"And so, you shall protect the populace I have made my servants."

Only the strange word *ʿumma* and its construction call for comment here. It certainly is cognate to CS *ʿamm-* and evidently has a specialized meaning here which can only be conjectured. Since it is equated by the verb with the predicate *ʿubudi*, it must designate some human collectivity, for which cf. Arab. *ʿamim*, pl. *ʿumum* 'anything collected together and abundant or numerous'.

The construction is especially interesting for it consists of a noun followed immediately by a finite verb in what has often been labelled as a 'construct chain'. The usage seems to be Common Semitic. It is frequent in Akk. (*awat iqbu*), and regular in Egyptian at the opposite extreme of geographical and linguistic range. It is an economical and easy way to convey a dependent relative clause. This is probably the construction underlying the much discussed introductory verse of Gen 1:1 in SC: a noun in construct state (with prefixed preposition) followed immediately by a finite verb. Unfortunately, it is difficult to translate the sense, but there is nothing at all grammatically objectionable to the received text.

The phrase *ʿu-ma a-ka-wa-na ʿu-bu-di* occurs in exactly the same spelling––the same signs––at D 21–22, and illustrates the pitfalls of relying entirely upon strings of identical signs in the process of decipherment. It is possible that the phrase is indeed the same––certainly the last two words are––but from everything we know of Semitic grammar, the first word is there impossible: *bi+ʿumma*, which would have to be *bi+ʿummi* with the gen. case after the preposition. It could be argued, perhaps, that the copula–verb had induced the acc. case ending to the first noun, but the interpretation of it as a *hendiadys* is more elegant and grammatically inoffensive.

L.28a: *[zu]-ku-ta la+ki-ti+ma* 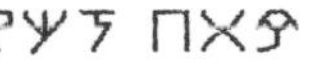

"Pure with respect to the covenant, and . . ."

zukuta: Here and in the next phrase is a word that involves two rare signs 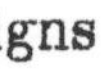 and ×. The first occurs clearly nowhere else, and the second at six other places scattered throughout the corpus. Among the unassigned syllabic values the present readings are those that yield the most reasonably satisfactory morphemes. The accusative singular case ending indicates that the word describes the collectivity *ʿuma* referred to in the previous phrase as the servants of the king, and who are here declared to be ‘pure’ by relationship to covenant. Thus there is a cluster of three different descriptions of the ‘populace’ who are the direct object of the main verb at the beginning of the sentence: *tisattaruni*, again illustrating the unbelievably complex syntax of this very archaic dialect.

The term *zukuta* probably illustrates much the same pattern of thought that underlies the Mari *tebibtum*, in which the recruiting process that involved the registration of the draftees is termed a "purification," that is, a ‘clearing’ of outstanding guilt or obligations to the king. The roots *ḥbb* and *zky* are thus semantic equivalents attested from two different linguistic dialect regions.

L.28b–29a: *zu-ku-ta d̲u ya-(29)ru-ni la+ki-ti* 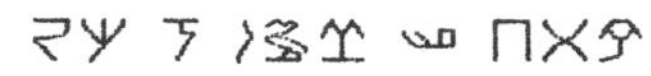

". . . pure, who are guided by covenant."

The verb *yaruni* has already been read at D 20, but with a significant variation of form. The  sign read certainly *ru* corresponds to a very simple sign that is essentially an elongated s–curve, and at first glance it would seem obligatory to assign a different syllabic value to it. It is conceivable that we might have in this contrast a phonetic contrast between different vowels, since the *ri* sign has not been identified in this text. It is also conceivable that the contrast signalled the difference between the long and short *u* vowel, but the context in D 20 is so completely obscure that little can be done at present with this hypothesis which unfortunately is not supported yet by any parallel case of a contrast in signs indicating such long and short vowels. It is a possibility that may be considered, however, where other unassigned characters are involved.

Fortunately, there is a parallel in this text for the alternation of the bird sign  and the s–curve. The verb form *tisattaruni* in D 26–7 is written with this same bird sign, while a different form of the same verb read *tatusataru* in D 16–7 has the *ru* syllable written with the s–curve sign. It seems virtually certain that the two signs are graphic variants, unlikely as that might appear at first glance. What is involved is simply the difference between the monumental, pictographic form and the much more cursive linear form for the same character. Analogies for such radical simplification have already been identified particularly concerning the  *hi* syllabic character, and the  *nu* sign that represents a bee.

The verb *yaru+ni* presents some interesting problems also. It is taken to be the impf. 3 pl. from the root *wry* that seems to be CS with a primitive meaning 'guide, direct'. The first syllable is the preformative *ya-* to be expected, but what happened to the first root consonant *w* that ought in this archaic dialect to be reflected in some way in the writing system? The first syllable theoretically ought to have been *yaw-* or even *ya-* followed by the syllable *wa* perhaps with a 'dead vowel'. It is possible only to observe that the first root consonant *w* is represented as zero, and to point out that the elision of both *w* and *h* is characteristic of quite a few different contexts in this corpus. It is quite certain that both were very weakly articulated in most WS dialects, and the writing system here and elsewhere simply reflects the **perceived** pronunciation of the words in question; that is, it is non–etymological.

The translation 'who are guided' is an attempt to render what is likely an intransitive stative usage of the Qal form, while the transitive form would be in a derived conjugation.

This is an interesting clause that further describes the populace to be protected. It makes a transition from a collective singular to a distributive plural in connection with a change of attention from that of status to that of function so far as the covenant is concerned. Thus the highly sophisticated character of covenant ideology already in the Early Bronze Age West Semitic culture is beyond question, and modern primitive ideas about the ancient "primitive" societies is badly in need of radical correctives.

L.29b: *ma-na-ma ṯi-ʿu-ʾu+ni* 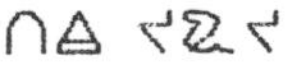

"Those who follow (i.e. 'look to') me . . ."

The verb *ṯiʿuʾuni* is impossible outside Egyptian in later Semitic, with its sequence of the root consonants *ʿayin–ʾaleph*. The vocalization is highly eccentric with the *i* vowel in the first syllable that ought to signal a D–Stem, but followed by an otherwise unparallelled *u* vowel after the second consonant. For this I can only suggest the frequently observed shift between the *u* in this dialect, and the *i* in similar locations in subsequent later Semitic dialects, which seems to have been a fairly gradual and progressive phenomenon. The best witness to this is Ugaritic that still in the 13th century preserved a fair number of what now seems clearly to have been more original *u* vowels.

The final *u* afformative to the perfect tense form of the verb is certainly the normal 3 masc. pl. ending, though one would expect the 3 sg. after the pronoun 'whoever'. Is the indefinite pronoun itself a plural form? It does contrast to the *ma-nu-ya-ma* of D 32f, and *ma-nu-ma* of C 12 that demonstrably have other grammatical contexts:

Nom. pl.	D 29:	*ma-na-ma ṯi-ʿu-ʾu+ni*
Obl. sg.	D 32–3:	*bi+ma-nu-ya-ma ša-du-da*
Nom. sg.	C 12:	*ma-nu-ma ša-du-da*

The verbal root is itself probably the most archaic form of a CS verb that in the course of time saw the ringing of the changes both in phonetics and semantics. The Ug. verb *ṯʿy* 'inspect' preserved the form most closely with the inevitable shift from final *ʾalif* to final *yod*, but with a highly technical meaning 'proofread'? Akk. *šeʾu* 'seek' shows the transition from 'look to expectantly' that is preserved in SC *šʿh* (Isa 17:7 and other passages), to induce the superior to act by 'offering': also Ug., but OSA *mṯʿyt* as well. The latter dialect saw also further development in form and meaning in the roots *šwʿ* 'sacrifice', and *šʿy* 'followers, allies', and *šʿw* 'take, acquire'. Outside SC the root nearly died out of usage in the Syro–Palestinian region, and was preserved in several forms in the complex of Arabian dialects.

For this political significance of the root in the Bronze Age note especially the Amarna passage in EA 266:9–15.

L.30a: *yu-du-ḫu tu-ʾu* 

". . . they submit, they are marked."

The verb is taken to be CS *dḫ* 'be submissive' (Arab.), in the D–stem, 'subdue'. SC has forms that presuppose both *dḥh* and *dḥḥ*. It is indeed probable that both forms existed in the various dialects of the various periods. The root is used almost exclusively in poetry, and often the meaning 'subdue' is quite appropriate. The root requires further study, but to judge from the present evidence the Qal form should be (as so often) intransitive, as in this passage, while the transitive forms would have to be either D–stem or causative.

The second verb *tu–ʾu* is simply a perfect 3 pl. like the preceding two verbs, and is again a stative probably meaning 'marked with a *tau*' (=+) sign, very likely a 'tribal' tattoo mark, for which note the old tradition of the 'mark of Cain' Gen 4:15. The function of a tattoo mark as signifying the protection (*tisattaruni* D 26) of an overlord is common to both the Genesis narrative and the present one. It seems that this verb ends the series of three traits of the ideal subject––an old ***Sklavenspiegel*** to match the numerous ***Fuerstenspiegeln*** that range from antiquity to recent times.

L.30b: *ʿu-bu-du-tu+ni ka-wa-[ta]* 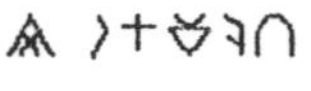

"Serving of me has become . . ."

ʿubudūtu+ni: an abstract (fem!) verbal noun with the objective 1 sg. suffix. It is in the nominative case with *–u*, and therefore the subject of the following verb which is unfortunately partly broken. The word is clearly identical to later SC *ʿbwdh*, which is used overwhelmingly of ritual services––the semantic origin of modern English (worship)–'service'.

The copula–verb has the final sign partly broken but the restoration offered here is the only reasonably possible one. The form is unique, but in view of the syntax, it must be a 3 fem. sg. perf. from the very frequent root *kawana*. The third consonant *nun* is evidently assimilated to the following *tau*, as is the case also in the cognate noun *kittu*. The verb is probably to be normalized as *kawatt*, and thus the final *ta* sign has a 'dead vowel'. What follows is that which is equated with the *ʿubudutu*.

L.31a: *bi-ra-ki ḥu-wu+ma du-ga-la* 

". . . blessings . . life greatly . . ."

biraki: oblique plural of the root *brk*, object of the preceding copula–verb. It is of course cognate to and doubtless the origin of SC *brkh*, 'blessing'.

ḥuwu+ma: specifies the content of the blessing, namely, life. The form is curious and unparallelled for one should have expected *ḥawwi,* with the gen. case ending and with the unpointed *ḥet*. The problem of the pointed and unpointed *ḥet* rises again, to which there is no answer, for shifting this sign to the unpointed *ḥ* simply introduces a larger host of paradoxes. Just as strange is the vocalization with *u* instead of almost universal *a* in later Semitic words for 'life'. The same sign is the ending of the verb form in the preceding line, which is part of a series all of which end in *u*. Consequently, it seems best to accept the unique form that may have been influenced by the following labial consonant *w*. This is the more probable in view of the fact that the shift from *w* to *y* had taken place in almost all Semitic dialects by the end of the Late Bronze Age. The enclitic *-ma* here also has nothing to do with a plural ending, but is rather a weak connective to the following clause that specifies the second most important aspect of ancient blessings.

It should be superfluous to point out that we have here the classic pattern of the blessings for obedience to superior political authority, which has been best known up to the present through the famous Hittite suzerainty treaties of the Late Bronze Age, nearly a thousand years later than this text. It follows also that the Hittites merely took over and formalized a pattern of political ideology that was perhaps centuries old even before they came onto the Near Eastern social and political scene. Note also that following the blessings there are curses or threats included as well.

duǵala: this word also presents difficulties that are not impossible to resolve. In the first place, the word almost certainly is the origin of later WS *ǵdl*, where metathesis of the first two consonants has taken place. Again there occurs the surprisingly frequent *quṭal* form. The problem is the case and number, for the ending in *-a* can be only acc. sg., while *biraki* can only be accusative plural, and *ḫuwi* must be a genitive in the 'construct chain' and probably plural also to judge from comparative usages in other semitic languages. The solution is probably to be found again in the surprisingly frequent usage of the 'adverbial accusative' and thus the translation 'greatly'.

L.31b–32a: *ha+bu-ʾa (32)bi+maʿ-bu-du sa-nu-bi* 
tu-ni-bi

"He who enters into the work of making flourish the fruit (of the land)."

ha+buʾa: The *ha-* could be a demonstrative particle referring back to the *mannu+ma* of line 29, but with change of number——now singular. It seems more likely, however, that it is the causative prefix to a passive verbal noun——the one 'brought in' to the working of the land. The accusative case can be explained only on the ground that this is also a part of the predicate after the verb *kawat*, and thus continues the series of 'blessings' consequent to submissive servitude to the king. I find it difficult to see how this accusative case verbal noun could be modified by the preceding *duǵala* which is also in the acc. sg., but certainly modifies the preceding phrase.

The contrast in form between *buʾa* here and the *baʾi* of D 5 would seem to support the interpretation of the former as a passive, particularly when it is in a series describing the benefits that will be conferred upon the faithful servant.

bi+maʿbudu: There are numerous problems in this word. First, the reading of the first sign is a measure of desperation since it introduces a type of syllable not elsewhere attested in the signary. It is here read as a CVC, where as all other signs are deciphered as CV. Further, it seems certainly to be not an independent sign, but a ligature of two other signs which are read as *mi* and *ʾi* respectively. This ligature occurs at two other places in the corpus, C 11,13, and the same reading yields satisfactory results. The argument for the process that produced this ligature is as follows:

1. The other *mem* signs do not have a form that readily is adapted to such a ligature, while the ⊤ *mi* sign asks for such a treatment.

2. It is a curious fact that this same sign does not occur elsewhere in Text D, though it is among the most frequent in the corpus.

3. The frequent occurrence of signs with 'dead vowels' readily explains the use of a syllabic form with an alphabetic, i.e. purely consonantal, value.

4. The use of the *ʾaleph* sign instead of the *ʿayin* is purely graphic: the signs are too large and cumbersome to fit, and as a matter of fact in C 13 at least there is a graphic contrast that may have been intended to distinguish it from the normal *ʾalif* sign. At any rate, the reading *maʾ* fits none of the contexts in which this ligature occurs. It is not surprising that syllabic signs of a type other than CV should be represented in the signary—quite the contrary. In view of the enormous complexity of both the Egyptian and Akkadian systems, it is surprising that the signary is characterized by such an economical and symmetrical simplicity.

For the meaning of the word, cf. SC *mʿbd* Job 34:25, a ***hapax*** for which there is hardly a parallel elsewhere. The word in this context of the "Elihu speeches" is definitely perjorative, and the question arises whether the word is not a learned neologism here. The Aramaic infinitive form *mʿbd* is hardly relevant directly, though those infinitives illustrate the 'nominalizing' function of the *m* prefix. The present form should be added to the list of 'verbal nouns' that seems characteristic of this dialect, and which was in the Iron Age dialects everywhere subjected to a ***Systemszwang*** that yielded the grammarians' extremely limited repertory of "infinitives" and "participles."

The second difficulty lies in the case ending. After the preposition the genitive case is appropriate and regularly observed in this corpus. The *du* sign is clear--and there is no reasonable explanation for the nominative case ending within the framework of present knowledge of WS historical linguistics. No problems are solved by interchanging the vowels of the *du* and *di* signs, and unless there is some other unknown grammatical order involved, it is best explained simply as a scribal error.

The last two words of this clause constitute another example of the ***figura etymologica*** that is so loved in this dialect. The root is SC *nwb* 'be fruitful' that survived only in poetry together with the derived noun *tnwbh* that occurs in the oldest sources Deut 32:13 and Jud 9:11. The first word *sanubi* is the *s-* causative verbal noun with the genitive case ending as the second noun in the 'construct chain', and the second is identical (except for vocalization and gender) to SC *tnwbh*, again with the *i/u* alternation. It also is in the genitive case in this double construct chain.

L.32b–33: *ma-nu-(33)ya+ma ša-du-da*
bi+ʾa-ḫu-sa-pa-yi

"Whoever has acted violently against the Ahusapay. . ."

mannuya+ma: The indefinite pronoun seems never to occur twice in exactly the same form. Here it must be nom. sg. as the subject of the following verb, but compare D 4–5: *ma-mu (5)ba-ʾi*, where it is the "subject" of a following plural participle in the oblique case.

šaduda: The meaning of the root involves little difficulty for a change. It is SC *šdd* 'destroy, ruin, slay', etc. In SC there is an exact (accidental) parallel to the form (Jud 5:27): *šm npl šdwd*, where *šdwd* is certainly a passive participle. The verb here must be a form that takes an object in spite of the thematic vowel *u* that usually indicates an intransitive in later WS. The same form occurs also in C 12 where it takes a direct object with the normal accusative case ending, while here the object is designated by a preposition. What difference in meaning if any is signalled by the contrast is not clear. Here the object is evidently a collective gentilic, while in the passage at C 12 the object is a woman individual.

In spite of the difficulty from the context of much later WS grammar, it is simplest to take the form simply as a classical "perfect" tense 3 masc. sg. of the *qatula* form. What corresponds to the infinitive absolute of later SC is of course a possibility, particularly since the vocalization fits precisely. The final *a* vowel would then be very difficult to explain, and translation extremely difficult. The identical form and vocalization in SC Ps 137:8 is probably pure accident.

The history of this root is also very strange. Except for the isolated occurrence in the Song of Deborah, the word is not attested in SC sources earlier than the eighth century prophets but very frequently later, especially after the destruction of Jerusalem. It does not seem to occur elsewhere than in Classical Arabic, where it is a very productive root with the primary meaning 'assault, attack' and the form is *šadda*, with *šin* in violation of the usual "linguistic laws," and therefore this obvious cognate is not cited in the dictionaries. The most reasonable explanation for this strange history is simply the fact that it is a remnant very little changed of the original Coastal Dialect that survived in SC colloquial speech, but was not taken up into the written language until the village prophets of the eighth century, and became very relevant at the time of the destruction of Jerusalem.

bi+ʾaḫusapayi: The preposition is vocalized according to the norm, and designates the object of violence or attack. The word to which it is attached has the gentilic ending *-ayi* with the genitive case ending obligatory after the preposition. In view of the "tribal" designations and names that occur earlier in the document, it is strange to find a completely new name suddenly the object of attention. Whether it designates a 'tribe', or a place name is difficult to say (cf. *śinay*).

It is startling to find the identical very unusual name turn up in the list of King David's mercenary soldiers (2 Sam 23:34): *ʾlyplṭ bn-ʾḥsby* (with the shift from voiceless *p* to *b* which is so frequent in the transition from the Bronze Age to the Iron Age). It is even more interesting that the person in question is identified as originating from Maacah in northern Transjordan. It is difficult to separate the name from Ugaritic *ḥšbn* (*PRU* II 64:7), and from the Transjordanian town of Heshbon. Both these latter place names illustrate the sibilant shift that began at least with the Amorite invasions at the close of the Early Bronze Age.

The prefixed *ʾalif* could be an elative such as in *ʾqht*, and *ʾlʾiyn*. Neither the name nor the root seem to have survived in later WS in a form that can be reasonably identified, with the probable exception of the place names cited above.

L.34a: */ʾi/-ba-ʿa-ti+hu* 

"I will assail him."

ʾibaʿʿat+hu: The first sign is missing but must be the 1 sg. preformative of the verb. Unfortunately, it is not possible therefore to determine the vocalization. To judge from later usage, the Qal stem should be intransitive, and the D–stem transitive. This is the form suggested here, since there is a suffixed pronominal direct object. There is no conceivable grammatical function for the *i* vowel of the *ti* sign, and thus again there is certainly a 'dead vowel' in which the *i*–series sign for that particular consonant is used to indicate the consonant only.

The root seems quite clear, though later preserved uses indicate that it was definitely archaic and even obsolescent. The verb occurs with certainty in SC and dependent sources only, so far as can be easily determined. Only with the tenth century monarchy does it first appear in biblical sources, and in connection with the kingship. The earliest occurrence is in I Sam 16:14 where it designates a subjective 'terrifying' of Saul by an "evil spirit." Roughly contemporary is the occurrence in the tenth century Psalm of David, II Sam 22:5, where also terrifying supra–mundane powers are the subject. It seems virtually certain that this verb was preserved in the local dialect of Jerusalem, and came into the biblical vocabulary only with the Davidic seizure of that city.

It is possible that this root was preserved in another form in OSA. The verb *bʿy* is regularly used to mean 'attack', and can easily be explained on the ground that the final *t* consonant was unstable and dropped with a compensatory *y* root consonant added. It is also very possible that in Classical Arabic this root fell together with *bʿd* 'behind' (Ug. and SC), for it is used in curse formulae, to designate 'death', and to designate unusual supernatural events.

It is important to note that in this Early Bronze Age text a violation of covenant obligations promises a human reprisal by political authority, over against the Late Bronze Age covenant forms where punitive action is taken by transcendent, divine power or powers. This tendency toward increasing appeal to supernatural powers is doubtless a reflection of the increasing inability of political organizations to maintain control directly through military and legal force. Parallel developments in the Late Bronze Age in both Egypt and Mesopotamia are quite clear——the increasing appeal to ritual religiosity is a fairly predictable social reaction to the recognition of the fact that society is faced with insoluble problems.

L.34b–35a: *ḏu ma-la-ki ṣi-(35)[ri]-ra pu-la* 7Ʊ 4[>]Ѱ Ѱ7< ᴗᴑ

"Who of my reign is made hostile, alienated . . ."

ḏu: This seems to be the classical usage of the particle: "the one of . . ." e.g. SC *ḏ sny* 'the one of Sinai'. It introduces further definitions of the person who is subject to the reprisals for action in violation of the social order that is created by this regime.

malākī: This is probably best taken as the classical form of the Iron Age 'infinitive absolute', and thus with a long *ā* in the second syllable. It is a verbal noun, of course, and though translated here as 'reign' it is better conceptualized as the function of 'ruling'.

ṣi(r?)ra: The missing first sign of line 35 is supplied from context and the fact that no other consonant yields a satisfactory sense in this context. The reading *ri* is based upon the probability that there are two verbs in sequence here. The first character read *ṣi* is almost identical to the *mu* sign that does not occur elsewhere in Text D, but several times in Text C. However, though the root *mrr* would be very appropriate here, the *mu* syllable in this text is preempted by the ᴍ sign (which in turn does **not** appear in any other text of the corpus). Accordingly, this is taken to be a variant of the *ṣi* = Ѱ sign that represents a growing sprout, SC *ṣyṣ*.

The root is common in Ug. designating especially hostility to the king, and is the regular word for 'attack' in OSA, which has also the root *ḍrr* meaning 'war'. The latter is the only form that survived in Classical

Arabic, since *ṣrr* was preempted by another root with an entirely unrelated meaning. The two forms with very similar meaning in OSA but semantically differentiated furnish a paradigmatic illustration of the process of 'root–doublet' formation, that is very often the result of the blending of originally distinct dialects. It is also most probable that the *ḏ* sign is not originally a distinct phoneme, but a dialect variant of the *ṣ* phoneme, until a semantic contrast made a graphic contrast necessary.

If the grammatical analysis of these two verbs is correct, it illustrates an ideological tendency to regard internal hostility as the result of unknown (therefore passive form!) external forces. It is an important contrast to the description of the *ʿapiru* band of David where the human cause and human agency are quite clearly described (I Sam 22:2).

pula: It is conceivable that this word should be read with the two following signs: *pu-la-ʾu+ma*, but two considerations make this very improbable. First, this would yield a noun in the nominative case which is grammatically incompatible with the context, and on the other hand the reading preferred gives a *hendiadys* that is entirely satisfactory. Second, there is another *ʾu+ma* in the following line, and therefore a well known sequence familiar in later WS, *ʾu . . . ʾu* results.

The verb is taken to be a passive from the root *plh* of SC that occurs at Exod 8:18 and 33:16 with the meaning, 'to make a distinction, separate'. Cf. Eth. ***tafalawa*** 'to separate', and probably OSA and Arab. ***falawa*** 'to wean––i.e. separate', a highly specialized semantic development.

Lines 35b through 41 seem to have a very complex syntactical structure which has not been completely deciphered, in part because key signs are again missing, but mostly because several words are simply not comprehensible:

L.35b: <u>*ʾu+ma*</u> *ha-ḫi-tu-yi [?](36)[?] ha li pi ma-ti-ma ra-ha-ʿa*
[ma]-ʾa-la du-ʾaʾi+ma yi-yi-ʾi-la

L.37c: <u>*ʾu+(38)ma*</u> *la yi-ki-ni-wi+ma+hu pi-ta+ni-ta*
(39)ḫa-wi-bu+ma ta-ḫu-ba+m ba-wa-ʾi+ni (40) ta-di-m?

<u>*ʾi-ma*</u> *la+ki-ti+ya+ma ha-(41)[?][ti]-ḫu-mu-pu [li ?*

It seems clear that there are two long clauses each beginning with

ʾu+ma, a following main verb, and a cognate accusative construction. In the second clause there is a conclusion introduced with the particle *ʾima*. There is a trace of what appears to be a  *li* sign after the lone word of line 41, but it is quite clear that there were no further words on this line, nor on the empty space at the bottom edge of the copper plate.

L.35b–36a: *ʾu+ma ha-ḫi-tu-yi(36)[-ma?] ha-li-pi* 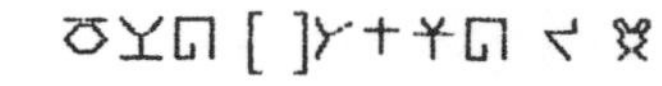

"whether causing to destroy [and?] causing to smite . . ."

ʾu . . . ʾu This construction needs no comment in the light of the frequency with which it occurs in later CS. The enclitic *-ma* seems to have no semantic function.

haḫtuyi: This normalization of the main verb seems both justified and necessary. The second sign with the vowel *i*, seems to have a 'dead vowel'. The causative with thematic vowel *u* is anomalous, but perhaps illustrates again the preference in this dialect for the *u* over against the later *i* class vowel in quite a few contexts. It is the *h-* causative of the CS root *ḫty* that occurs in so many forms with closely related meanings that it is not possible to choose among them. The problem is that none seem to favor the causative stem in normal usage, and most languages presuppose the *ḥ* rather than the *ḫ* consonant. The various meanings attested range from 'destroy', 'strike down', 'snatch away'——objective acts, to 'fear' in SC and Akk.——which is a semantic change shifting from the objective cause to the subjective effect, beautifully illustrated in SC *mḫth* that is translated both 'ruin' and 'terror'.

There can be no doubt that this verb designates some action inimical to the well-being of the state, or at least of the king. The only question is whether it designates an act of instigation of evil, hence the causative, or whether the causative is merely the transitive form of a root that is intransitive in the Qal stem. The context is so broken and enigmatic that further conclusions are not possible. The important sense of the sentence is that a cause-and-effect relationship is established between some kind of violent wrongdoing and a suffering as a consequence.

halipi⟨ʾ⟩ Causative from the root *lpʾ* attested in Arabic: 'peel, beat (with a stick)', and in Ugaratic with probably a similar meaning. This, together with the preceding word, describes two types of anti-social behavior at any rate. The forms are verbal nouns with genitive case endings, of the sort discovered fairly recently: *qatāli ʾanaku*, in which the genitive case ending results from a preposition such as *b-, k-* originally prefixed to the verbal noun, but in idiomatic usage simply dropped from the spelling, and no doubt the pronunciation. The infinitive ending in *i* is thus probably a temporal or circumstantial clause in origin, as in this passage.

L.36b: *ma-ti-ma ra-ḥa-ʿa* 

"whenever he has done evil . . ."

mati+ma: CS *mty* is usually an interrogative 'when?' but here it would seem to mean 'whenever', like *man+ma* 'whoever'< ʿ*man*ʾ 'who?'

raḥaʿa: This is a surprise. The root appears in the perfect tense form with a medial *ḥ*, which evidently shifted (as almost always was the case) to medial *w* to yield forms such as SC *roʿ*. In forms in which the shift to *w* did not take place, the medial consonant was simply dropped, yielding *raʿ* The root *rʿʿ* is purely a figment of the grammarians' system-building. Medial *ḥ* verbs were preserved in unusual numbers in OSA, just as in this dialect. The use of the perfect tense here is interesting, for it stipulates that a completed act will have consequences that are described with the preformative (imperfect) tense.

L.37a: *[ma]-ʾa-la du-ʾa-ʾi-ma yi-yi-ʾi-la* 

"with the curse of sickness he shall be cursed."

The grammatical construction of this sentence is much easier to describe than it is to render it into English in a way that reflects accurately the grammar.

[ma]ʾala: Accusative of specification in the ***figura etymologica.*** The nominalizing prefix *ma-* is analogous to the *ta-* preformative in the ***hapax leg.*** *tʾlh* in SC, Lam 3:65. However, the prefix is here supplied, and the noun could well have had some other form.

It is quite clear from the following verb that the root is *yʾl*, which again seems to be CWS, though in various forms since the root consonants are especially unstable, surviving in NC (Yaudi), SC and Arabic (curiously absent in Ugaritic), and coming into East Semitic with a semantic base that is probably primitive: 'to bind'. Cf. the discussion of the root *skr* above at line 12. Cf. OB *iʾlu* 'pact, covenant'. The oath(=the curse) **is** the covenant.

du-ʾa-ʾi+ma: The root is clearly a very archaic form of later CWS *dwy*. The form is the frequent *qutal* structure, in the genitive case of the 'construct chain'. The enclitic *-ma* again seems to have no semantic function. The noun specifies which of the many deleterious "acts of god" it is that will result from violation of covenant.

The history of this root is especially illuminating for linguistic "areography" as plant taxonomists have labelled the phenomenon. The root is so archaic that it cannot have survived unchanged with two *ʾalifs* in later WS. It is clearly a Coastal Dialect word that was the semantic equivalent of the Common East Semitic root *mrṣ*. It survived in SC with a fairly specialized semantic range ('menses'), and fully in the southern regions even as far as Ethiopic. It came into the Inland Dialect region probably with the Persian Empire, and thence in Late Babylonian as a loanword. Meanwhile, the CES *mrṣ* word came into all the WS languages, no doubt as a result of the EB–MB Amorite invasions. The form in Arabic with *ḍ* is almost certainly attestation to its Inland Dialect original habitat.

yiyiʾʾila: The normalization reflects the analysis of this verb form as the impf. optative/precative of the D–stem. The Qal form of the verb would presumably have meant 'to swear (an oath)' as it does in later WS. Here, it is the imposing of the curse that is the topic in consideration, and this would require a derived stem, transitive with the accusative of specification. The repeated *yi-* sign violates the rule that *y* and *w* at the end of a syllable are represented by zero, and therefore there is no 'dead vowel' in this form. The only usual verb form in which there is a vowel after the first root consonant is the D–stem.

Even the ending in *-a* is significant, for it illustrates the 'optative' *yaqtula* form that is quite well attested in the Amarna Letters, and survived as the so–called 'cohortative' in SC. The subject of the verb is possibly the relative clause beginning with *d̲u* in D 34b, but there are no formal or semantic grounds for regarding the verb as a passive––it is simply a verb form that designates the fate of the subject that meets certain conditions. The fulfillment of the curse is clearly the function of deity universally, but the deity is not named. More's the pity, for it would be most interesting to know what personal names of deities were in common use in Byblos toward the close of the Early Bronze Age. The self–conscious religiosity of the closing days of the Late Bronze Age was evidently not a cultural trait at the time these texts were written.

In this respect, the 'secular' nature of the SC 'Covenant Code' is an interesting and very significant parallel phenomenon. The reason for this is historically quite simple. As anthropologists have pointed out ritual is a universal social means for maintaining the social boundary line and social solidarity. When the historical situation (such as the formation of a state) demands a larger unity, the adherence to traditional ritual religious forms is an enormous burden upon the larger unity, and a hazard to its successful functioning. Consequently there seem to be only two responses to the dilemma: either the 'establishment' of virtually all existing ritual traditions, and their subordination to the overarching ritual tradition of the royal court (='polytheism', but actually Baal–worship), or the functions of religion are successfully concentrated on those obligations that are essential to the operation of the larger unity——norms of social ethic, which is of course covenant. It should not be surprising that this sort of religious structure was regarded by its opponents as "outlawry" in the Early Iron Age, and as "atheism" in the period of the Roman Empire.

Still another phonetic feature of this verb form needs comment, even though there is no clear answer. The thematic vowel *i* between the second and third root consonants is, to be sure, characteristic of the D–stem impf. in later WS, but there have been repeated cases where the contrast between the *a* and the *i* thematic vowels can correspond to the contrast between present–future and preterite 'tenses'. If such a contrast did really exist, the use of the preterite here would be a case of the 'precative preterite' the existence of which is debated. The least that can be said is that this archaic dialect had a remarkably complex morphological and syntactic structure, and this is only to be expected. The sequence of verb forms in this sentence is remarkable: (1) Verbal noun: *qatali*. (2) Suffix tense: *qatala*. (3) Prefix tense: *yaqtul*, possibly preterite, certainly precative.

L.37b–38: *ʾu+(38)ma la yi-ki-ni-wu+ma*
hu-pi-ta+ni-ta

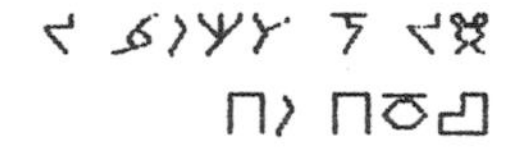

"Or whether he does not do uprightly, fulfilling obligations to us"

ʾu+ma: The second of the *ʾu+ma* . . . *ʾu+ma* series that began at line 35. The first describes evil deeds, and this clause seems at least to describe failure to fulfil obligations.

la yikinniwu+ma: The D–stem of a root *knw* that is probably the remote origin of much later WS *knh/y/ʾ*: 'give a name (of honor)'. SC occurrences are found only in exilic literature and later, Job, II Isaiah, Sirach. Possibly Ugaritic uses the root in much the sense as here: Aistleitner translates it as ***tadellos***, and compares Akk. *kunnu* ***'rechtmassig'***.

hupita+nita: This strange looking form is the *h* causative verbal noun of some sort from the root *wpy*, or a suffix tense verb in the second person. This latter suggestion does not commend itself, for it would yield two verbs in sequence, with a shift from 3rd person to 2nd person. The *-ta* afformative is much more easily interpreted as the feminine ending to a verbal noun, and according to rule, in the accusative case. As a verbal noun, it receives the oblique first person plural suffix, *nita*. According to rule again, the first *w* root consonant is represented as zero in the orthography, but probably influenced the vocalization with the vowel *u*.

For the meaning, cf. OSA ***wfy***, *h*-causative: "pay, grant, fulfill obligations, render s.o. his due." Possibly it is cognate to SC *yph* 'beautiful'.

L.39a: *ḫa-wu-bu+ma ta-ḫu-ba+m* 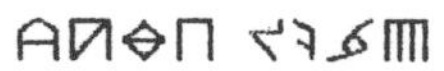

"you have incurred guilt."

ḫawubu+ma: This form shows that there was not a single structure used in the ***figura etymologica***, but rather there was a variety of grammatical constructions possible. It is most likely that this is a *qatul* form of the verbal noun with two short vowels, a stative parallelling the *qatil* form that is much more frequent, in words such as *malik*, *ʿapir*, and the like. The case ending suggests that this is a sort of 'nominative absolute' similar to the *-umma epešu* construction known elsewhere in the Bronze Age.

taḫuba+m: for *taḫwuba+m*. The *w* is represented as zero when it is not protected by a vowel both preceding and following this weakly articulated consonant. The verb form is the classical prefix tense *yaqtul* with the optative/precative *-a* ending, and what is treated in this decipherment as a final alphabetic i.e. vowelless *m* sign, for lack of a better solution. The sign is quite common in the BS corpus, though this is the only occurrence in Text D, unless the third sign of line 40 is a mere graphic variant--a suggestion that does not seem very probable. With one exception, the sign occurs only at the end of a word, both with verbs, as in this construction, and with nouns. The problem of its reading arises from the fact that its position demands its identification as a grammatical affix, but virtually all of the consonants thus used are represented by the complete series C+*a,i,u*, and thus this sign almost certainly is a fourth--and therefore vowelless--representative of a consonant that is most probably the most frequent in the signary--the *mem*.

This solution of the problem then yields another feature of this writing system that made possible the much later transition to a purely alphabetic signary. The quite frequent use of syllabic signs in contexts where the vowel was not 'read', i.e. the 'dead vowels', is then paralleled by at least one consonant-only sign. Thus it is easy to understand how a subsequent period of very minimal literacy (EB IV to MB II) could reduce the writing system to the bare bones of consonant representation only. The fact that there is no parallel to the transition from a syllabic system to an alphabetic system of writing is entirely irrelevant to the historical process, for there is no ancient parallel to the development of any independent alphabetic system at all. Furthermore, to argue that the subsequent Canaanite alphabet is a "syllabary" simply flies in the face of fact, and classifies together two radically different writing systems.

The use of the the prefix-tense in this context is intriguing, for it is preceded by another prefix-tense verb that clearly refers to some future contingency--the failure to fulfill obligations--but this verb seems at least to illustrate the normal 'narrative' tense, though with a precative force. The 'pluperfect' is almost demanded in this context: "you shall have become guilty." It is clearly the origin of the frequent phrase in the Hittite suzerainty treaties, "you act in disregard of your oath."

The root *ḥwb* has an interesting semantic history. Its presence here and in Classical Arabic *ḥwb*: 'commit a crime', indicates that it is CWS in the EB period, but it became obsolete in 'Canaanite' of the MB-LB period. It does not appear in Ugaritic, nor in early sources of SC (its reading in I Sam 22:22 is mere conjecture, and furthermore, the dating of this particular segment is far from clear). The root survived with a primarily financial meaning in Aramaic, and it is very probable that it came into Arabic from Aramaic a second time under the Aramaic form *ḥwb* 'be poor'. The grass roots colloquial usage of the root to indicate both economic and moral deficiencies is illustrated vividly in the old controversy over the liturgical translation of 'forgive us our debts/transgressions' in the protestant churches: the Greek word is a translation–loan of a Semitic word (certainly this one) that merely indicated unfulfilled obligations.

L.39b–40a: *ba-wa-ʾi+ni-(40)ta di-m?* 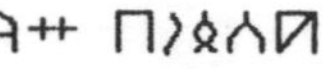

"entering into us is? ??"

bawaʾi+nita: Again the *qatāli* verbal noun form with the genitive case ending that is grammatically unmotivated by anything that precedes. As we have seen, the previous two sentences evidently conclude with the final verb of the ***figura etymologica***, and therefore this word introduces a new sentence with two phrases. This first phrase is evidently a two word noun sentence, and it is followed by a conditional clause introduced with the particle *ʾ+ma* 'if'.

di-m: The second sign is the problem. It is a ***hapax*** that closely resembles the *m* A sign discussed above, but it has an extra vertical stroke suspended from the crossbar, and it does not seem at all justified to treat it as a mere graphic variant, particularly since the resulting word *dim* is meaningless. It also has some affinity with the second character of D 32, and it could also be analysed as a combination of the T *mi* sign plus the ∩ *ʿi* sign. Unfortunately, the resulting reading *di-mi-ʿa*, does not commend itself in the context, and the phrase will have to await some new bright idea. If the analysis of the general context is not too far from the mark, the phrase ought to mean that the incorporation of the group or person into the society is 'void, if––'.

L.40b–41:*ʾi+ma la+ki-ti+ya+ma ha-* 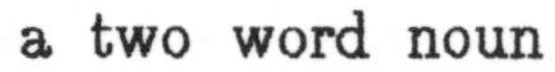

(41)*[?-ti] ḫu-mu-pu[li?* 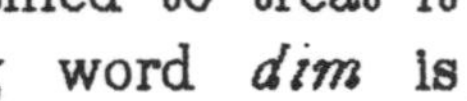

" . . . if against my covenant you act ruthlessly."

The conditional clause needs no further comment beyond the observation that the particle *ʾima* 'if' occurs in its classical SC form deriving from the EB Coastal Dialect, over against the Inland Dialect form with *h* as in Ugaritic and Aramaic. Cf. also the use of *ʾim* in OSA as a strong asseverative, 'indeed'. This is also a possibility here that should be considered, for it would enlarge the range of potential meaning for the obscure two–word phrase that precedes: ' . . . verily, you have acted ruthlessly'.

[ti-?]ḫmupu [li?: The first part of this final line is broken, but traces of a diagonal stroke are visible on the photograph, which can be identified as either a ∢ *ma* or a ⌖ *ti* sign. The latter seems far preferable, since it continues the second person address found in *taḫubam* of line 39. For the meaning compare Amarna 288:8, *ḫa-an-pa ša iḫ-nu-pu* "the ruthless deed which they committed," and note the continuation of this usage of the root in Ugaritic, SC (though not earlier than the eighth century prophets), and even Ethiopic. It is clearly a WS loanword in the Amarna letters. The representation of the root in Arabic and OSA is far from clear.

The archaic source of this root and its text is clearly indicated by the medial *m* which is virtually impossible in all later WS, where there was a dissimilation to *n*, and it is not impossible, to *l* in Arabic.

6

BYBLOS SYLLABIC TEXT C

L.1a: *ha-bu-la ni-ni-ti ru-ḫi-ma-tu ṯu-tu-ni ba-ti-mi-m*

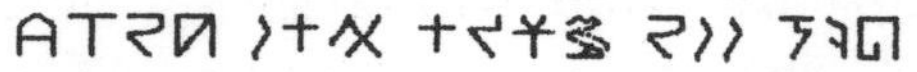

L.2: *ba+ḫi-ti+ma ta-la-[bi]-sa+ni ka-yi-na-tu+m*

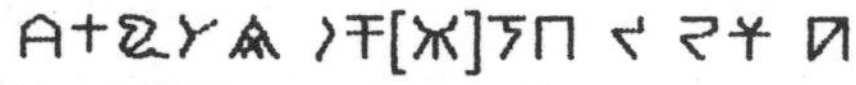

L.3 *ma-ʾi-ma wi-ṯu+ni bi+hu-ʾi ʾa-ka-yi-na+ma* 

L.4 *ba+yi-li ha-ra-ra-ti ta-ka-yi-na+ma ba-yi-ta+hu*

L.5 *pa+ma-ta ba-ḫi-mu ḫu-li-ta-ti bi+ma-li-ha-m*

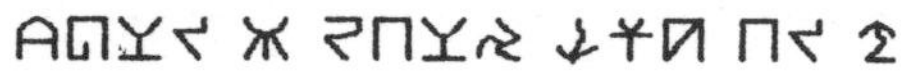

L.6 *ṯu-tu-sa-ru bi-ni+hu-mu sa-ba-ru ka-yi-na-tu-m*

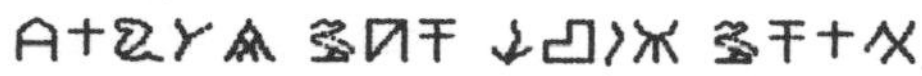

L.7 *ʿu-bu-du-wu+ma du-ga-wi+ma ya-ta-sa-ʿu-bu-du+ma+ni-ni*

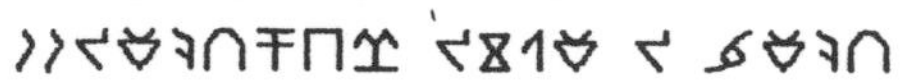

L.8 *pa+ti-ru-ni-tu yu-ḫu-bu-ba ta-ta-ʿu-bu-du+ma+mi*

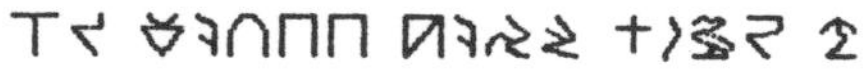

L.9 *ba-ti-ya+ma ba-yi-ti ba-ri-ri za-hi-ru+ma hi-li-ni*

L.10 *ma-ni bi-ni-hu-mu sa-ba-ru ka-yi-na-tu-m*

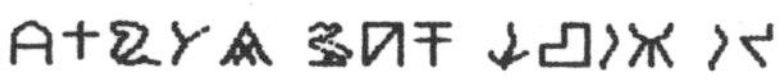

L.11 *pa+ha-ḫi-ni+mi maʿ-bu-du bi+ʾa-ha-sa-sa-nu-tu-ʾa*

L.12 *bi+ma-nu-ma ša-du-da ra-ḫi-ma-ta ʾi-ba-li-gu+hu*

L.13 *maʿ-pu-tu-m ma-ʿu-ta-ma ʾi-ḫi-lu ti-li-ḫa pa+ḫi*

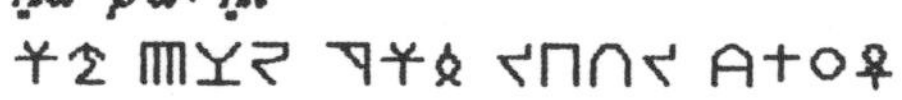

L.14 *-wa ḫi-du bi+hu-ʾi ʾa-ba-ḫi-mu ḏu* 

L.15 *[ ]ba+ḫi-ti+mi 1 1 1 1 1 1 1* 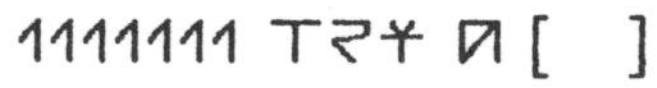

L.1a: ha–bu–la ni–ni–ti ru–Hi–ma–tu 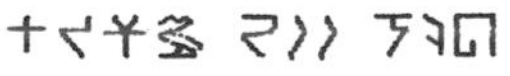

"Habula my daughter is the 'beloved' . . ."

habula: The text begins with the personal name of the woman who is being betrothed in this marriage contract. The name is very archaic and appears nowhere else in Canaanite sources, but it is reported four times in Old North Arabic inscriptions. It is certainly the same name as *hbl* in Gen 4, and evidently falls into the rather large class of personal names that can be given to females as well as to males.

niniti: The first sign read here *ni–* shows traces in the IR slide of a stroke toward the bottom and could be read *bu–*, thus yielding *buniti* with the archaic preference for the *u* vowel that seems characteristic of this dialect. Cf. also the Amorite PN *bunu-ištar*. The word as read is the feminine form of the word that survives only in an idiomatic expression in SC: *nyn wnkd*. The final long *i* vowel is the 1 sg. pronominal possessive suffix.

ruḥimatu: Nom. case passive feminine verbal noun. It is the subject of the noun sentence of which the PN and appositional identification are the predicate. The translation 'beloved' renders the meaning, but in the context it is the Coastal Dialect semantic equivalent of Akk. *ḫawir* lit. 'chosen', but meaning 'spouse' particularly in view of the following prepositional phrase.

This usage in the context of a marriage contract illuminates the famous SC passage of Hos 1:6,8 and 2:3,25, where *lʾ rḥmh* derives from a Qal passive, not D–stem passive as traditional grammars would have it. Exactly as *lʾ ʿmy* means 'illegitimate' with regard to a child, so *lʾ rḥmh* means, with reference to a female, 'not a legitimate spouse'. The parallelism is perfect.

L.1b: *ṯu-ṯu-ni ba-ti-mi-m* 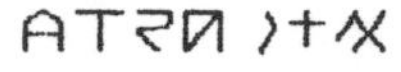

" . . . of Thutun in legitimacy."

ṯutuni: The reading of the first sign is not certain, but this is by far the most probable. The only conceivable alternative to the X = *ṯu* sign is the X = *ku*, but the upper right diagonal stroke seems quite clear. It is significant that this same sign recurs in lines 3 and 6, and all three of these forms have a stance that is the reverse of that which is used in Text D, lines 14 and 23, further indication that this writing system was not rigidly fixed, but was perhaps still in process of evolution when the culture that produced it was destroyed.

The PN of the bridegroom, for which cf. Ug *ṯty* with the *-ya* hypocoristicon ending instead of the *-un* suffix here. Compare SC *zbwlwn, yšwrwn*, both archaic forms. In SC the name *ṯut-* could only become *šet.* It is a hair-raising fact that in this document we have the record of a marriage or betrothal of a bride named Abel to a groom named Seth. I would draw no further conclusions from the data.

ba+timmim. The vocalization with *i* instead of *u* is somewhat surprising, in view of the fact that this dialect seems to have a considerable preference for the *u* vowel elsewhere. The final sign read *-m* is a problem, but no alternative reading has recommended itself. It may be a conventional enclitic that later became a mimation or nunation, but nowhere does there seem to be any discernable grammatical function.

The meaning, however, is clear here, for the phrase clearly defines the status of the woman as a legitimate spouse over against the status of concubine, paramour, or slave-girl. For the usage, compare especially the archaic narrative of Jud 9:16: *ʾm-bʾmt wbtmym* "if in good faith and legitimacy . . . ".

L.2: *ba+ḥi-ti+ma ta-la-[bi]-sa+ni ka-yi-na-tu+m* 

"In fear you shall clothe her in perpetuity."

ba+ḥitti+ma: Literally, 'in fear', but the meaning corresponds to English 'conscientiously', i.e. fearing to fail in fulfilling voluntarily accepted obligations. The construction is straightforward enough: the prep. *ba-*

with *a* vowel is followed by a syllable with *i* vowel in accordance with the almost invariable rule, and the noun has the genitive case ending after the preposition. The noun is preserved in SC *ḥitt–* (Gen 9:2), where the fear of man is upon the animal world. By analogy the *ḥtt ʾlhym* in Gen 35:5 describes the objective source of an internal state that determines behavior. It is, of course, the ancient semantic equivalent of the later frequent *yrʾt ʾlhym* 'fear of God'. The enclitic *–ma* has here as usually no clear semantic or grammatical function.

tala[bbi]sa+nni: The supplied syllabic sign ㅈ *bi* is of course not certain. There is no observable trace preserved, but there is hardly any other known Semitic root that fits in the context. The reading with the vowel *i* instead of *a* is preferred simply because the following two verbs have the same vocalization, and probably the same grammatical construction. The verb is the D stem and therefore has the doubling of the second root consonant. The ending in *–a* signals the 'optative/precative' mood that has been observed a millennium later in the Amarna and Ug. sources: Amarna *ia–di–na*. The direct object of this transitive verb is the 3 fem. sg. suffix *–hi* that has been assimilated to the *–ni* impf. ending: *talabbisa+ni+hi* > *–anni*.

kayyinatu+m: This normalization is far from certain, and is based partly upon a similar usage in the OB and esp. Mari adverbial acc. *kayyantam*, 'perpetually'. It could be read *kaynatu+m* exactly as *ba–yi–ta* must be read *bayta* in line 4b. The nom. case ending is intriguing as a sort of 'nominative absolute' where we would expect the adverbial accusative as in OB and elsewhere in these texts. Cf. the later *–umma epešu*. The form is taken to be a D–stem verbal noun from the root *kwn*. Since this stem demands a themative vowel in *–i–* after the second root consonant, it seems that the vowel has influenced the shift from *–w–* to *–y–* here as well as in the verb forms of the following two lines. We thus have the EB phenomenon underlying the SC verb forms of the Iron Age in another grammatical context: *yakun / yakin*.

After the statement of the change in status of the bride, the father of the bride speaks directly to the bridegroom concerning his prescriptive obligation, which is the economic support of the bride, symbolically described as 'clothing' her in perpetuity. A millennium later, the same description occurs in the old SC 'lawcode' at Exod 21:10, where it appears as one of a trio of the normal obligations of a husband.

L.3 *ma-ʾi-ma wi-ṯu+ni bi+hu-ʾi ʾa-ka-yi-na+ma* 

"Any defect existing in her I establish."

The translation is uncertain, and is ***ad hoc*** based upon the proposed etymologies of the first two words. The clause is taken to be a guarantee on the part of the bride's father that there is no physical defect or other hidden disease or shortcoming. Similar clauses are attested quite frequently in the case of transference of slaves in antiquity.

maʾima: This is probably SC *mʾwm/mwm*. The reading is not certain, but it is nearly impossible to assume that the 'ears' of the 𐎀 = *ʾu* could have been present on the copper plate. The surface erosion at the top of the existing *ʾaleph* sign is not that extensive. It would seem that here is another case in which the *u/i* interchange has taken place, as in *ba+timmim* in line 1.

wiṯu+ni: The etymon of SC *yš*, Arab. *ʾiṯay* and Akk. *išu*, complete with the *i* vowel. It illustrates once more the very frequent preservation of the *w* consonant, over against later WS dialects. The particle seems to govern the acc. case ending in *−a*, as does the negative particle *ianu* in Amarna Akkadian, though the noun *maʾima* could also be construed as the dir. obj. of the main verb at the end of the clause. As usual, the enclitic *−ni* has no observable function or meaning.

bi+huʾi: The form is anomalous in every respect. In the first place, the prefixed preposition should have the vocalization in *a* before the following *u* vowel. The form of the supposed 3 fem. sg. pronoun is also very curious. The final *i* vowel is taken to be a gen. case ending after the preposition, and thus is not likely a feminine marker. Could it be that the 3 sg. pronoun was not gender differentiated, like the 1 sg. pronoun that remained so?

ʾakayyinama: The transitive 1 sg. optative−precative impf. with final *−a* that occurs in all three verbs in lines 2−4, and in all three persons: 2nd, 1st, and 3rd fem. The translation in this particular context is difficult because of the uncertainty of meaning of the first two words in the clause. 'Establish' is general enough and justified by later usages of the verb in derived conjugations. At any rate, there can be little doubt concerning the intention of the clause. The enclitic *−ma* again is opaque. It could be taken as a weak conjunction marking the shift of attention to the obligation of the bride, but the same enclitic *–ma* occurs in the main verb of that clause.

L.4 *ba+yi–li ha–ra–ra–ti ta–ka–yi–na+ma ba–yi–ta+hu* 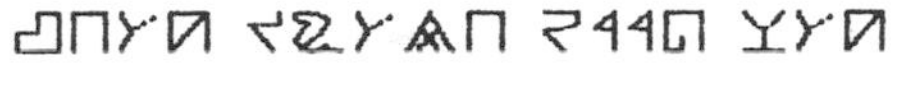

"With desirable offspring she shall establish his house."

ba+yili: The preposition has the proper vowel *a* before the following *i* according to rule. For the main word, Ugaritic for once seems to preserve the only clear descendant in the archaic poetic parallelism *ṯr ʾaḫyh // ṯr ylyh*. If Aistleitner is correct in seeing here a cognate to Arab. *wali*, then the present form would represent the elision of the second *yod*: *yi–li–yi > yili* with a final long *i* vowel. This word seems clearly to be a collective noun: 'siblings'?

hararāti: In form the word is a gen. pl. collective/feminine modifying the preceding noun that is therefore similarly collective. For the meaning of the word that seems to have no cognates outside Ug., cf. again the archaic/poetic parallelism of *hrr // ḥmd*. Professor Ward has suggested that the word is cognate to Eg. *hri* 'be content, pleased'. In certain forms the verb geminates: *hrr*: 'One who satisfies'. It is very intriguing that both of these words with cognates only in Ug. occur in the same text (BH 51–52 and BH 38–39), though rarely elsewhere as well. Whether the offspring was 'desired' or 'desirable' is probably an irrelevant semantic issue.

takayyina+ma: 3 fem. sg. optative D–stem parallel to those of the two preceding clauses. For the concept of 'establishing a house' cf. the advice of Shamshi–Adad to Yasmakh–Adad in the Mari letter ***ARM*** I 52, and also Psa 127:1,3.

bayta+hu: As expected, this dialect preserves the diphthongs and writes them necessarily as though they constituted two syllables. The form is a textbook illustration of that which underlay the Iron Age form of noun plus 3 masc. sg. possessive suffix.

L.5 *pa+ma–ta ba–ḫi–mu ḫu–li–ta–ti bi+ma–li–ha–m* 

"And when they are numerous in progeny in their fulness . . ."

pa+mata: The conjunction *pa–* as usual introduces a new subject or sentence, and is here prefixed to a temporal conjunction. This is identified with the CWS *mati* that occurs from OB and OA to OSA.

baḫimu: The reading *mu* for the sign ↓ seems necessary. The corresponding sign in Text D ʌʌʌ never occurs in this text and the sign read *mu* here does not occur in Text D. It is another indication that this syllabic system either had not become canonically fixed, or possibly the texts cover an extended period of time during which changes of the syllabary were introduced.

This word again has a phonetic structure that is virtually incompatible with any later West Semitic phonological structure, and was not preserved in this form. It is to be identified with Arab. *faḫuma* 'be great'. The inital voiced stop has become voiceless, and the back fricative cannot be now defined in terms other than historical, i.e. etymological. The subject is presumably the persons involved in this marriage contract, and the verb is thus a classical 3 pl. perfect tense form with a presumed final long *u* vowel. It is interesting to note that again for the third time in five lines this text illustrates the interchange of the *u* and *i* vowels, in contrast to Semitic dialects of the Iron Age.

The 'perfect tense' form here is of particular interest because it posits some (necessarily future!) situation as a precondition for another complex verb form that does not have the *ya–* preformative. The intent of the sentence should probably be translated as 'when they will have become great with respect to progeny, then (as a consequence) . . . '.

ḫulitati: This word is the oblique plural feminine form of an abstract or collective noun with the *–t–* suffix. It is cognate to later SC *ḫld* and Arab. *ḫld*. Its function is as an accusative of specification that describes the situation in which the previous verb is operative. The semantic shift between this very old usage and those of the Iron Age Semitic dialects is of special interest. In both Arabic and SC the shift has been toward a more abstract sense of 'perpetuity', instead of something like 'continuity through progeny' that is the meaning in this context.

Note again that this dialect seems to have voiceless where later Iron Age Semitic dialects have voiced consonants. The environmental influence of the liquid *l* can easily be cited as the 'linguistic law' to account for the shift. It may be irrelevant, but the exact consonantal structure of this word occurs in Ug. as the name of a month *ḫlt*, and it occurs also as a personal name in ONA.

bi+mali(ʾ)+ham: Lit. 'in their fulness', an idiomatic expression that is CWS from Mari to OSA in varying form and construction. This is the only occurrence of the 3 fem. pl. pron. suffix in this corpus, and is formally and semantically according to rule, referring back to the fem. collective noun *yili*. Also according to rule, the preposition takes the *i* vowel before the following *a* vowel.

Though the following lines are very difficult if not impossible to interpret, it seems that this clause introduces a sort of 'blessing' formula in which the future well-being of the married couple is described. It seems strange to us that it should be part of what we regard as a legal document, and this merely points out the inadequacy of imposing our modern concepts of literary 'genre' upon ancient writings that stem from a radically different cultural milieu.

L.6 *ṯu-tu-sa-ru bi-ni+hu-mu sa-ba-ru ka-yi-na-tu-m* 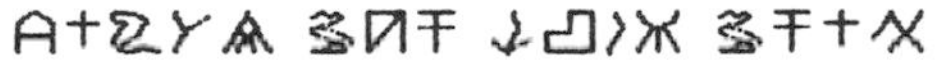

"Well-being is forwarded among them in perpetuity."

ṯutusaru: Shafel-causative reflexive-stative perfect of the verb *wasāru*, in which again according to rule the first root consonant *w* is represented as zero after the *u* vowel in a closed syllable. The verb is of course the later *ʾ/yšr* of Ug. and EA, as well as SC and CWS. The translation reflects the actual usage of the verb in the Bronze Age that is attested in both the Amarna Akkadian and in OSA, as well as in the archaic WS name *yiśra-ʾel*. This name as well as its normal 'Canaanite' form attested in Ug. *yšr-ʾel* and also in the SC hypocoristicon *yšrn* belongs to the large class of archaic 'tribal' names that stem from a stage of the language antedating the biblical Israel by perhaps half a millennium or more, and therefore they were all subjected to 'popular etymologies'. If as this line suggests the verb was already toward the close of the Early Bronze Age used as a blessing formula, the significance of the name receives a considerable illumination.

The causative preformative of this verb form is an anomaly and not paralleled elsewhere in the corpus. The reading of the sign as one of the *samech* series instead of the *ṯa* creates more difficulties than it would solve, and the only reasonable solution here is to see it as a deliberate dissimilation before the following *samech*--the opposite to that attested in such Ug. forms as *yṯṯbn*.

The meaning of the verb at this early date is not ascertainable beyond the vague semantic range reflected in the translation. In Amarna Akk. it definitely is used of the installation in office of a subordinate within the framework of the Egyptian imperial government structure, and therefore the legitimate exercise of authority is based upon the fact that one is 'sent' into an office by a higher power. What the authority does is described with the same linguistic label, and thus EA 306:25 *a-na šu-ta-ši-rim* 'to set matters right' or the like. This Amarna usage is still preserved in OSA, where 'send' is the normal translation. It is the concept of legitimate agency that gave rise, then, to the semantic shift represented in the Iron Age usage translated as 'upright, straight'.

bini+humu: *bini* is most probably the very archaic source eventually of the later Iron Age separable preposition *min*. It is the preposition *b*– plus the enclitic –*ma* that has been dissimilated to –*ni*. The vowel with the preposition was fixed, and therefore did not shift with the change from –*ma* to –*ni*. Thus we have in OSA the regular form *bn*– as well as the unassimilated form *b+mw* just as in Iron Age SC *bemo*. There seems to be no reason to question that this form *bn* became further assimilated to become *mn* in Iron Age SC. Phonetic shifts from *b* to *m* are not very common, but are well enough attested to make this virtually a certainty.

The differences in meaning between SC *b*– and *mi*– are a result of progressive semantic specialization that accompanied the phonetic shift.

The 3 masc. pl. pronominal suffix is particularly interesting in contrast to the suffix read –*ham* in the preceding clause. Here it must refer to the betrothed couple, while in the preceding clause the referent is a still theoretical and hoped for posterity.

sabaru: The translation 'well–being' is the reflection of a complex process of semantic as well as phonetic reconstruction that is necessary in order to identify the word here and its continuity into much later Semitic languages. In view of the sibilant shift for which we have such massive evidence in the contrast between this dialect and the 'Canaanite' of the LB and Iron Ages, it would seem very probable that later cognates would have the *š* where this has the actual *samech* ₸ sign. There is no SC root *šbr*

(*šbr* 'break' derives from *ṯbr* and does not fit at all into the context here). Again the voiced/voiceless shift yields the SC *špr* 'beautiful' which is itself a semantic specialization. Classical Arabic may preserve this root in both forms: *spr* 'to shine', cited by the dictionaries is certainly relevant, but compare also *sbr* that seems to be preserved only as a derived noun *sibrun* or *sabrun* 'goodly form or appearance.' It also exhibits the semantic specialization in which the aesthetic aspect has become predominant in the usage of a root that originally like CS *ṭwb* and Akk. *damaqu* designated 'good' of all sorts

The noun is nom. sg. masc., the subject of the sentence that begins with the verb form *ṭutusaru*. Should this latter form be regarded as the derived stem verbal noun also in the nom case? We simply are not in position to explain these extremely archaic forms on the basis of Iron Age grammatical 'rules'.

kayyinatum: Exactly the same spelling as in line 2, and with the same meaning: 'in perpetuity'. Its interpretation as an 'adverbial nominative' is entirely in keeping with the context in both places.

L.7 *ʿu-bu-du-wu+ma du-ǵa-wi+ma* 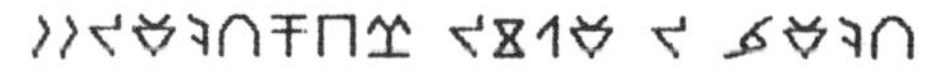
ya-ṭa-sa-ʿu-bu-du+ma+ni-ni

(Translation not yet possible.)

This is a strange sentence. In form it appears to be a noun from the CS root *ʿbd* with an augment in the nominative case, followed by a modifier in the genitive case, ending with a reflexive—causative verb from the same CS root *ʿbd*, with probably an enclitic *—ma* and a suffixed double *—ni*. The verb is in 3 sg. or possibly masc. pl. reflecting the number and gender of the noun—subject with which the sentence begins.

ʿubuduwu+ma: For the noun suffix *—uwu* cf. again Arab. *ʿubudiyyatun* which has the fem. ending, and the meaning is given as an abstraction: 'obedience with humility or submissiveness', esp. in a religious sense.

duǵawi+ma: Cf. the **hapax** in SC (Gen 48:16) *dǵw* 'be numerous', and Arab. *djw* used in several idiomatic expressions meaing 'abundant, ample' or the like. It is suggested that we have here a word that barely survived into later times, and is possibly the origin of the very old WS deity Dagon, and of the later designations of both 'grain' and 'fish', neither of which is then primitive.

yatasa'budu+ma+nini: The verb is the most complex of the corpus, and little more can be said about it, other than the fact that it is a finite imperfect form with the normal *ya–* preformative that fits with the noun subject that does not have the fem ending. The thematic vowel is in *u* that contrasts with the *i* and *a* vowels attested in similar forms in Text D.

The problem is semantic. It is diffidently suggested that later CS *'bd* in a multitude of forms designating a state of slavery cannot be the primitive meaning, if only for the simple reason that legal slavery is a sophisticated political concept that can exist only in the presence of a highly developed political territorial state. The noun and verb must certainly go back to prehistoric times before the development of the EB states, and therefore its primitive sense would have been something like 'to be of service or benefit to', or as here probably 'to be submissive and obedient'. That the term was already used in a political sense is guaranteed by repeated occurrences in Text D. All that is argued here is the historical necessity of the conclusion that such political use is a transferred meaning that cannot be the original sense. Perhaps the sentence here means something like 'Benefit in abundance shall be beneficial to them', taking the final suffixes *–nini* as pronominal indirect objects.

L.8 *pa+ti–ru–ni–tu yu–ḫu–bu–ba*
ta–ta–'u–bu–du+ma+mi

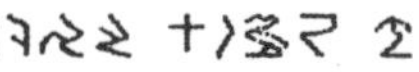

(Translation not yet possible.)

The clause seems to be introduced with the usual *pa–* that indicates a change of subject, for there is no root *ptr* that yields any usable meaning or context. The main verb then is *tirunitu* which is again impossible: no root *rnt* exists. It is most probable that the final two syllables are a 1 pl. pronominal suffix, and it is possible that the root is *rwn, rnn,* 'rejoice' or even Arab. *rhn* 'be enduring' though this would hardly be compatible with a pronominal suffix. Still another possibility is *tir'u* 'you shall see . . .' with the elision of the *'aleph*, but the following finite verb in the 3 masc. sg. makes the syntax difficult. A new idea is necessary, especially in view of the fact that the clause seems to consist of three finite verbs, the first in the 2 pl., the second seemingly in the 3 sg. and the third in the 2 pl. reflexive (or is it dual?).

yuḫubbuba: This is taken to be a D stem——possibly passive? The Arab. root *ḫbb* 'to love' would seem appropriate, but if it is correct the back fricative is wrong——as usual. It is tempting to see it as a noun *ḫu-bu-ba* with acc. case ending, the direct object of the preceding verb, which then would have to have an indirect pronominal object of the form *nituyu*.

tataʿbudu+mami: This is an interesting form in the light of the form with causative *s* in the line above. This would seem to be a simple Qal reflexive/middle form, and thus the vowel after the first root consonant would likely be silent——another 'dead vowel'.

L.9 *ba-ti-ya+ma ba-yi-ti ba-ri-ri* 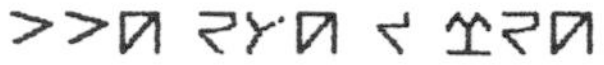
za-hi-ru+ma hi-li-ni

(Translation is not now possible.)

batiya+ma: No plausible root or cognate has presented itself. Together with the following word, it looks very much like a cognate accusative formation that is so frequent in these texts, thus 'building my house' or perhaps better 'the builder of (my) house' reading the form as an active participle in the accusative case. 'House' here is of course used in the sense of 'dynasty' so familiar from much later SC usage. This interpretation would strongly support the interpretation of this text as the record of a (then) very important royal marriage covenant.

bariri: This is certainly the root preserved in Ug., SC, Arab. and Amorite with a extraordinary range of meanings, most of which can be derived from a primitive base meaning such as 'pure'. Cf. *brh kḫmh* in Cant 6:10. The sign read *ri* is not frequent in these texts, and is thus not certain. However, among the unassigned syllables there is no other that fits comfortably into this context, and here it yields perfect sense——as in Cant 6:10 it describes the 'pure' status of the 'house' under discussion.

zahiru+ma: This is another *qāṭil* participle form, evidently, but this time in the nominative case. The syntax is evidently very complex in this sentence, and no solution has yet been found. The root is clearly the later *zhr* 'shine' that is a very productive root in Classical Arabic, and is the base for a variety of proper names (individual and tribal) in pre-Islamic

Arabic, notably Sabean and Safaitic. At the time of the Exile, it comes into SC (Ezek and possibly Job). The homonym 'to warn' is also late in SC and is certainly an Aramaic LW, that is unrelated to this root.

Note that the *hi* = ✻ sign has an extremely cursive form. It strongly suggests that this writing system was used with considerable facility on other materials such as papyrus, and emphasizes the fact that almost any writing system at any given time is likely to exhibit a rather considerable variety of forms depending upon the materials used.

hilini: This is an extraordinarily intriguing word. It is the same as Ug. *hl*– 'this' > *hln* 'then' and *hlny* 'here', but which of the latter two with suffixed *n* is appropriate here it is difficult to say, because the context is so unclear. The word is a demonstrative adverbial in all probability meaning 'here' or 'now'. It is of course the ancestor of later CWS demonstratives and definite articles, with very frequent shift from this original *h* to the later *aleph*. Note also the preservation of the original *i* vowel in the SC plural *ʾlh*.

L.10 *ma–ni bi–ni–hu–mu sa–ba–ru ka–yi–na–tu–m* 

(Translation is not now possible.)

mani: In view of the obscurity of the entire passage the meaning or function of what appears to be a particle of some sort is entirely unclear. It can hardly be a suffix to the preceding word if the interpretation of the latter is correct. In view of the various forms of *mnm* already observed in these texts, it is tempting to see here a pronominal adjective––that is a related form without the indefinite suffix *–ma*, but it is difficult to see how such a reading would fit into the larger context.

bini+humu sabaru kayyinatum: Cf. the identical sequence of words at line 6. It evidently is a formula which would be entirely appropriate as a part of a blessing.

L.11 *pa+ha–ḥi–ni+mi maʿ–bu–du* 
bi+ʾa–ha–sa–sa–nu–tu–ʾa

(Translation is not yet possible.)

pa+haḥinni+mi: The conjunction *pa* introduces another main clause, it would seem, just as at the beginnings of lines 5 and 8. The following verb evidently is a *h*– causative preterite, possibly from the root *ḥnn* 'be gracious'? If so, its meaning in the context is not retrievable because of the entire obscurity of the rest of the sentence. Because of the quite clear threat in line 12, it is quite tempting to see in this clause introduced with the particle *pa*+ a curse formula. In such a context, the OSA root *ḥny* 'destroy' or Arab. 'be corrupt, destroy, break covenant' would be entirely appropriate, especially since the verb is regularly construed with a preposition *ʿly* or *fi* which corresponds to the preposition *bi* prefixed to the second following word. It is not surprising to find the enclitic –*mi* appended to the verb.

maʿbudu: If the reading of the first sign is correct, as also at C 13 and D 32, as a ligature, then this would be a verbal noun from the root *ʿbd*. It would have to be the subject of the verb because of the nominative case–ending. The word is simply a semantic equivalent of the later SC *mʿsh* 'deed'.

bi+ʾahassanutuʾa: This sequence of signs is grammatically impossible and inexplicable. The prefixed preposition would demand a gen. case ending in the first place, which does not exist in the cluster of signs. It is entirely possible that the readings are not all correct, but no rectification is possible because a crucial part of the line was 'cleaned' out of existence some years before I had opportunity to inspect and photograph the text. One possible solution to this impasse would be to see a proper name in this sequence of signs, perhaps of a collectivity. This name could be a diptote or indeclinable, and therefore does not take the required genitive case ending after the preposition. For the form with a prefixed *ʾa*– compare the name at D 33: *ʾaḥusapayi*, and Ug. *ʾqht*.

L.12 *bi+ma–nu–ma ša–du–da ra–ḥi–ma–ta* 
ʾi–ba–li–gu+hu

"Against anyone who assaults the young lady, I will overcome him."

bi+mannu+ma: The indefinite pronoun is evidently indeclinable, though the variety of forms in which it occurs suggests that there may have been morphological features other than case endings that distinguished varying grammatical relationships. Note the vocalization with *i* before the following *a* vowel, according to the usual rule.

šaduda: This verb is particularly intriguing for a number of reasons. In the first place, it seems to be a classical perfect tense form and its function as a 'completed action' indicator is entirely appropriate, for it is followed by an 'imperfect' form that indicates action subsequent to that posited by the first verb. What is curious about this verb, however, is that the form in later grammar ordinarily designates a stative verb, but this is clearly a transitive verb with a direct object. It is most tempting to see in this clause an archaic grammatical construction that in later times was no longer in use or understood. It actually **is** a stative to be translated 'Whoever is violent . . .' but it is followed by the accusative of specification: 'with reference to the young lady'. In other words, the acc. case ending does not necessarily mark the 'direct object', but rather the limit of activity that will result in the action specified by the following verb. Thus violence with reference to any other person or persons is not within the range of interest of the speaker.

raḥimata: This is the same word as the SC *rḥmh* of Jud 5:30, and contrasts beautifully to the passive participle form of the same root in line C 1. It is an indication of the extremely archaic usage that this meaning for this form is attested only in SC, including the Mesha stele, though it is possible that it survived in the mythological texts of Ugarit. In pre–Islamic Arabic, the derived meaning 'compassionate' is already dominant. The history of the term strongly suggests a very archaic usage that survived in local colloquial usage, but it was doubtless regarded as too gross in later educated elevated language circles.

ʾiballigu+hu: This normalization is speculative, but very probable in view of the *ʾi* preformative, and the *i* thematic vowel after the second root consonant. The form is thus considered to be a D–stem, and in the context refers to an action subsequent to that posited in the first verb of the sentence. In spite of the contrast between *i* and *a* thematic vowels in Text D, here there is clearly a future reference, and the verb has the regular indicative *–u* ending instead of the *–a* ending that regularly occurs in the prescriptive sections of this marriage contract, lines 2–4.

For the meaning, compare the obscure SC phrase (Amos 5:9) *hmblyg šd ʿl–ʿz*, 'who brings retribution for violence upon the mighty'. The cognates to this root have not been searched, because a later (Exilic) homonym 'shine' seemed adequate. Actually, the later descendant of this root is Arab. ***flj*** 'overcome, conquer' and also 'divide, distribute' and even 'impose a tax'. Note also that in Classical Arabic there is at least one form cited of the later SC cognate: ***ʾinfalaja***, which is simply a variant of the normal *blj* 'the daybreak shone brightly'. It illustrates the tendency toward the shift from voiced to voiceless in the presence of both a liquid and a voiced fricative. It is clear that this root is connected to the larger CWS complex associated with the root and name *plǵ*, 'divide', and like many other semitic roots it is associated with the concept of the distribution of just deserts.

The pronominal suffix at the end of the verb form is also curious. It is evidently a reference back to the prepositional phrase with which the clause began: *bi+mannu+ma*. This type of construction seems peculiar after a prepositional phrase, and no parallel from later inscriptions or literature comes to mind.

L.13a *maʿ–pu–tu–m ma–ʿu–ta–ma* 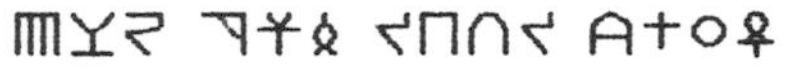
ʾi–ḫi–lu ti–li–ḫa

(Translation is not possible.)

maʿputu+m: Again there seems to be an adverbial nominative form that probably is a modifier of the preceding word or phrase. It is strange that the word is indented from the right side of the plate by the width of at least two signs, and it is quite clear that there is only blank space here. In contrast to other texts, in this text each line seems to end with a sentence or a phrase stop, except in this and in the following two lines.

The reading of the first sign as the ligature read also in line 11 is particularly insecure here, though no other reading has recommended itself. The root could be *ʿpw* that occurs with a range of meaning in Arab.: 'be effaced, obliterated, perish, forgive' and others. It is hardly rewarding to engage in further speculation as to the meaning.

maʿuta+ma: This is taken to be a *ma–* preformative noun possibly a ***nomen agentis*** from the Arab. root *ʿtw* 'behave proudly, be immoderate, corrupt'. The case ending in *–a* indicates that it is apparently the direct object of the following verb.

ʾiḫillu: This word is parallel in both form and meaning to the *ʾiballiǵu* of line 12, and is taken to be from the CWS verb *ḫll*, for which cf. Sabean *ḫll* 'harm, destroy', and SC 'be defiled, profane'––and therefore no longer forbidden. Classical and pre–Islamic Arabic use the verb in very similar fashion: that which is not *ḥrm* 'sacred' is *ḥll* i.e. 'profane', and therefore permitted, such as 'legitimate booty'. A similar sense can be seen here: such action as that previously specified means that the covenant relationship implied in this marriage contract no longer affords the culprit any protection from the consequences of his own behavior, and therefore subjects him to the harm or destruction of which the injured party is capable.

tiliḥa: This word is taken to be possibly a *ti*– prefix adverbial accusative noun form with –*a* case ending from the root *laḥḥa*, in the IVth form in Arabic meaning 'persecute, harass'. It goes with the preceding words as a continuation of the curse formula, but that is all that can be said for this attempt at indicating the meaning of this very difficult clause. Note, however, that there is evidently a deliberate play on sounds with –*ḥilu* contrasting or comparing to –*liḥa* in this word. It is entirely possible that this adventure in stylistic elegance makes its own contribution to the difficulty of interpretation, but at any rate it should serve to warn against the absurd idea that any stylistic elegance––or attempt thereto––automatically removes the document from the real world to enshrine it in the sacred world of "literature." After all, an honest survey of the evidence would lead to the conclusion that long before "*1984*" politicians and their bureaucrats had perfected the art of "Creative Writing."

L.13b–14a *pa+ḥi*–(14)–*wa ḥi*–*du bi+hu*–*ʾi* 

(No translation is possible.)

pa+ḥiwwa: The word divisions here, and as a matter of fact in all of line 13 as well as the first half of line 14 are extremely uncertain. The word division given above is based partly upon the fact that *pa*– occurs in this and other texts almost exclusively as the conjunction that introduces a new sentence or even a new subject, and what little that can be elicited from these lines at least fits in with that interpretation also here. It is curious that in every other occurrence of the conjunction in this text, it stands at the beginning of a line. Furthermore, in all the preceding lines the end of the line marks also the end of a sentence or a main clause––it is for this reason that the line length is extremely ragged in sharp contrast to Text D where even words are 'wrapped' across lines.

The word is taken to be an otherwise unknown form from the root *ḥwy* 'live' in the accusative case, but it is difficult to see any syntactic relationships, since the following word that could be a perf. tense verb seems to have no subject.

ḫidu: As noted above this word could be a perfect tense or stative hollow verb. As a matter of fact, the Sabean *ḫwd* is used in a sense that would be appropriate here, i.e., 'grant' a favor or oracular response, but it takes a direct object. The fact that the 'wrong' *ḫi–* (instead of *ḥi–*) appears in the OSA verb is no obstacle, in view of the entire unpredictability of these fricatives in relation to their cognates in the much later WS languages and dialects. Since there is no possible candidate for the subject of the verb, it must be taken as a stative or a passive, and again the associated noun in the accusative can be only the accusative of specification. 'And life there is granted with respect to him'?

bi+hu'i: The original publication read this sequence of signs as *ḥi hu 'i* = ♁ ⊐ ᛉ which is more impossible than the rest of these two lines. Fortunately, the Infra–Red Ektachrome slides clearly yielded the reading *bi* = ⋊ which gives a fairly fixed point in the text as the preposition *b–* plus 3 masc. sg. pronominal suffix.

L.14b *'a–ba–ḫi–mu ḏu* ᗜ ⅄ᛉ◸♁

"I will honor (him) who . . . "

'abaḫḫimu: In line 5 the same sequence of signs occurs, but there the verb is a stative with a following accusative of specification, while this is evidently a D–stem transitive imperfect followed by a relative pronoun *ḏu*. Unfortunately the following word which should be a verb is lost.

L.15 / */ba+ḫi–ti+mi 1 1 1 1 1 1 1* 1111111 ⊤⥽ᛉ ◸[ ]

" . . . in fear."

ba+ḫitti+mi: 'Conscientiously' repeats the phrase with which the obligation of the bridegroom is described in line 2. Some action on the part of the lucky man is presupposed in the lacuna that precedes. The fact that something like 'honor' is conferred upon him by presumably the father of the bride further strongly suggests that this contract preserved on a copper plate records no ordinary marriage but is rather an important royal and political document that marks an event of considerable significance for ancient Lebanese politics. If this interpretation and the dating are both correct, the marriage preceded by a few years or decades the complete destruction or collapse of this Early Bronze Age city state and its ruling dynasty.

Though details of grammatical and semantic relationships are far from clear, the vocabulary that can reasonably be established in these final lines almost certainly indicates that this legal document concluded with a formula for a threat of future evil to a malefactor, and similarly a promise of good to one who acts 'conscientiously'. It is just as interesting, however, that the formula invokes no supra–natural action by divine beings, but is to be carried out by the speaker himself. This observation is in keeping with the trends in ancient and more recent societies as well––the increasing insecurity of a culture approaching a crisis with which it cannot cope tends strongly to create an ideology and dependent patterns of behavior that rely increasingly upon supernatural forces both as 'explanations' and as hope for succour.

1 1 1 1 1 1 1: The seven hooked vertical strokes can only be the 'marks' of the traditional 'seven witnesses' to the marriage contract. It is tragic for us that their names were not inscribed for posterity upon the document––there would have been plenty of room for their names together with their patronymics, and we would have had invaluable information concerning EB age onomastics and linguistics.

Free Translation:

1. "Habula, my offspring, is the legitimate betrothed of Thutun.
2. Conscientiously you shall clothe her in perpetuity.
3. I guarantee that there is no defect in her, and
4. with beautiful offsprint she shall establish his house.
5. Furthermore, when they have become numerous in progeny,
6. (may?) well–being be assured them in perpetuity.
7. Abundant mutual benefit will be beneficial to them.
8. Furthermore, (??)...beloved, you shall benefit each other, and
9. (building?) a pure house, they are 'shining' hereto.
10. (?)...well–being between them perpetually.
11. Furthermore, an act of corruption in ...(?);
12. anyone who does violence to the young lady I will assail.
13. I will destroy the one who acts corruptly (?)
14. Furthermore, life is granted him, I will honor who
15. [. . .] conscientiously. (Marks of 7 witnesses)

7

MONUMENTAL INSCRIPTIONS

Text A

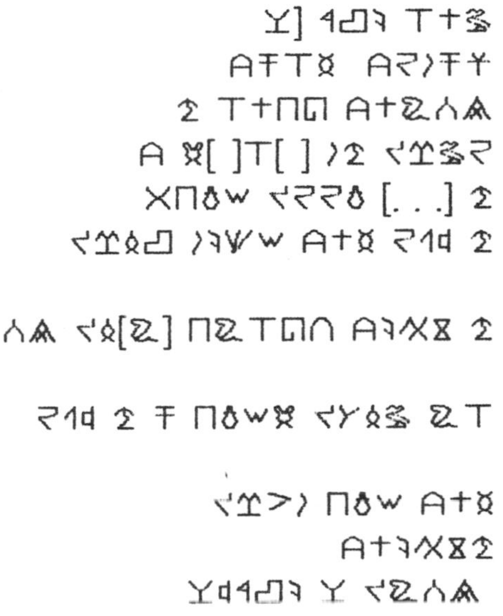

L.1 *ru-tu+mi bu-hu-ra [li]*
L.2 *ḥi-sa-ni-ti-m ʾa-mi-sa-m*
L.3 *ka-wa-na-tu-m ha-ta-tu+mi pa-*
L.4 *ti-ri-ya-ma pa-ni [ ]-mi ?-ʾu-m*
L.5 *pa+[. . .] qa-ti-ti+ma ša-qa-ta+ku*
L.6 *pa+da-ga-ti ʾa-tu-m ša-ṣi-bu+ni hu-ʾi-ya+ma*
L.7 *pa+wi-ṯu-bu-m ʿu-ha-mi-na-ta [na]-ʾi-ma ka-[*
L.8 *mi-na ru-ʾi-yi-ma ʾu-ša-qa-ta+sa pa+da-ga-ti*
L.9 *ʾa-tu-m ša-qa-ta ni-ri-ya+ma pa+wi-tu-bu-tu-m*
L.10 *ka-wa-na+ma li+bu-hu-ra+da-li*

L.1 *ru-tu+mi bu-hu-ra [li]*

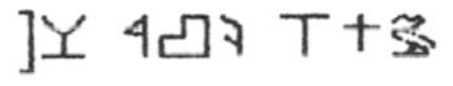

"Dedication of Buhura to [?. . .]"

Rūtu+mi: The few words that can be read with confidence strongly suggest that this is a building inscription possibly for a temple, and it is therefore most probable that the OSA *rt(m/n), ryt* 'obligation', 'penitential offering' is the later descendant of this word. Cf. also *ryt* that designates some kind of offering to the deity in the Moabite stela.

The word is here analyzed as nom. fem. sg. from a root *rw* with an enclitic *–mi*. Though the use of this enclitic at so early a date is not an entirely comfortable solution, the interpretation of the word as a triliteral root *rtm* is much more difficult since there is no explanation for a gen. case ending. Moreover, the enclitic *–mi* does seem to appear elsewhere in the corpus.

Buhura li-?: The second word is certainly a personal name that actually occurs in ONA inscriptions, and survives in both Arabic and SC as a primitive root alongside the variant form *brr*. Such root doublets are far more frequent in the Semitic languages than has been realized, and constitute extremely valuable evidence for historical linguistics. Probably in the majority of cases the variant forms are preserved because they have undergone a historical process of semantic specialization. The name is appropriate for a royal personage 'brilliant, shining', and thus is very near semantically to the other royal name of Text D *ḥūru+baʿil*.

The traces of a sign that is most easily read *li* fit very well with the grammatical structure, for it is the preposition that indicates the deity to whom the dedication was made. In accordance with the general rule, the name of the deity would begin with a syllable containing the vowel *a*, or *u*, possibly *baʿalat* in view of the remarkable persistence of the cult at Byblos of the "Lady of Byblos." There are at least six and perhaps seven characters missing at the end of the line.

L.2 *ḥi-sa-ni-ti-m ʾa-mi-sa-m* 

". . . the benefactions daily. . ."

ḥisanitim: The translation is taken directly from the Classical Arabic lexicon (Lane) where this meaning is given to the fem. noun *ḥasanatun*. The distribution of this root is curious, and probably illustrates beautifully the interrelationship of phonetic and semantic change, involving an extremely archaic root. It is not attested in Ug. in this form at all, while there are three different noun forms plus a denominative verb in SC, all from sources closely associated with the city of Jerusalem and its immediate environs. It is not attested in OSA in this form, though there are several PN formations derived from the root, largely though not exclusively attested in ONA. On the other hand, the root is enormously productive in Classical Arabic.

Probably what happened in the second millennium was the superimposition of the Inland Dialect root *ḥṣn* 'embrace, protect' upon this unrelated root. SC *ḥṣn* shows the resulting semantic gamut: 'strength, stored wealth', (cf. Arab. 'stored grain') and the obscure usage in Ps 89:9 proves that the word still had close connections with the divine benefactions to the king under the impact of the 'Divine Charter' theology. Subsequently there was a re-borrowing of the other root *ḥṣn* 'bosom' (post-Exilic only). Except for isolated PNs, OSA preserved only the velarized form of the root with the extended/derived meaning 'protect, protege, client'. Classical Arabic alone exhibited considerable elaboration of uses of both roots, with some semantic transference between them.

ʾamisam: 'Yesterdaily'? This adverbial accusative referring no doubt generally to the past benefits received from the deity proves beyond doubt the archaic distribution of this concept of the benefit : response theology that underlies much later covenant theology. At the end of this line there are at least four and perhaps five signs missing.

L.3 *ka-wa-na-tu-m ha-ta-tu+mi [pa]-* 

"Perpetually they have been brought to completion. And . . . [ ]"

kawanatu+m: This word is treated here as a nom. adverbial as in text C–2, where it reads, however, *kayinatum*, and the contrast has no clear explanation. An alternative interpretation would recognize in the form the classical 'Proto–Semitic' 2 masc. pl. perfect tense form, and this is made even more attractive by the repeated occurrence of the *ʾa-tu-m* sequence in lines 6 and 9, which can hardly be anything other than the 2 masc. pl. personal pronoun. In this case the dedication would presumably be to a collectivity of divine beings, possibly the *[ʾ]ʾimu* of D 12? It would be delightfully appropriate if this were the commemoration stone for the building of the Obelisk Temple––to the deified ancestors whose steles were the main feature of that temple. Against this analysis of the verb form is the difficulty of the syntax: "You are . . ." what?

hatatummi: This is taken to be a causative–reflexive verbal noun from the root *tmm* in the oblique plural case agreeing then with the main noun *ḥisanitim* (exc. for gender). There are two or three signs missing at the end of this line.

L.4 *ti-ri-ya-ma pa-ni [ ]-mi ?-ʾu-m* 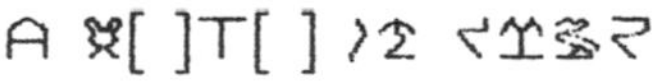

Untranslatable.

Only the first word of this line is well enough preserved to be reasonably certain, and the second character that appears elsewhere only in Text D is of uncertain reading (taken to be a variant of the  sign). Further speculation is useless, other than the observation that there is probably a *ti–* verb preformative, and an afformative in the precative *–a* that occurs so frequently in these texts. It is tempting to see here a strange form from the root *rwm* 'be high, exalt'. Alternatively, it could well be for *tirʾiya+ma*, which would again be a precative with the dir. obj. *pani/ya?/* '(my?) face'.

L.5 *pa+/. . . / qa–ti–ti+ma ša–qa–ta+ku* 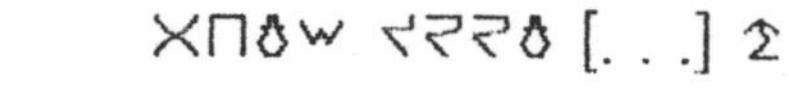

"And . . . . ? ? he has made you tranquil."

qatiti+ma: The context is so broken that it is difficult to make any reasonable suggestion either concerning the form or the meaning of this word.

šaqata+ku: If only this word and its context were more certain it would be of enormous importance for historical linguistics. The readings of the signs seem to be quite secure, but the meaning is not. It is here suggested to be the etymon of the SC *šqṭ* 'be tranquil, at peace, rest' that has no convincing cognate, though Akk. and Arab. *šqt* 'fall down' is the usual etymology suggested. What is significant if this etymology is correct is the fact that both SC and Arab. illustrate the velarization of the final *ta* under the influence of the *qof*, while both Akkadian and this dialect exhibit the original unvelarized *ta*. This is the more important since there is no trace whatever of the *ṭet* consonant in this syllabary, and the conclusion can only be that there was not at this time a phonemic contrast that required an epigraphic signal.

The final suffix *–ku* is interesting if it is indeed the 2 masc. sg. pronominal suffix. Though the top part of the sign is broken, the traces allow no other reasonable possibility. The verb form would then be the classical *qaṭala* perfect, though the reading of the second sign as *qu* cannot be ruled out. It seems terribly far–fetched to analyze the word as an Akk. permansive 1 sg. form: *kašda+ku*, even though the form is letter perfect, and it would yield good meaning in what little context is available: 'I am at peace'.

L.6 *pa+da–ga–ti ʾa–tu–m ša–ṣu–bu+ni hu–ʾi–ya+ma* 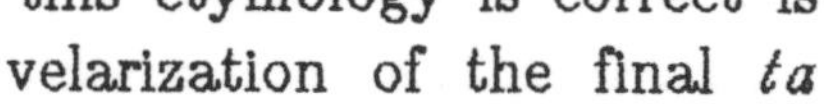

"And you having given good fortune, they have established him . . ."

pa+dagati ʾattum: This represents perfectly the later inf. abs. with personal pronoun of the *qaṭāli ʾanaku* formation, and here with a 2 masc. pl. pronoun that has no visible antecedent in the preserved and readable portion of the text. The verbal root does not exist in this form in later dialects, and it is probably metathesized as is also *dgl* = *gdl*, thus yielding the common root *gdt* > *gdd* 'decide, determine' in OSA and 'be fortunate' in classical Arabic.

šaṣibu+ni: The traces are too obscure to yield certainty, but the readings given are the most likely. The form read as a *qof*  in *BG* is actually a beautiful monumental pictograph of the *ṣiṣ*  =*ṣi* sign, as is clear on all of the IR color slides. The sign after the *bu* is far from clear. The Egyptian palm leaf shown in *BG* does not exist in other texts. It is the monumental form of the cursive  *ni* sign. The form is then a *šafel* of the root *nṣb*--'to set up', evidently in the 3 pl. perf. The causative prefix with *ša* instead of the usual *sa* is no doubt the result of dissimilation, for in WS an initial *sin/samek* is never followed by a *ṣad*.

huʾiya+ma: This curious form can hardly be anything other than the 3 masc. sg. pronoun with enclitic *–ma*, and from the context available it has to be interpreted as the oblique case form of the pronoun--the direct object of the preceding verb. If so, then it is dramatic illustration of the very archaic structure, and early date of the texts, for only Akkadian has preserved the oblique cases of pronouns otherwise. Compare and contrast the form *bi+huʾi* in Text C 3 and 14, where it has a feminine referent.

L.7 *pa+wi-ṯu-bu-m ʿu-ha-mi-na-ta* 
na-ʾi-ma ka-/

"And your dwelling eternal and glorious . . .??"

Though the morphology and syntax of this statement are far from clear, the sense is historically and semantically appropriate to this building inscription.

wiṯubum: Noun form in nom. case from CS root *wṯb*.

ʿuhaminata: The form and syntax are both very difficult, for the root can only be *ʿhm* and the suffix *–nata* is unparalleled. To start with the semantic aspect of the word, it can be identified with OSA and Classical Arabic *ʿwm* 'year, duration of time', but also in all probability with Cl. Arab.

ʿhn 'to remain, stay, abide' and the verbal noun *ʿāhin* 'lasting, enduring'. The fem. ending in the acc. case is probably to be interpreted as the adverbial accusative.

naʾīma+ka: The transcription indicates the reading of the first sign in the word as the serpent ᘔ, in which the lower right part is entirely eroded away. The upper part is identical to the well preserved serpent sign two spaces to the right. This word is to be identified with the SC *nʾh, nʾwh*, 'beauty'. It survived in the Palestinian colloquial, and evidently nowhere else except in the post–biblical dependent literature. The form is again difficult, unless the final *mem* is a nominalizing suffix, and therefore the word is in the acc. case like the preceding word. Though the copy in *BG* shows part of a following ∧ sign, no trace can be seen on the photographs, and I take the *-ka* to be the 2 masc. sg. possessive suffix.

L.8 *mi-na ru-ʾi-yi-ma ʾu-ša-qa-ṭa+sa* 
pa+da-ga-ti Untranslatable.

mina: Indef. pron. If it means 'whoever' it contrasts in form to the various spellings found in other texts, usually with *man-*.

ruʾiyi+ma: Probably an active verbal noun from the CWS root *rʾy*, 'see'. The readings are considerably improved over the hand copy of *BG*. The first sign is clearly the bird with barest traces of the feet visible on the slides. The second is not at all clear, but most probably to be read, for no other character of the signary fits the traces at all. The third sign is surely the monumental form of the ⅄ character, and a very welcome addition to the list of pictograms––even though it is far from possible to say what it is supposed to represent.

ʾušaqata+sa: The first sign given in *BG* as × is clearly, with the horns showing at the top of the broken area, thus yielding the 1 sg. preformative of an impf. verb form, probably in the D–stem, of the same root that occurred in line 5 in a very broken context. The sign ǂ can only be a pronominal suffix, in view of the strong conjunction *pa-* that introduces the next phrase. There is no parallel for this usage in the rest of the corpus, but there are no clear pronominal suffixes to finite verb forms attested at all elsewhere. It is anomalous, but if it is a pronoun, it should be a fem. form, and it is most interesting to see it spelled with the *s* rather than with the *š* consonant.

pa+daġati (L.9 ʾattum): The same idiom discussed above, L.6.

L.9 *ʾa-tu-m ša-qa-ta ni-ri-ya+ma* 

"And you having given good fortune, let us see tranquillity."

The inf.+ pronoun construction has been discussed at L. 6 above.

šaqata niriya+ma: Obj. noun from root *šqt* discussed also above, in the acc. case as direct object of following verb, which is taken to be from the root *rʾy* with elision of the *ʾalif* at the beginning of the syllable: *nirʾiya > niriya*.

L.9b *pa+wi-ṯu-bu-tu-m* 

And a dwelling place. . ."

pa+wiṯubutu+m: This introduces a new clause as is usual with the conjunction. The contrast between this fem. form and the word without the fem. suffix in line 7 is not at all clear, but the translation has attempted to give some idea by contrasting the concrete 'dwelling' in the former case to the more abstract 'dwelling–place' in this passage. At any rate, the noun is in the nom. case and just about has to be the subject of the following verb even though it does not have the feminine ending.

L.10 *ka-wa-na+ma li+bu-hu-ra+da-li* 

"There has been for Buhura–Dali."

kawana+ma: 'There has become ?'. The verb is in 3 masc. sg. form and the only nom. case noun in the vicinity is the preceding fem. word.

li+buhura+dalli: Prep. followed by the personal name, no doubt of the king whose inscription and building project this commemorates. The final two signs are clearly a distinct morpheme in view of the name in line 1, but they have no syntactic function in the sentence and are therefore taken to be part of the compound name which is given in only the shortened form in line 1 above. The word is from the root *dll* 'guide, direct': 'my guide is majestic'?

Stele G

L.1 *yi-qa-wa-ru ʿi-ǯa-/qa?*
L.2 *ba ta ti ʾu tu ʿi-ǯa-qa /*
L.3 *ba li+ṯu-tu-sa-li+hu ti/*
L.4 */ba tu li ta ti ʾu-ya-tu-ti/*
L.5 */ʾu nu ti ʾu ya/*

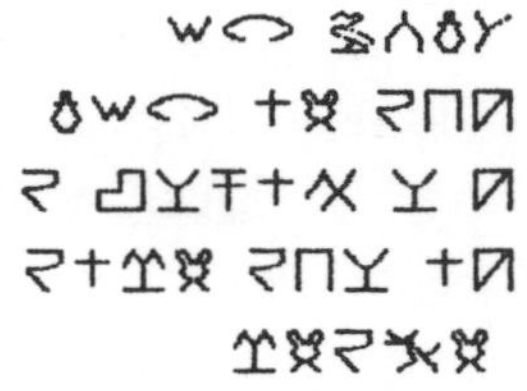

Little can be done with this fragment. It is unfortunate, for the monumental and elegant carved inscription furnishes beautiful pictographic forms that underlay the much more cursive forms used in the other texts. Word divisions are particularly difficult, for it is probable that at both tops and bottoms of the lines there are word fragments only. The vocabulary used is also largely, it seems, archaic and probably obsolete in later WS dialects. The few words that can reasonably be identified suggest that it is another dedicatory inscription of a type familiar from some OSA monumental inscriptions.

L.1 *yi-qa-wa-ru ʿi-ǯa-/qa?* 

yiqawaru: The root is not a common one in WS, but it is useful for illustrating the fact that the "hollow verbs" are true triliteral roots at this early period, like *kawana*. The verb is used in OSA with the meaning 'engrave', and in Classical Arabic with the meaning 'be wide'.

ʿiǯa/qa/: The third sign is restored on the basis of the repetition in line 2. The only cognate readily found is Arab. *ʿǯq* 'to love excessively'. The meaning of neither root seems particularly appropriate to a monumental stele such as this.

L.2 *ba ta ti ʾu tu ʿi-ǯa-qa /* 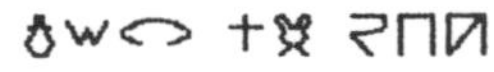

The first sign is particularly intriguing, for it can hardly be anything other than a monumental form of the *bayt* with the 'door' closed, and therefore the form anticipates by more than half a millennium similar forms in the Proto–Sinaitic corpus. The same form is found in line 1 of Spatula e. Unfortunately, *batati* does not make sense, nor does any other sequence of signs in the line.

L.3 *ba li+ṯu-tu-sa-li+hu ti/* 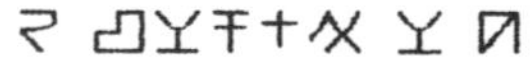

Again the square *bayt* occurs at the head of the line, and it must belong to the preceding word, the rest of which is lost. What remains of the line is mostly a single word: the *li+* preposition plus a *s–ṯ* infinitive causative–reflexive with pronominal suffix. It is phonetically significant that the causative prefix is written with the *ṯu* sign, which is probably to be explained as dissimilation before a following *sa* phoneme. The root is probably Arab. *wsl* 'seek favor', and OSA 'make a propitiatory offering'. The meaning may be something like 'to seek favor for himself'. The importance of the line is exhausted by the observation that the Ŧ *sa* sign is a monumental form that certainly derives from the Egyptian *djed* pillar, and therefore the meaning 'support, pillar' for *samek* seems demonstrated beyond reasonable doubt.

L.4 */ba tu li ta ti ʾu-ya-tu-ti/* 

Nothing meaningful emerges easily from this collection of signs. It is conceivable that the sequence *ʾuyatuti* may be derived from the root underlying Arabic *ʾāyatun* 'mark, sign'. Cf. *ʾuyatata* at D 24.

L.5 */ʾu nu ti ʾu ya/* 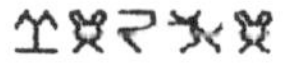

The word *ʾunuti* may be cognate to Arab. *ʾwn* 'be at rest, repose, calm', but there is little point in further speculation. Most notable is again the monumental, pictographic form of the  *nu* sign that is a faithful representation of a bee, WS *nubtu*.

8

THE MINOR TEXTS

Spatula b

Obverse

L.1: *pu-sa yi-pu-yu ha-ga-*
L.2: *-ra+ma / yi-la-ṣu ʾi-ma*
L.3: *la+pi / ka-yi-nu sa-*
L.4: *ra+ma ti-[?]-pu*

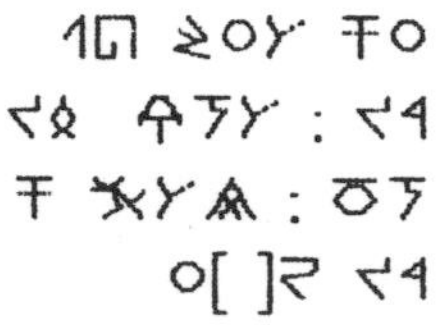

Reverse

L.5: *nu-ta-ka-pi-la*
L.6: *sa-nu-ta / ʾi-la*
L.7: *mi-ku ḫu-ga-ra*

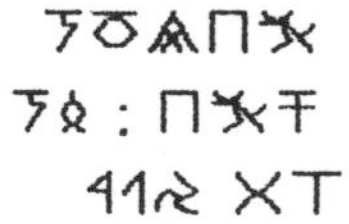

1. 'Adze' that Yipuyu and Hagara
2. make binding. Verily,
3. in accordance with that which Sara
4. and Ti[?]pu established
5. we will be surety.
6. Further: with Miku is the pledge."

The numerous uncertainties in this brief inscription need not be dwelt upon. They speak for themselves. Notes on the frequent dubious readings will be included in the discussion of each relevant word. The rendering yields at least a plausible text that is evidently the record of some very important legal transaction or agreement concluded between two local citizens Sara and Tipu. Each presumably has a guarantor and these two draw up the text of the document, for it is they who are assuming responsibility for the performance of the agreement. Still a third party, Miku, holds something of material nature which is the 'gage' or 'pledge' involved in the transaction.

pusa. Punic *ps* 'tablet'. This word can furnish a remarkable explanation for the peculiar 'spatula' shape of the copper plate on which the document is written, for it is a miniature *fa's*——a mattock, actually, that has a pick on one end and a mattock/hoe blade on the other. Note the translation 'spade' for Aramaic *passa'*, and the cognate *pista'* 'palm of the hand'. For some strange symbolic reason this shape was evidently regarded as appropriate to an important document, and its designation as an appropriate writing material was then transferred to other media such as wooden boards and tablets. It is most tempting to see this as the symbol of the ax wielded by the storm–god, the word for which is *ps* in Ugaritic, and which Aistleitner already (1974: 262) translated as "Axt (als Symbol des Blitzstrahls)."

The vocalization with *u* presents some difficulty, but it is exactly parallel to that which has been reconstructed above for the history of the word for 'fish'. Originally *dugg*– then *digg*–, as indicated in the Ugaritic rendering with the syllable *di* of the name or sound of the alphabetic letter *d*, by Philippi's law it would have to become *dag* in South Canaanite. The Aramaic forms have preserved the second and third stages of the process, though admittedly in different lexical items.

For the form it is most probable that the writing represents an original or even pronounced *pu's*, since the *'alif* at the end of the first syllable had no following vowel and therefore was represented as zero in the orthography. It was preserved only in Arabic. The noun is in the acc. case, and is thus the object of the very obscure verb *yilaṣu*.

yipuyu: This is taken to be a one word name, which is the first element of the later compound royal names: *yp–šm–'b*, 'fair is the name of the father'. The root is usually associated with Arabic *wfy*, and the form here would then be an impf. with preformative *yi*– and the *waw* is represented as zero at the close of the first syllable. In the form without preformative, this root is very productive in pre–Islamic onomastics: *wfy*, *wfym/n*, *yf*, etc. This reading of the text as well as the interpretation of the personal name is powerfully supported by the Ug. name *ypy*.

hagara+ma: The first sign on line 2 is read here as *ra* ⏉ instead of *ga* ⏉ of the original publication because the traces on the Infra–Red slide seem to justify the emendation. It is a personal name that is quite common in pre–Islamic Arabic inscriptions (identical to Hagar in SC traditions), but not attested in Ugaritic or Phoenician. It is curious that only five personal names in Ugaritic begin with the consonant *h*, and one of them is uncertain.

Only 9 Phoenician names begin with this consonant and two of those are certainly late Punic misspellings for *ḥ*. In sharp contrast, there are 26 pages of names beginning with this consonant in Harding's index.

I know of no accepted interpretation of the name (Harding [1971] does not offer even a tentative translation), and if it is a name already in use in the EB period, it is not surprising that the meaning is opaque. If this interpretation is correct, the final *–ma* enclitic functions here as a conjunction linking the two names so that the following verb is in the plural (or dual?) number.

It is interesting that this name is followed by a word–divider that consists of a short vertical stroke, as also in lines 3 and 6. This ought to lay to rest the idea that inscriptions can be dated by means of the presence or absence of word–dividers, since other inscriptions of the corpus also use word–dividers.

yilaṣu: The form is impf. 3 pl. of a verb that is identified with Arabic *laṣṣa/raṣṣa*, the latter being clearly a dialect variant since an extraordinary number of identical meanings are listed by Lane under both verbs. It is well known that the *l/r* interchange is very ancient and very common in Semitic as well as in many other languages. The verb is used of anything 'made firm and joined together', and is here taken to refer to a binding agreement involving the two persons named probably as guarantors of the legal action described subsequently.

It is strange that the sign read here as *ṣu* is virtually identical to : *zu*, the only significant contrast being in the sharp bend to the left of the bottom vertical stroke, that may correspond to a similar bend in the vertical shaft of the *za*= sign. This character appears elsewhere only in Spatule e, line 1 with the same syllabic value.

ʾi+ma: The meaning given to the particle *ʾi* in Lane fits perfectly: ". . it does not occur otherwise than before an oath. It is a word preceding an oath. . . ." It is clearly a strong affirmative followed by an oath, and for this we have an excellent antecedent in Ug. (I Krt 201: *ʾiʾiṯt ʾaṯrt ṣrm*). The enclitic *–ma* is used with it here, and probably we have the origin of the later WS conditional particle *ʾim* that continues to be used as the introduction to an oath formula. Note the cohortative particle *ʾi* in Akk. from OB on––probably an Amorite introduction into Akkadian, and thus a common West Semitic vocabulary item, but with a different nuance in the

Coastal as contrasted to the Inland Dialect. It is curious that in SC the particle seems to have obtained a negative sense as in the PN *ʾi-kbd* Ichabod, and probably also in the usual oath particle *ʾim*. This particle should be clearly distinguished from the interrogative particle *ʾay* 'where?', which is also CWS.

la+pi: This idiomatic expression continues in use as late as Neo–Punic *lpy* 'in accordance with'. Cf. SC *ʿal pī*. Here it seems to refer specifically to the oral agreement which is here being guaranteed.

kayyinu: This is a D–stem transitive without a direct object named other than that implied in the preceding prepositional phrase. It is a perf. tense form indicating that which had already been established by the two subjects of the plural (or dual) verb form who are named in the following line.

sara+ma: Perhaps to be read *sarra*. It is extremely common in Safaitic inscriptions, and in other forms (with suffixed *m/n*) also in other regions of pre–Islamic Arabic. As in line 2 the enclitic *–ma* seems to be a conjunction joining the two names of principals to the legal action. This could be identified with several names in Ug., but *šr* is a most likely equivalent, in view of the sibilant shift that had taken place at least a half–millennium before the Ugaritic texts were written.

ti-[?]-pu: This reading is very improbable and yields a name that does not otherwise occur. The surface of the spatula is badly eroded, but the *pu* seems quite clear. The *ti* sign is backwards in orientation, and between the two signs there is a clear remnant of the bottom of a vertical stroke, so there may well have been a second syllable––possibly a *ra* sign, yielding *tirapu*, cf. OSA PN *trft*, *trfm*.

nutakappila: This interesting form is an infixed *t–* impf. 1 pl. with the final optative/precative ending in *–a*, that is appropriate in what amounts to an oath formula. It corresponds to the Arabic Form V, and in meaning exactly to the Arab. *kpl* 'be or become surety, guarantee for'. It probably is historically related to the Amor./OB root *kbl* meaning 'to bind' that appears also in SC as 'fetters', but probably originally had nothing to do with the later WS *kpl* 'double'. It raises interesting questions concerning the original meaning of the name Machpelah at Hebron. The questions cannot at present be answered.

sanuta: The translation 'further' is a measure of desperation inspired by the very frequent usage of *šanitum*, literally 'secondly', at Mari, OB and OA to introduce a change of subject. The sibilant is wrong, but the sibilant system is far from clear——as usual. It is possible that certain signs may have been used to indicate more than one consonant element, a practice which is very familiar from Akkadian, and may well have been known to the scribes of Early Bronze Age Byblos. Furthermore, the possibility cannot be excluded that the etymological *ṯ* may in certain words have been actually pronounced as an *s*: it could well be that the contrast between *ṯ* and *s*, phonemic in later West Semitic, was only allophonic in this early dialect.

ʾila: The preposition *ʾel* common to WS.

mikku: The last three signs of this line are reversed, and therefore the line is read from left to right. No sense at all can be made if the opposite reading is followed. Spatula f also includes lines that read from left to right, though all on the reverse side are so read.

This normalization presupposes the etymology that is suggested by Harding for the name *mk* as well as for the cluster of pre–Islamic Arabic names that include this word. The name *ʿbd-mk* is particularly suggestive since a comparison with *ʿbd-wd, mk-ʾl* and *mk-wd* strongly suggests that this word is either the name or the appellative of a deity ('destroyer'?). The name *mi-ka-ʾil* would thus be another illustration of popular etymology.

ḫugara: This word is identified with Arabic *ḥǵr* 'be surety for'. Occurring as it does in the same text with the root *kpl* that has the same range of meaning, its function in this document would appear to be fairly certain. The root is semantically similar to Latin *'sacer'* and Arabic *ḥaram* 'forbidden'. Note again the frequent verbal noun form of *quṭal* vocalization noted so frequently in this corpus.

The consonant *ḥ* of the etymon does not as usual correspond to the reading of this sign, but it should be clear that later linguistic 'laws' simply do not correspond to usage in these texts of this particular dialect of West Semitic, and other regularities were probably in operation.

Spatula e

L.1: *pu-sa ra-ba-ṣu-ti pu-ta-*

L.2: *-ma pi-di-ʾi*

L.3: *1 1 1 1 1*

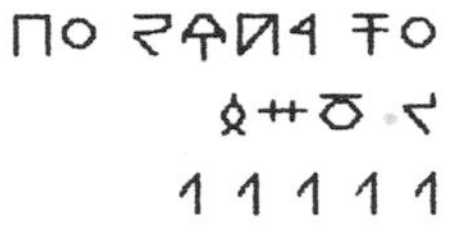

"'Adze' of the *rabaṣu*-ship of Putama Pidi'i."

This intriguing little inscription contains a surprising number of implications for cultural history. The first word has been discussed above and need not be further elaborated upon here, except to observe that the acc. case ending has no syntactic relationships that would explain its presence, but almost certainly is to be explained as the predicate of the understood verb *kawana*, whose subject would then be an implied demonstrative pronoun: '<This is> the adze of . . .'.

The 'spatula' is taken to be the written document that formally witnessed to the fact that a certain citizen of Byblos had been elevated to the status of *rābiṣu*, a term that is well known from the Amarna period, designating the governor under the Egyptian Empire of a fairly large provincial territory, a thousand years after this inscription was chiselled on a copper miniature mattock. The SC Iron Age opinion of the *rābiṣu* is preserved in the archaic phrase in Gen 4:7

rabāṣuti: The sign read here as *ba* is identical to some forms of the consonant *bet* that occur in the Proto-Sinaitic inscriptions, a fact that is not without historical significance. This form does not occur elsewhere in this corpus.

The word is the abstract fem. verbal noun form that underlies the later SC 'absolute infinitive' *qaṭāl* form with the *-ut-* ending. Here it designates the official position to be occupied by the person named.

putama: There does not seem to be any reasonable alternative to the interpretation of this word as the personal name that is required after the two preceding words. For the name cf. Ugaritic *ptm*, and Saf. *ftn*. In view of the fact that there is no evidence at all for a sign designating the CS consonant *ṭ* as a contrasting phoneme in this corpus, it is most tempting to suggest that it is a cognate to the very famous later feminine name ***Faṭima***. Harding lists no names at all with an initial *fṭ-* sequence. The name has the CuCaC form that is so frequently observed in this dialect, and also in Amorite.

*pidi*ʾ*i*: This is the common WS name *pdy* that occurs in Ug. both with this original ʾ*alif*: *pd*ʾ*u*, and in the later form in which the ʾ*alif* has shifted to a glide: *pdy, bn pdy, pdyn*. Cf. pre–Islamic Arabic *fdy, fd*ʾ*l*, ʾ*lfdy*.

The problem here is that the inscription as interpreted has two personal names in sequence with no connective. This is characteristic of much later OSA onomastics, and perhaps elsewhere as well. The second name may be a cognomen or a patronymic without the connecting *bin–*, for which many later parallels are known.

The last line of the adze consists of five vertical strokes that are certainly the five 'signatures' of the witnesses to the legal act, just as Text C has the 'signs' of seven witnesses at the end of that marriage contract. It is probable that a similar significance for the series of seven strokes or dots very frequent in inscriptions especially of the desert regions a couple thousand years later may occasionally be relevant.

Spatula f.

Obverse

L.1 *pu-sa [ti]-ri-ʾi-ta+ni*
L.2 *la+ti-nu-ta : yi-tu-sa-*
L.3 *pu-li-yi pu-la-sa*

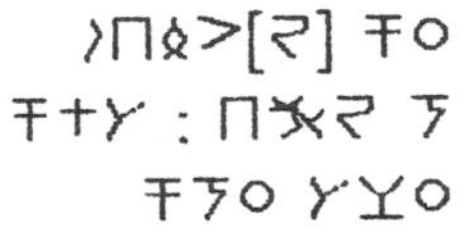

Reverse

L.4 *ta-yi-mi wi-ḫu-?-ti*
L.5 *mi-ku ti-pu-ṣa pu-sa*
L.6 *ta-yi-mi ḫi-di-nu-ta 1 1*
L.7 *yi-tu-pu li+ta-yi-mi 1*

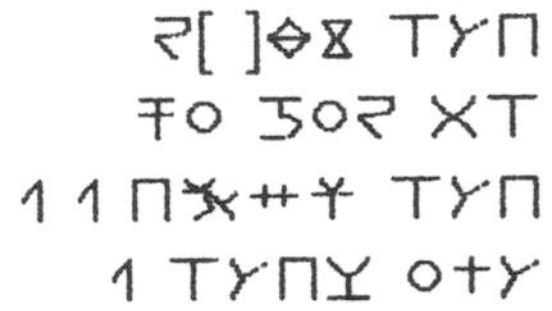

It is extraordinarily difficult to interpret this text, largely because the surface is badly eroded, but also because of eccentric sign forms that do not appear in other texts. This variability of form is, however, only to be expected in such archaic inscriptions. What meaning can be obtained from identifiable words is compatible with the functions of the other 'spatula' texts as important legal documents. The reverse of the spatula is quite clearly written from left to right, but the text is reproduced above in the order normal in the rest of the texts, not that in which the signs actually occur on the original. Lines 4–7 should be read from right to left as usual.

A number of forms are quite peculiar and no doubt represent a different 'hand', and it is of course difficult to identify these forms with those that appear in other and probably more carefully inscribed texts of this corpus. The character forms give every indication that they are reflections of a much more cursive writing habit appropriate to other writing materials, and certainly justify the opinion that this writing system must have been much more widely utilized than this tiny corpus of documents would indicate.

L.1 *pusa tirʾītāni*: "Adze of divination . . . " This attempt at the translation is based upon the identification of the second word as derived from the root *rʾy* with the *ti–* nominalizing preformative, a fem. abstract ending in *–t* and a second, abstractive, CS suffix in *–ānu*. Here it is in the gen. case which is appropriate to the second member of the construct chain that identifies the function of the 'adze' itself.

The first sign of the word *pusa* is very curiously written like an open sided figure 8, but there can nevertheless be little doubt as to the reading.

The second word begins with a broken sign that can be identified as *ti* , though the traces are very uncertain. The *ʾalif* sign is preserved at the top barely enough to guarantee that it can be neither the  nor the  sign, and therefore must be read as *ʾi*.

Regardless of the reading of the first sign, it seems clear that the word is a derivation from the root *rʾy* that has associations with augury and oracles in every language that uses the root. The *ri* sign is evidently used to indicate a consonant, and the vowel is a 'dead vowel'. Note Arab. *tirʾiyyatun* 'a man who practices artifices', and OSA *rʾy* 'oracle', as well as archaic SC (I Sam 9:9) *rʾh* 'seer'.

L.2a *la+tinuta*: "To Tinut." It is next to impossible to see in this word anything other than the famous Punic goddess Tanit. The signs again are eccentric, to say the least, but the suggested readings are by far the most probable within the framework of the known syllabary. These readings are supported by visual collation on Jan. 25, 1956 and again in 1968, and confirmed to large extent by the Infra-Red color photograph.

The vocalization is peculiar, at least from the point of view of traditions nearly two thousand years later, though it could easily be the base for a later *tinnit* that has been suggested. In this case, there would be still another example of the *u>i* vocalic shift that is illustrated so frequently in this dialect. The form does not, unfortunately, immediately suggest an etymology for the name or appellative. The name ends with the accusative case ending which is anomalous, but could easily be explained either upon the assumption that this proper name is diptote, or upon the assumption that the final sign has a 'dead vowel'.

The preposition *la–* is also peculiar: the literal translation given above certainly does not render the meaning, which should designate the goddess as the source of an oracle. Do we have another case where the preposition means 'from' or 'by' instead of 'to'?

Following the name there is a possible word divider––two dots do appear on the surface, but they are too low on the line compared with occurrences on other texts, and there are no further word dividers in this text at all. It is probably preferable to disregard the dots as accidents of the casting process.

L.2b–3a *yitusapuliyi*: A reflexive causative impf. preterite (?) from the root *ply*, for which compare OSA *fly* 'seek or obtain an oracle (*bʿm*) from a god)', and also Arab. *tafāwala* 'consult omens'. The verb ending *i-yi* probably represents the colloquial pronunciation of the final long vowel without a following vowel after the verb root consonant *y*. Note again the thematic vowel *i* after the second root consonant, that may indicate a preterite tense form.

The actual reading of the verb is a complex problem. The corrosion at the end of the line renders certainty unlikely. There seem to be clear remains of a horizontal *tu* + sign, and underneath it there may possibly be remnants of a *sa* ∓. If this should be mistaken, then the verb form is actually easier to construe, for it is difficult to see why a causative is called for in the recoverable context.

pulasa: This is an accusative of specification after the reflexive verb preceding. The first sign is quite clearly the normal circle representing the *pu* syllable. The identification of the noun is difficult and crucial, unfortunately, to the understanding of the entire text. There does not seem to be a cognate that immediately fits into the context. Arab. *fls* 'bankruptcy, poverty' is hardly appropriate in the circumstances of a divination. It is probably simplest to identify the noun as derived from the Coastal Dialect cognate to Akk. *parāsu* 'separate, decide', and thus SC *prš* 'divide, explain, decide'. A trace of this root with a very specialized meaning may have survived in OSA, where *fls* is used, as also in Ethiopic with the meaning 'expel'. Here it then merely designates the 'oracular decision' that pertains to the PN following, and so furnishes no information concerning the substance of the proceedings.

L.4a *taymi*: "of Taym." Extremely common PN in pre-Islamic Arabic both alone as here and in very many compounds. The gen. case ending is appropriate in the construct chain.

L.4b *wiḥuf /ti*: No explanation for this sequence has turned up. The readings of the last three characters are quite insecure. The emendation of the *BG* reading ○ to ⟠ is fairly certain, and therefore the word *wi-ḥu-ti* instead of *wi-pu-ti*, for the photograph as well as collation showed traces of the horizontal crossbar, and the circle is not at all like those of the following line. It is simply a very poorly incised diamond shape. From the photograph the sign read between ⟠ and ₹ by *BG* is not discernable, and it seems unlikely due to the spacing. The function of the word in the sentence is not at all clear. I suspect it is a preposition or a designation of the other party in the case, who is the same Mikku who appears in Spatula b as the bearer of a 'pledge'. 'Vis–a–vis Mikku' would be appropriate.

L.5–6a *mikku tipuṣa pusa taymi*: It is possible that this line is the first of three that render the judgment of the oracle. First there is introduced the same Mikku whose name appears on Spatula b as the bearer of a 'gage' or something similar, but this name probably is grammatically linked in some unknown way to the preceding word, and the new sentence begins with a normal word order with the verb in initial position.

The following verb is most intriguing because the *ti* preformative can only be feminine unless there is direct second person address here, but this is highly unlikely. The ending in *–a* is the 'optative' that has appeared so often in legal documents, notably in the marriage contract, Text C. The verb is not preserved with a meaning that fits well here, telling what Mikku is to do with the 'adze'. However, most of the Semitic languages share a semantic range 'remove, separate', and even 'smash' for the root *pwṣ* that strongly suggest that Mikku shall 'break the adze of Taym'. The phrase could well be analogous to OB *ṭuppa ḫuppu* 'break a tablet' of debt. At any rate, it seems quite clear that the document that Mikku holds becomes invalid, whatever it may have been.

For a change all the readings are quite clear and unambiguous. The only question might be raised concerning the *ta* ⊓ near and slightly below the PN Mikku. It fits neither at the beginning of the word, nor at the end of the preceeding word *pusa*, and is necessary at the beginning of line 6 as the first syllable of the repeated name Taym. The drawing in *BG* would give a reading *ta–ni–mi* but again it is clear that there is a curved extension of the diagonal line to the right and a short line to the upper left at a right angle, yielding a character virtually identical to the two *yi* ϒ signs in line 7. Again the name has the genitive case ending appropriate in a construct chain.

L.6b–7 *ḫidinuta yittupu li+taymi*: The grammatical construction appears completely simple and clear: dir. obj. + impf. 3 pl. verb + indirect object PN. It is the lexicon involving both form and semantics that is far from clear. The verb has an internal subject or is an 'impersonal' since there is no subject in the environment that can be identified. Very diffidently it may be analyzed as the Gt stem of a root *nwp* and thus representing **yintupu*. For this a usage in OSA may very well be directly applicable: 'DN ***hnfhmw*** a territory H.' 'The deity ***granted*** them the territory of H.' (The translation 'enrich' does not highly commend itself under the circumstances, Biella ***ad loc***).

The noun object remains open to speculation. It is strange that a root *ḥdn* of any conceivable relevance does not exist in later Semitic lexica. If, therefore, this word and its cognates continued in usage it had to be in a form subjected to phonetic change, and it is quite conceivable that two different forms are actually known and attested. Closest in time and perhaps meaning is the otherwise entirely obscure etymon for the Mari royal name *Yaḥdun-Lim*, but this name is itself entirely obscure. The Mari form is of course 'Amorite' or Inland Dialect, and the *ḥ* is no obstacle to its identification with this word. It is suggested that the Coastal Dialect did preserve the word with a shift from voiced to voiceless dental, and the dissimilation of the liquid from *n>m*, thus yielding the well–known Arab. root *ḥtm* 'decree, ordain, render firm, establish'.

Thus the final verdict of the divinatory procedure is that the judgment is granted to Taym, whose name as usual ends with the genitive case ending after the preposition.

Three additional characters have been tacitly ignored in this discussion until now. At the end of line 6 stand two 1 1 signs that are usually read *ga*, though the sign is rare. At the end of line 7 is a third identical sign, and none of them, if read *ga*, makes any sense at all. They constitute the witnesses' marks that are found also on Spatula e and on the marriage contract, and are on two different lines simply because the last line ran on too close to the right edge of the 'adze'.

Though there are extraordinary numbers of uncertainties of reading and semantic interpretation, the nature of the document seems reasonably clear. A legal claim against a certain local citizen named Taym was brought 'before the god(dess in this case)' and the finding was in his favor with the result that the document held by Mikku (who may also have been the plaintiff against Taym) is to be voided. If Mikku was a lady as the feminine ending of the verb strongly indicates, it does raise the interesting point that the goddess cannot be deemed guilty of sexism.

Spatula i

This spatula which is the fourth longest inscription in the corpus is unfortunately beyond any reasonable possibility of adequate treatment, because the original text had disappeared from the collection in the Beirut Museum some time before 1968 when I first had opportunity to study and photograph the inscriptions. The hand copy in the original publication contains a number of forms that do not occur elsewhere in the corpus, and there are also a number of other very peculiar features that must remain inexplicable, notably the occurrence of two initial A signs that elsewhere are placed only at word or syllable–final position. At least 20% of the characters are either unreadable or extremely uncertain. Other sign sequences yield gibberish, and the readings are likely the cause of failure to obtain much more than isolated words.

To judge from the words that can be retrieved in the text, it would appear that the document is another marriage contract possibly involving the same Mikku who is involved also in Spatulas b and f.

L.1 *ḫu-ʾi / m-ba-ti / ra-?-ta ʾi*
L.2 *ḫu ḫu-pu hu-mu / ta-ḫu*
L.3 *ra-ḫu-mu+ka / ta-m-mi*
L.4 *nu-ḫu-m / ḫu-[ ] / ha-yu-ti ?*
L.5 *pa-ḫu-wa / m-ra-ḫu-mu+ka / mi-ku[*
L.6 *hi-ta-ʿi-? / ka-pi-ḫu / mi-ku-yu-ni /*
L.7 *pu-ḫu ḫa-ma ḫu-ri ḫu-bu-ta bi-ni*
L.8 *ṣa-mu-li ʾi-na / ḫu-wu-mi-li / nu-ka*
L.9 *m-ḫu-ṭu-? / ri-?-ka-tu-m*

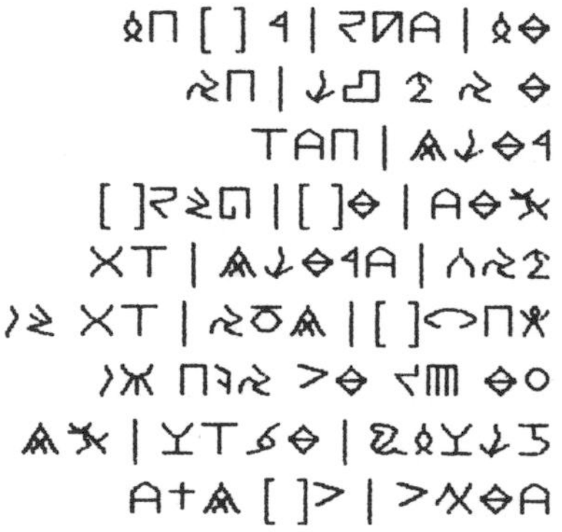

L.1 *ḫu-ʾi*. This is the only word that can be read with any certainty in this line, and the second sign is itself uncertain. There is no diacritical mark on the *ʾalif*, and the left leg of the sign is evidently indistinct, so that it could possibly be a cursive form of the *wu* sign, which would actually yield a better form and meaning. To judge from the openings of the other spatulas, it should designate the nature of the inscription, and it is here taken to be cognate to SC & Aram. *ḥwy* 'to show, declare' and thus also Arab. *wḥy* 'reveal'. The initial sequence *ḥ ʾ* does not occur in later Semitic roots, but it is by no means impossible here: the noun form could well represent *ḫuwʾi* with the final *ʾalif* shifting to *yod* in later dialects. Compare D 1 *ʾtʾ = ʾty*. The meaning here would be something like 'record', or 'declaration'.

L.2 *ḫa-pa+hu-mu*. The *ḫu* sign at the beginning of the line must belong to the preceding word, since the sequence *ḫu-ḫa* is too implausible to accept even for this dialect. The context is too uncertain to venture a translation, but there several cognate roots that could be relevant here. The form is evidently a noun object or predicate in the acc. case with a following 3 pl. pronominal suffix.

L.3 *ra-ḫu-mu+ka*: This is evidently a verbal noun subject of a verb or noun sentence, in the nom. case with 2 masc. sg. possessive suffix. In later times this would be a passive participle, but that interpretation seems to be ruled out by the occurrence of *ruḫimatu* in C 1. Very diffidently, I would suggest we have here the EB form of the active participle with an original *u* vowel that later shifted to *i* to yield the theoretical *qāṭil* form that underlies the still later SC *qōtēl* form. This *u/i* shift is attested so frequently in this corpus that no apology is needed for this suggestion. It would thus mean 'the one who loves you'.

ta-m-mi-(L.4)*nu-ḫu-m*: Seems clearly to be delimited by word dividers, but the result is most curious, for it yields a unique example not only of a graphic representation of a closed syllable by use of the vowelless ⋂ *-m* sign, but also the representation of a doubled *-mm-* consonant, which can only be interpreted as the result of an assimilated *n* of a *niſʿal* verb form. The root then has to be *mnḥ*, whence Arab. and SC *minḥa* 'gift, loan': 'The one who loves you has been given'?? The sign read *nu* is taken to be a very cursive form of the 'bee' sign ⋇, though there are other more remote possibilities. The problem is complicated further by the form *mraḫumu+ka* in line 5 which should be a derived stem participle written with an initial consonant cluster.

ha-yu-ti?: At first glance this would appear to be the common root *hyh*, but it almost certainly is not, for the copula-verb in this dialect is *kwn* and the semantic equivalent *hwy/hyh* is certainly Amorite that did not come into the coastal dialect until the Amorite invasions of the 21–20th centuries. Could it be the 3 fem. sg. personal pronoun? The traces of another sign at the end of the line suggest an entirely different interpretation, but it is impossible to determine.

L.5 *pa-ḫu-wa/ m-ra-ḫu-mu+ka*: This line should be quite straightforward: 'Pakhuwa is your spouse', but the first word does not occur as a PN in any reasonable variant form in either Ugaritic or Old South Arabic, and as pointed out above the participle form is unparalleled. The first two signs of the first word are, however, quite uncertain and no further speculation is appropriate under the circumstances.

L.6 *ka-pi-ḫa / mi-ku-yu-ni*: This word is clearly marked off by word dividers, and is another example of the survival into Classical Arabic of an extremely archaic root that appears nowhere else in attested literature, except possibly in OSA. For the meaning here in the context of a probable marriage contract, cf. Arab. *kafīḥ* 'husband'. The word is followed probably by the name of the bride Mikkuyuni.

L.7 *pu-ḫu ḫa-ma ḫu-ri ḫu-bu-ta bi-ni*: Each word in this line can be explained individually on the basis of later WS survivals, but the syntax is entirely obscure at present, and translation is not possible.

pu-ḫu: The root *pḥ* occurs with the meaning 'breathe, hiss' in CWS, but again in Classical Arabic there is a completely unrelated and isolated reduplicated form *faḥfaḥ* for which Lane gives: "He (a man) was, or became, true and sincere in love or affection."

ḫama: A derivative of the CWS *ḥm* 'be warm' for which cf. especially Ug. *ḥmḥmt*. The acc. case ending is probably 'accusative of specification'.

ḫuri: 'Free, noble, pure'––note the royal name *ḫuru-baʿil*, and Ug. *ḥry*. Why it has the genitive case ending is obscure.

ḫubbuta: Though the fricative is wrong, it seems likely in this context that the word is cognate to OSA and Arab. *ḥabba* 'love'.

bini: Probably the same preposition that occurs in the marriage contract Text C with the suffix *-humu* referring to the married couple.

L.8 *ṣa-mu-li ʾi-na / ḫu-wu-mi-li*: Except for the name *ṣml* of the 'mother of the eagles' in the Aqhat epic, the root *ṣml* does not appear in the usual Semitic lexicon. Since the word is evidently the object of the preposition at the end of the preceding line and must refer to the principals of the marriage contract, it is probable that this word reflects a local dialectic interchange of *d>l*, a phonetic shift that is particularly well attested in later Anatolian languages. The word then is derivative from *ṣmd* and simply refers to the 'yoked pair'. In view of the fact that the later Arabic word is spelled with the *ḍaḍ* instead of the *ṣad*, it is tempting to speculate that the shift from *d* to *l* may have been a case of dissimilation. At any rate, there is no reason in this dialect to regard the *ḍaḍ* as anything other than an allophone, not a contrastive phoneme.

The following two signs that may possibly be *ʾi-na* are indicated in the hand copy as indistinct, and it is difficult to see any meaning or grammatical function for them as read. If the second sign is correct, it would be a very archaic cursive form of the ☡ *na* serpent sign that anticipates the later common WS alphabetic form.

ḥuwumili: The word dividers again demarcate this strange form, that corresponds to no known formation. The second sign is likely the cursive form of the ≤ *wu* character, and its function here must be simply to signify a long vowel, probably of the Qal active participle. The third sign is the ⊤ *mi* character rotated 90 degrees, as is also the + *tu* sign in the following line below. The identification with the root *ḥml* 'carry, bear, be pregnant' is possible, but one wonders whether this is not the same root that appears with reference to offspring in the marriage contract Text C, *ḥmd* again with the dialectic *l* instead of *d*. It is in the same genitive case construction as the preceding word, and probably is an adjectival modifier of the former.

L.9 *m-ḥu-ṯu-ʔ / ri-ʔ-ka-tu-m*: None of the words can be securely read or be plausibly derived from known Semitic lexical items.

9

Grammatical Observations

In view of the numerous uncertainties of readings, identifications, and interpretation in this meager corpus of texts, it hardly seems justified to attempt a systematic grammatical description of the language. For further discussion the treatments of the texts themselves should be consulted, for it is not infrequently the case that a given word or construction could be construed in at least two different ways, because of the obscurity of the word or of the context. The purpose in this chapter is rather to collect some linguistic phenomena that have been observed repeatedly, and especially those that seem relevant to the understanding of linguistic phenomena that appear in much later Semitic languages. Also it will be a purpose to point out those isoglosses that demonstrate close ties to that language group that has heretofore been relegated to the separate classification of "South Semitic." This modern academic classification actually results from a classical process in linguistic history that took place in stages from the Early Bronze age to the Iron Age in remote and relatively isolated regions. It began with the separation of population groups from the Coastal Dialect region beginning already with the collapse of civilization at the end of the Early Bronze Age. The process was complete by the beginning of the Iron Age.

1. Phonology.

a. Vowels: The writing system allows notation of only the three classical "Proto-Semitic" vowels *a, i, u*. There is no evidence for the resolution of diphthongs. It is interesting, however, that there is a strong tendency to omit notation of the half-vowels *y, w, h* when they are not 'protected' by a vowel both preceding and following: e.g. **taḥwubam > taḥūbam*. It is obvious also that long vowels do not produce changes in the writing system, though one or two instances have been observed where a special spelling may possibly have been used to specify a long vowel. It also seems clear that vowel length is a **phonemic** feature of the language for there is no other marker of the singular/plural contrast, even though the writing system does not systematically signal the long vowels.

There are numerous words in which this dialect prefers the *u* vowel where later dialects have shifted to *i*. Otherwise, the simplicity of the system makes further discussion of the vowel notation otiose.

b. Consonants: At present only 24 consonants have been identified in the signary, and of those two are isolated, i.e. they are represented by only one sign of a series of three possible, and may not be separate phonemes. Since the writing system permits only historical, etymological comparisons, it is not possible to say whether the language itself had so unexpectedly few consonants, or whether the writing system does not signal some consonant contrasts. The hypothesis here preferred is that the enormous social and cultural changes that attended the transition from the Early Bronze Age to the Middle Bronze Age resulted in the introduction of new consonant phonemes, and the 'splitting' of others, almost certainly under the influence of Anatolian sub–strata that are powerfully attested in the northern regions by 1500 B.C., and very probably even in the Hyksos period.

Most surprising is the infrequency of identified signs for the velarized consonants. Of those usually posited for "Proto–Semitic" only the *qof* and the *ṣad* have been found. Even the *ṭeth* is missing. It is most probable that the elaboration of the velarized consonants is the result of the historical linguistic processes of later stages in the Bronze Age. At present it seems that "Geer's Law" represents a primitive trait in Semitic, not a peculiarity of East Semitic, namely, that a velarized consonant will not cause velarization of an adjacent one. This assimilation to velarized consonants, on the other hand, became almost standard in later WS. An extreme example from Ug. is the spelling *ṣṭq* for *ṣdq* that certainly derives from actual colloquial speech of the time.

An important feature of the language is its systematic preservation of the consonant *w* where it is protected by both a preceding and following vowel. This is a sharp contrast to all other WS except the OSA and ONA languages. As Huffmon pointed out (1965, p 14), the *waw* is vestigial in Amorite already by the 18th century, and by the Late Bronze Age the Ugaritic evidence proves that the shift to *yod* was virtually complete, with only a few archaic (?) survivals attested. This is taken to be highly significant for both the dating of the texts and their relationships––a topic discussed further in Chapter X.

The consonant *h* is surprisingly frequent, relatively speaking. It is preserved in a number of verbal roots especially in medial position where later dialects show a shift to *waw/yod*. This also is an isogloss with the proto–Arabic dialects, in contrast to NWS where again only isolated survivals have been preserved such as in PN ***Ab–raham***. There are also, however a number of Aramaic roots that exhibit the *-h-*, and at present it is not possible to determine whether this results from the preservation of an archaic CWS trait, or is a much later reintroduced glide sound to be explained only from internal structure.

Startling is the appearance of the medial *h* in the verb *raha*ʿ*a* elsewhere cited as ʿ*ayin*—doubled. This introduces the most intriguing possibility that the late SC roots *r*ʿ, and *ršʿ* are actually doublets, both of which are derived from the very archaic phonetic shift or interchange *s* > *h*. By the MB period, the sibilant shift had taken place in Canaanite, resulting in the *šin* instead of original *s*. This *s/h* shift is attested also in the fact that both consonants are used in this dialect as causative preformatives, while in later OSA dialects the contrast became a dialect marker. Compare also WS *hu*ʾ and ES *šu*, and, I would suggest the Eg. numerals with *ḫ* where WS has *s*. The similar dialect contrast between much later Lycian A and Lycian B illustrate the fact that this shift is an 'areal phenomenon'. The shift can thus be posited for a period reaching back before the Early Bronze Age so far as the Semitic languages are concerned.

The later contrast between ʿ*ayin* and *ǵayin* is not attested. It is significant that Gelb (1982) also has not identified the *ǵayin* in his corpus of 'Amorite' personal names, or in Old Akkadian, and it is worth considering that this particular consonant was introduced into Semitic in the course of the Middle Bronze Age (with the 'Hyksos'?) from Anatolian sub—strata, since so many of those names are spelled with this consonant in Ugaritic.

The contrast between the *ḫ* and *ḥ* is very poorly attested, since the sign read as *ḫu* is very infrequent, and therefore the identification of the consonant phoneme is uncertain. The usages of the respective consonants do not correspond in any systematic way to those of other dialects where this contrast is epigraphically represented or can be reconstructed (e.g. as in Akkadian). It is entirely possible that the later graphic representations are the result of a shift from a positional variant to a phonemic contrast, and thus there would be a classical illustration of phonetic change by the process of 'splitting'. This situation likewise calls for a socio—linguistic solution to be found in the enormous changes that took place in all known NE languages in the transition from the EB to the MB period.

The sibilants, as always, are a confused mess. The signs read with the consonant *ṯ* are much more frequent than the *šin*, and are slightly more frequent than the *samek*. The sibilant shift argued for in the text discussions seems beyond question, though its systematic nature has been greatly over—exaggerated in earlier comparative studies——another example of ‘linguistic laws’ as "highly useful hyperboles." It is most tempting to speculate that in this dialect the various sibilants may have been at least in part positional variants that later became re—organized into phonemic contrasts. I have not attempted to pursue this hypothesis further, but in any case it is necessary to emphasize that linguistic laws tend to be chronologically bound. They are even more bound to the modern idea that there was an undisturbed socio—linguistic continuity from prehistoric times that resulted in Iron Age dialects’ preservation of "proto—Semitic" traits and regularities. Few would defend that thesis now.

There are a number of sequences of root consonants that are impossible in later Semitic: *ʾtʾ, ḥmp, ḥḥš* to cite a few, as well as evidence for voiceless/voiced shifts that seem strange (and are sometimes even denied) to Iron Age Semitic. Since many of these phenomena are not at all strange to Egyptian, it would appear that this dialect is considerably closer to the common Egypto—Semitic origins than any other Semitic dialect thus far known. Furthermore, the phonemic structure of the consonant system is quite different from that known in LB Canaanite, even though the details are far from clear.

2. Morphology.

a. The Noun: An incalculable asset to the decipherment process is the fact that the three noun case endings are used almost perfectly in accordance with that predicted by comparative philology, and preserved in Classical Arabic. This fact helped both to establish the vowel quality of numerous signs, and also to establish the syntactic relations between verbs and associated nouns. The cases have the same function and form as in Ugaritic: Sg. *u, i , a* for the nom. gen. and acc. respectively, and Pl. with *ū, ī* for nom. and oblique cases with presumably long vowels, though the writing system of course does not mark them. The very frequent enclitic *—ma* strongly suggests a relationship to the later *m/nunation*, that is attested in WS only in the southern group that became Arabic. There is evidence also that an earlier final *mim* later shifted (possibly under Aramaic influence in the North) to *nun*. As in Old Akkadian (Gelb, 1961) no observable function can be observed for this enclitic.

Noun forms are somewhat surprising. In the first place, the *qutal* form is surprisingly frequent, as it is also in Amorite——a fact that seems not to have been noticed in comparative philology. It is difficult at present to determine the form this became in later successor dialects other than in the notorious SC *molech*, and the archaic PN *noʿam*. In most cases it would appear that *qutal* became assimilated to the segholate class with the *u* vowel. In view of the *u>i* shift noted above, many of these could have become *i*–class segholates in the Iron Age SC.

A further unexpected, though not inexplicable, feature of nouns is the frequency of forms that can only be explained as 'collectives', and some of these may be ancestors of the otherwise entirely isolated 'broken plurals' of later Arabic.

As has long been known, prepositions govern the 'genitive' case with the vowel *i*, but there is one curious feature that could not have been predicted: the vowel dissimilation involved when the inseparable preposition is prefixed to a noun whose initial syllable contains the vowel *a*, for in this case the preposition will have the vowel *i*, otherwise it is normally *a* as expected.

b. The Verb: This aspect of the language is evidently very complex, and has a structure that does not easily fit into even LB WS. I have the strong impression that it is just as different from Ugaritic, as Old Kingdom Egyptian is from that of the New Empire. There are too many uncertainties of interpretation to justify speculation and over–systematizing, but the following aspects of verb morphology seem to be relatively secure:

i. Suffixed tense: Completed action. The *qaṭul* form *šaduda* appears as a transitive verb taking a direct object in both occurrences.

ii. Prefixed tense: There is a contrast between forms ending in *–u* and those in *–a*, which I identify as the old 'optative' form that survived into LB dialect.

There seems also to be a contrast between forms with thematic vowel in *a* and those with *i*, which corresponds to a contrast between the present–future and the past, as in Akkadian.

iii. Verbal nouns: There is an extraordinary variety of these, much more than the traditional 'infinitive' absolute and construct, and participle' active and passive of the traditional Iron Age WS grammars.

Unusual are the following:

ruḥimatu: Fem. pass. part. that has the normal form of the Qal passive in later Arabic.

qaṭāli: This infinitive form known from Amarna and Karatepe at least seems also to occur here as a substitute for a finite verb. I have long regarded it as an idiomatic truncation of a prep. + verbal noun, functioning as a dependent clause, whether temporal or circumstantial. The preposition is omitted, but the verbal noun retains the appropriate genitive case ending.

The ***figura etymologica*** is remarkably frequent, so much so that it can be regarded as an evident stylistic attempt at elegance. The ancient taste is such matters serves as a warning that modern aesthetic and literary criticism may well go far astray in assuming that modern canons of taste and style can be taken for granted as applicable to ancient literary works.

3. **Syntax**

This is an aspect of the language that seems to have been very complex, and no systematic attempt at description is feasible at present. The one feature that is quite certain is the unusual frequency of constructions involving the ***figura etymologica*** in such a small corpus of texts. The frequency of the suffixed particles *-ma, -mi -ni, -nini* also calls for attention in view of their survival even into the Iron Age.

10

Prolegomena to a Linguistic History of the Semitic Languages

It is a truism to observe that all languages were and are undergoing a process of constant change, and it is an even worse platitude to observe that languages are created and used by human beings. Yet the traditional philology that calls itself "comparative Semitic linguistics" exhibits tendencies that can easily be identified with the ancient constant process by which social and cultural conventions are hypostatized and mythesized. In other words, language is treated as though it were some sort of supernatural entity that is independent of all non–linguistic factors. The correlation of language change with the constantly changing cultural, political, and social scene is a problem which academic specializations have rarely faced and with which they cannot cope when they deal with ancient history, though such matters are commonplace in contemporary society. It is ironic that the greater the claims to "scientific" status any discipline dealing with humanity pretends to, the less is that discipline able to cope with the facts of unpredictable cultural change in periods of historical discontinuities.

After delving into standard works on the recently emergent sub–discipline of "historical linguistics" I have been forced to the conclusion that the term is misused, for only rarely is there much more than a bow in the direction of historical processes and social reality involved in such works. For much of the history of languages there is hardly an alternative, for the relationships as well as the changes that are preserved in the linguistic records took place at a time that far antedated the production of usable historical sources. It would much better be termed "evolutionary linguistics" for it deals with language change largely within the framework of language itself, isolated from the constant connection between language and the non–linguistic external real world.

There is no language family group that is attested over so long a period of time with such an extensive and historically grounded body of evidence tying linguistic realities to specific time and place as is now available for the Semitic language family group. Yet little or no attempt has even been made to place that linguistic history into the framework of what is known about population history and the processes of cultural history. Instead, there has been interminable argument over the classification of languages, using very traditional nineteenth century categories of "East Semitic, West Semitic, and South Semitic" as though they had been let down from heaven at the Tower of Babel. Note the argument concerning the use of the label "Canaanite" for Ugaritic, and the vehement rejection by some scholars of the idea that extra-biblical evidence could and should be used for the understanding of materials in "Biblical Hebrew." A similar argument is brewing over "Eblaite" which consists merely of the scribal habits of an ancient bureaucracy under powerful influence from prestigious Mesopotamian urban centers with their mixture of Sumerian and Akkadian, which was superimposed upon the local West Semitic linguistic inventory precious little of which can yet be identified.

1. Horizontal Differentiation

It would seem obvious that major language families derive from major population density regions, and we now have sufficient direct and indirect evidence dating to the Early Bronze Age to engage tentatively in the correlation of those regions with their respective linguistic reservoirs, so to speak. The direct evidence comes from three of those areas of population density, and the fourth can now safely be inferred.

a. Akkadian =Akk. Proceeding from East to West, the first major dialect region was the Old Akkadian of the Early Bronze Age, and the Akkadian language family showed considerable continuities from that time until it died out. This belongs to the Mesopotamian region, and especially the trans-Tigris area where some scholars believe the Old Akkadian language to have had its specific origin. This is so well known that it need not be further discussed here. Grammars and lexica for the language are available, and have been for quite some time.

b. Amorite =J(ezireh)D. This region constitutes the NE Syrian Jezireh with the adjacent steppe lands that furnished (in good years) vast pasturage for large scale sheep herding. The extraordinary high density of village population already in the EB period and extending back to the Neolithic is attested by the hundreds of *tells* that extend for many miles in the flatlands South of the Anatolian mountains. The language is known, of course, only from proper names, and indirectly from its impact upon the Eastern dialect region that took place with the establishment of Amorite dynasts all over Mesopotamia proper during the 20–19th centuries. Though extremely meager evidence exists for the EB period proper, there is no good reason to believe that there was major language change between the EB and

MB period in that region, any greater than that which took place in the Akkadian dialect or the Coastal dialect discussed below.

c. **Inland Dialect** =ID. This region extended from Damascus at least, if not further South, to the Anatolian mountains North of Aleppo, Syria. The portion from Hama northward particularly had a very high density of population, which has been attested to by any number of scholars who have travelled in the region and observed the large number of ruin mounds. Though relatively little archaeological work has been done in this region, compared with the regions of Palestine and Transjordan, sufficient evidence is available to establish it as a major dialect area. For the EB period, even less evidence is currently available than for the Amorite region. The texts from Ebla have demonstrated the existence of a local Semitic dialect, but the difficulties involved are so great and so controversial that at present, I prefer not to attempt any conclusions. Theoretically, this region should be the homeland of a linguistic group that later evolved into Aramaic. To term the Eblaite dialect 'Canaanite' on the ground of etymological isoglosses is just as anachronistic as it would be to call Latin 'Middle English' because the latter has a considerable inventory of Latin–derived vocabulary items.

At the present time, the contrasts between Eblaite and the Amorite dialect area to its East, and the Coastal Dialect to its West are not at all satisfactorily available. All that can be said is that within the framework of what we do know about the processes of linguistic history, there is no possibility that the entire region from the Mediterranean coast to the Tigris River was a homogeneous linguistic entity. The probability is that the Inland Dialect was much more closely related to the Amorite than it was to the language of the Coastal region.

d. **Coastal Dialect** =CD, or OCS (Old Coastal Semitic). The high density of population in Palestine and Transjordan in the EB period is well attested archaeologically. Furthermore, the EB cultural continuities illustrated by the archaeological evidence indicates that the Coastal region was closely interrelated from the border of the Sinai at least to the Anatolian mountains. At this same time the contiguous regions of the Arabian peninsula are "an archaeological blank." If there were any population there it was so sparse as to leave no identifiable remains.

There is now no escape from the conclusion that with the enormous cultural and social changes and disruptions that attended the transition from the Early Bronze to the Middle Bronze Ages, the older cumbersome syllabic writing of Byblian OCS was discarded in favor of a much simpler system that signalled only the consonants. In this process, a signary consisting of 70 to 80 signs could be and was reduced to a much simpler inventory of less than thirty, and thereby literacy became theoretically possible to any person of average intelligence whose social situation furnished a motivation for literacy.

2. Vertical Differentiation

In addition to these four major language population areas differentiated linguistically by geographic location, another factor that seems to be a constant in linguistic history is what is termed here 'vertical differentiation'. This may be assumed to hold true **within** each of the areas. Of course it is true that not much can be known directly, particularly in comparison with the elaborate dialect maps that can be and have been drawn for modern language regions. It is important as a working hypothesis for ancient languages as well, however, for very many puzzling aspects of many ancient inscriptions may well be explained within this theoretical framework, and many tendencies of modern scholars to engage in the anachronism of reading modern canons of uniformity and precision into ancient societies may be avoided.

Vertical differentiation takes two major forms:

a. The first constant is the contrast between urban and village dialects that can safely be assumed to hold true throughout the recorded history of Semitic, as it is everywhere else. Whether it be ancient Rome where the urban sophisticates ridiculed the crude and oldfashioned speech of the country bumpkins, modern Yemen where the population of Hodeida say *bēt* while villagers five miles away say *bayt*, or Tell Toqaan in modern Syria where some of the villagers can even speak the 'Aleppo dialect' of Arabic, this contrast must always be considered as a possibility for the explanation of linguistic change, particularly when there is also evidence for political 'reforms' or other social disruptions that often enough stem from non—urban grass roots sources.

This observation is especially relevant to the ancient biblical prophets, almost all of whom are attested as natives of otherwise unknown and insignificant villages. It is not surprising that their language is often difficult. Correlated with this is the fact also that village thought as well as language is very frequently 'archaic', preserving important aspects of tradition long after they had been discarded by urban sophisticates as outmoded.

b. The second constant is the contrast between what my late colleage Professor Ernest Abdel–Massih termed "educated elevated Arabic" and the colloquial language that a generation ago was called "kitchen Arabic." It is this aspect of ancient language that has introduced a very large and smelly 'red herring' into all sorts of pseudo–historical comparative philology. In the ancient world and extremely frequently elsewhere, the educated elevated language was often entirely foreign to the man on the street. The language of the Amarna letters from Palestine and Syria is an excellent example, as is also that of the Akkadian archives of Ugarit, and a thousand years earlier the Ebla texts. The existence of Proto–Literate tablets from the Euphrates Valley in Syria a thousand years earlier than the Ebla texts is sufficient witness to the antiquity and the constancy of this contrast. The very fact that the urban bureaucracy on the walls of beseiged Jerusalem in the late eighth century B.C. could request the Assyrian general to carry out his negotiations in Aramaic that they alone understood further illustrates this process in the Iron Age.

One wonders how many textual 'emendations' both ancient and modern have been motivated by precisely this inability to recognize authentic dialect contrasts. It is true that the resources of native speakers so important to modern linguistics are not accessible to us, but at least one starting point is to recognize the fact that these internal differentiations did exist, and the ancient people were entirely aware of them. As at the modern time, those differentiations were also socially significant, and there can be no doubt that the much–vaunted 'democratic' tendencies of ancient Israel were a function of its origins in the vehement rejection of those ideologies of pre–Mosaic paganism that were called the worship of the 'baals'. They were actually political ideologies that worshipped the political state as the value that took precedence over every other moral and ethical consideration. In addition, there can be little doubt that the political centralization of economic and social power is itself the primary means by which social stratification takes place. The linguistic significance of this fact is well illustrated by someone's ***bon mot*** that "a language is merely a local dialect with an army and a navy."

In the absence of native speakers what practical significance or use do these theoretical considerations have for the modern scholar? In addition to the sensitivity to linguistic contrasts mentioned above, it is possible that an entire new world of possibilities can open its doors. Over against the old assumption that biblical Hebrew was a homogeneous entity that can be described in the traditional normative grammars (a tendency that was precisely paralleled by the proliferation of "Old Testament theologies"), this sensitivity to the relationship between preserved **texts** and the real world **context** within which they were produced can and should be highly productive.

3. Historical Processes

The often reiterated idea that it was the invention of the alphabet that facilitated or even made "democracy" possible is, in all probability, the opposite to the actual historical process: it was the disruption and destruction of the urban political and bureaucratic hierarchical social structure that made the scribal specialists unnecessary and their elaborate syllabic system disvalued and outmoded. In other words, it was an already levelled society in which some unknown descendant of the old scribal elite found that a much simpler writing system actually could and did work. After all, there is no reason whatever to think that King Solomon or his scribal elite were any more "democratic" than Sennacherib or Sesostris.

The surprising fact about the process was not the discovery of the alphabetic principle, for this was already implicit in the syllabic system itself as well as in the ultimate model of the Egyptian hieroglyphic system. What is surprising is that there was any continuity at all, for a similar process in the Aegean world brought about a total discontinuity of literacy and of the old Linear B system. On the other hand, though written documents in Cyprus are absent for some six centuries, it is clear that there was not a complete discontinuity of the old Cypriote syllabic system. It is also entirely clear, that in spite of the complete absence of evidence for six or seven centuries, there is an important continuity between some inscriptions from Byblos to the Sinai of the Bronze age and those of Iron Age Yemen.

This argument correlates very well with the little historical and archaeological evidence available at the present time. It was noticed many years ago that the earlier corpus of Execration Texts exhibited very little evidence for the sort of centralization of power and the consequent development of hierarchies that must attend political elaboration of society, while the later corpus of Execration Texts showed considerably more chiefdoms or kingships. By the MB II period at Byblos itself there was a kingship and probably a dynastic succession, almost certainly "Amorite." The disvaluation of centralized political, social and economic control systems, which was so characteristic of the pre–monarchic Israelite tribes can now be seen to be an ideologically based recurrence of a process that had already happened some eight or more centuries earlier in the EB IV and MB I periods that also constitute a "Dark Age". In both cases there were no doubt very compelling social and economic grounds for that devolution.

That writing and writing systems are just as closely related to and dependent upon social and cultural relationships as is language itself ought to be self–evident. Unfortunately, scholars in the nineteenth century with extremely meager information concerning the realities of the ancient Near Eastern world began working with inscriptions and newly deciphered languages on the basis of what was available, and inevitably had to treat those texts and languages as though they were some sort of metaphysical entity entirely independent of the social processes that produced them. Of those social processes the nineteenth century scholars could have known extremely little, but they did an amazingly good job working with what they had available. The juncture periods of ancient culture were, and still are, largely inaccessible to us, for those chaotic periods of extremely rapid change were also those in which the services of professional scribal elites were in little supply and probably even less demand.

The evidence of language, and of writing systems where there is some continuity, constitutes a powerful means for obtaining access to those juncture periods that mark the end of an old era and the beginning of a new. It is for this reason that the relationship between the syllabary and the alphabet takes on a unique significance especially since it took place at a time when an equally powerful discontinuity of language itself was occurring. The fact that the society of the coastal region was decentralized, and simple in comparison with the later, and––it may safely be assumed––in comparison with the prosperous and populous culture of the EB II to EB III ages was mentioned above. The survival of writing at all must be assumed in the light of the many connections between the syllabic and alphabetic systems. It is justified to engage in some speculation concerning the process since there are material facts that illuminate that process.

The simplification of the writing system was already inherent in the old syllabic system. Throughout this discussion of the texts there are repeated references to 'dead vowels', a term borrowed from the specialists in the Linear B texts of Mycenean Greece. Since the syllabary had no means by which to write a closed syllable, and since from all comparative evidence and common sense this ancient language must have had closed syllables, the scribes had no alternative but to write a final, vowelless consonant with a sign that normally signalled that consonant with a specific vowel. In the process of reading the text, that vowel would simply be ignored, and thus some signs in some contexts were known to be vowelless. From this practice, it would not take any outstanding genius to realize that **all** signs could be alphabetic; in fact, it is even more likely that some person or group of persons with pretensions of literacy but little talent or energy for mastering complex systems couldn't remember the rest of the signary and settled on the minimum necessary for some sort of permanent record——which probably wasn't very important anyway in a survival level, poverty stricken, and fragmented society. It would not have been the first time and it certainly was not the last time that highly significant innovations for human culture were "started as a makeshift, and continued through an oversight" as someone described the origin of the ***London Times Literary Supplement*** decades ago.

The evidence available indicates that the simplification of the system was accompanied also by a simplification of the forms themselves, though this was by no means a systematic, unilinear process. It is curious to observe antithetic directions in the alternation of pictographic and linear forms between the BS signary and the earliest corpus of known alphabetic inscriptions from the Sinai (of all places)! The evidence cannot yet be presented, since the work on this latter corpus is not yet near completion, but anyone can see the sharp contrast between the abstract BS ♉ and the *ʾalif* of the Proto–Sinaitic. The same is true of the *rēš*, and the *bēt* probably belongs in the same category of the pictographic over against the more abstract/linear of BS.

What is of more immediate relevance here is the fact that many of the linear signs of BS became even more simplified in the alphabetic forms, by the simple device of omitting strokes that were not necessary for the identification of the letter or for its differentiation from others. This process is also clearly evident in the variety of forms already present in the BS corpus itself, and has extremely close parallels in the Sino–Japanese writing systems (*ryakuji*). It is predictable in any writing system that has multi–stroke complex symbols as language signals, and has a large number of users or usages of the written system. Note a similar contrast between hieroglyphic and hieratic systems in ancient Egyptian, though this is also not really analogous, since such systems were created by highly trained and professional scribes. The syllabic–alphabetic transition took place in a period of minimal literacy and minimal socio–economic stratification.

For present purposes it is necessary to emphasize the fact that nowhere in this transition period from EB IV to MB IIA is it likely that any social organization existed in this coastal region that could or would have supported any professional scribal group with its esoteric writing system. Any literacy that existed would have been a non–professional type of a village or small town society, similar to the non–professional village 'experts' in carpentry, tanning, or the casting of spells. All that can be said is that literacy was extremely limited socially and minimal in productivity, so that no evidence has been found so far that bridges the gap between EB IV and MB II C in the Near East, unless some of the texts from Byblos itself that do not conform to the main corpus of syllabic texts may fall into this category.

The same gap, however, exists a millennium later between LB II and the sixth century in Cyprus, between Late Mycenean and the eighth century in Greece, between the LB and the eighth century in Anatolia, and between the fifteenth century and the eighth century in Sinai and the Arabian Peninsula. Certainly those gaps will narrrow in the future, for the Palestinian evidence for the continuity of writing in that area exists simply because of the extremely intensive archaeological work that has been done there for many decades, while many other parts of the Near East have only recently been explored in any depth at all. Yet, curiously enough, as soon as evidence for literacy again becomes available, in **all** of these widely separated cultural regions there is not a single writing system, but an astonishing variety of alphabetic local systems, or, in the case of Cyprus, syllabic systems. Only in the North (Aegean and Anatolia) is there a complete discontinuity of epigraphic tradition, but even in North Syria the Hieroglyphic Luwian bridges the literacy gap between the cuneiform Hittite and the alphabetic systems of the 9th century and later.

The same diversity was true of the Levant in the Middle and Late Bronze Ages. The idea that **the alphabet** was invented at one time and place and then diffused is patently simplistic, and not compatible with the evidence. It is belied not only by the Ugaritic alphabetic cuneiform system, and the Kamid el–Loz and Tell Jiṣr ostraca, but also by the Deir'alla tablets, and by those aspects of Proto–Sinaitic that have continuity in the Eastern Alphabets, but not in the Central Alphabet. The history of writing was roughly analogous to that which took place centuries later in the Hellenic world, where the 32 local alphabets gradually died out in favor of a single, unified alphabet diffused by an educational system. The same process took place to some extent by the tenth century in the coastal region, but by that time there was a parallel alphabetic tradition in the inland and southern regions that later is attested in an indefinite variety of epigraphic traditions that we term OSA and ONA.

Of the possible 28 to 30 characters of the 'Central Alphabet' used in the Coastal language area, it is argued that no fewer than 23 are derivations from the syllabic system forms. The evidence for the Inland or Eastern Alphabet tradition is not so striking, probably because at present there exists no comparably early corpus of inscriptions for evidence. Nevertheless, probably 18 out of the 30 signs represent a continuity from BS characters, and they are not always the same forms represented in the Central Alphabet. In this respect, the Proto–Sinaitic inscriptions are a sort of local hybrid between the two epigraphic traditions, and this is exactly the sort of phenomenon to be expected at this early date. It appears also that some of the signs used in both alphabets were innovations subsequent to the BS texts simply because of the fact that phonetic changes had taken place, resulting in new consonantal phonemes that were not present in the BS dialect.

In the evaluation of these statistical results, it must be observed that the parallel evidence for massive linguistic change in the Coastal Dialect must also be taken into consideration. For those changes required signs for the notation of phonemic contrasts that did not exist, so far as the evidence now available indicates, in the Old Coastal Semitic dialect of Byblos. It is therefore inevitable that innovations in the signary would have to take place, and it is those innovations that almost always have no explanation or visible origin, simply because they took place at a relatively late time when the reliance upon the pictograph/acrophony process was no longer necessary. The best illustration of the invention of new abstract forms is of course the Ugaritic cuneiform alphabet itself, but even there the old tradition was preserved in the names and probably some order of alphabetic signs, and curiously enough, also in a preservation of vowel indicators for the consonant *ʾalif*.

It is no accident that virtually all of the preserved cuneiform syllabic equivalents for the Ugaritic alphabetic signs are identical to the phonetic value of the corresponding BS character, allowing for sound changes that we know to have taken place during the centuries–long interval that separates the two systems, e.g. *ba* > *bē* in the case of the *bayitu* sign. It is important to note, however, that neither the relationships between the BS signary and the later alphabets, nor the virtual identity of the BS phonetic value and the Ugaritic syllabic equivalents were even noticed until **after** the vast majority of the BS signs had been read and had yielded meaningful linguistic data.

The Proto–Sinaitic system is crucially important to the present study in various ways. It is ironic in view of the present state of our knowledge, that it furnished a very disturbing obstacle to progress in the analysis or understanding of the BS writing system and context. The paradox consisted of the fact that the language emerging from the syllabic texts was turning out to be so archaic that a post–Hyksos date was inconceivable, but the Proto– Sinaitic inscriptions, dated to the early fifteenth century on quite secure archaeological grounds, exhibited a writing system that in many respects was more 'archaic', pictographic, and 'unevolved' than were the equivalent signs of the syllabic system. The paradox was a problem only because I also had inherited from the past the idea that there was a unilinear evolution from pictograph to linear that is a function of time. The inadmissibility of the thesis now is guaranteed by the presence of the Egyptian pictographic hieroglyphics at the same site——and its preservation as one kind of writing system until the demise of the entire system itself.

It is inherently very probable that the Proto–Sinaitic inscriptions are a result of the same deliberate concern for an elegant monumental quality that we observe already in the Byblos Syllabic as well as in the Egyptian hieroglyphic system. The impression of crudity received from the published copies is in part a function of the erosion of the stone surfaces, for certainly some of those inscriptions give every indication of an attempt in the direction of pictographic elegance, though there is no comparison, of course, between them and the products of the trained professional scribes of the Egyptian culture. The Egyptian model present at *ṣerabīt el–Khadem*, however, may suggest to us why the Proto–Sinaitic appears to be so 'archaic' in its preservation of pictographic forms——and why simplistic ideas about the history of writing or of language should be left to the nineteenth century as part of the history of the discipline.

The impression of rapid language change that one receives from the written documents of two adjacent cultural periods in the Near East is largely an illusion: e.g., there is hardly more than a 50 year gap between the latest Ugaritic documents and the earliest poetry of the Hebrew Bible, such as the Song of Miriam (Exod 15) and the Song of Deborah (Jud 5).

The enormous linguistic gap is, to be sure, partly the function of geography (North Canaanite vs. South Canaanite), but much more important is the social and political function: the contrast betweeen the language of a political bureaucracy and the lingua franca of the grass roots population. At epochs for which we have more abundant documentation the marvellous diversity of the population in the Eastern Mediterranean area is most impressive. One can only imagine the kind of daily communication that took place at Ugarit, for example, where the population was almost equally divided between native speakers of diverse Semitic dialects, no doubt equally diverse Hurrian dialects, and Hittite/Luwian Indo-European tongues. When significant aspects of those languages are even isolable in the Ugaritic written documents, it doesn't take much imagination to reconstruct the linguistic mayhem that was happening to all those languages in the ***suqs*** and kitchens of ancient Ugarit. Meanwhile, the elite literati in the palace and temple continued to produce their documents in "King James Canaanite", loftily contemptuous no doubt of the vulgar jargon in the streets below, though they too no doubt had to speak it if they wanted to talk to the help when they came home at night.

The time came when the palace and temple were destroyed, and the city virtually deserted. There was no need and no one to pay for the services of the highly specialized scribes, and their writing tradition as well as rigidly ordered literary language ceased to be used. Survivors, however, continued to talk, to form new social communities in which the broad linguistic inventory was sorted out in the process of daily conversation, and very rapidly language became again standardized in any number of localities. Since the base of the new language was already the ***lingua franca*** of the cosmopolitan city, it is not surprising that when political organization again called for a literate elite bureaucracy, the language was fairly uniform across the eastern Mediterranean region. Scholars conclude that the old Canaanites were wiped out and "fresh new blood" came in to create a new civilization, for the new language was so radically different from the old that they couldn't imagine any other process. This is especially true because the new society very often took a new tribal name, understandably, for the old was in most cases regarded as evil and as having suffered the just consequences of its own atrocities, probably not without abundant reason in most cases.

Even though it is not necessary to posit a new migration of foreign populations into the East Mediterranean littoral at the close of the Late Bronze Age in order to account for the radical linguistic change that took place at the time all over the ancient civilized world, such evidence does exist in abundance. It is entirely possible that a similar situation or a similar process was involved in the similar period of transition from the Early Bronze to the Middle Bronze Age, but it is too remote to be certain. At any rate, both North Syria and the North coastal region had for several centuries contained very diverse populations before the urban destructions took place and during that period+ the popular language was undergoing the changes that did not show up in the writing system, except rarely, until the next epoch finally emerged into the light of day.

The new linguistic synthesis was then systematized and ordered by a new cadre of professional scribes on the basis probably of the dominant urban population, but the colloquial language kept changing—as did that of the scribes, whose position put them into contact with their counterparts in other language areas.

While these changes were happening to the LB Empire and City States, an entirely different process was operative in more remote areas. We know that during the hiatus at the end of the EB period, there were surprisingly large numbers of people who eked out a precarious livelihood in the remote fastnesses of the Sinai Peninsula, and evidently succeeded in adaptating to this very hostile environment. The motivation was doubtless what was going on in the former urban and Imperial regions. The breakdown of social controls and the radical reduction of population to a quarter of what it had been is sufficient guarantee that anyone who didn't enjoy causing the mayhem had the best chance of surviving in a region that had no attractions. They took their language along with them, of course, and the language escaped the radical changes that characterized the LB urban speech and the LB/EI destructions.

The Proto-Sinaitic inscriptions are thus a direct descendant of the EB language of Palestine proper, and a direct ancestor of the language of the desert fringe that itself evolved into the dialects of Old South Arabic and Old North Arabic. This is not to argue that the Arabic dialects were preserved only among desert bands. It is virtually certain that until the end of the Bronze Age, the distinction between the proto-Arabic dialects and the "Canaanite" dialects was no greater than the internal contrasts in each group. It is inherently probable that the greatest contrast was simply that of urban/village cultural and linguistic tradition. After all, even the old educated language of the Ugaritic scribes is structurally closer to Arabic than any other ancient language except the Byblos Syllabic, and the language of the Palestinian Amarna scribes can best be reconstructed on the model of

Arabic, as was actually done by Bőhl back in the days before WW I.

As in the time of troubles at the close of the EB period, so also in the LB period, peoples again took to the desert. The result was the formation of a loose–knit federation of tribes that collectively was called Midian in the northern Hejaz. With the help of the camel they rapidly spread across the Arabian Peninsula and created new cultural, political, and linguistic syntheses on the foundation of preserved traits that they brought with them from Palestine, Transjordan, and the Sinai. In the remote mountains of Yemen, and many other places, these peoples continued and developed the language base of the Early Bronze Age in a wide variety of local dialects until the rise of a new educated elite on the basis of a single unifying Sacred Book, the Qur'an, developed an amazingly adaptable and flexible language known as Arabic.

The report of the Greek historian Herodotus that the Phoenicians claimed to have derived from the Red Sea region may well have been true of the "Phoenicians" who were his informants, but those sources and that information is entirely irrelevant to social history and social processes of nearly two thousand years earlier.

APPENDIX I

Concordance to the Texts

Text	Line No.	SYLLABIC	TRANSLITERATION
			ʾa ʾi ʾu
C	14		*ʾabaḥimu*
C	11		*ʾahasasanutuʾa*
D	33		*ʾaḥusapayi*
D	21		*ʾakawana+ma*
D	27		*ʾakawana+ma*
C	3		*ʾakayina+ma*
A	2		*ʾamisa+m*
A	9		*ʾatum*
A	6		*ʾatum*
D	1		*ʾiʾituʾuni*
D	19		*ʾiʾutati*
C	12		*ʾibaligu+hu*
D	34		*ʾibaʿati+hu*
D	6		*ʾiḥidi*
C	13		*ʾiḥilu*
b	6		*ʾila*
D	11		*ʾilila*
D	14		*ʾilila*
b	2		*ʾima*
D	40		*ʾima*
i	8		*ʾina*
D	17		*ʾiya*
D	35		*ʾu+ma*
D	37		*ʾu+ma*
D	15		*ʾubaru*
D	20		*ʾuḥa*
A	8		*ʾušaqata+sa*
D	24		*ʾuyatata*
			Ba Bi Bu

D	5		*baʾi*
D	7		*baʾu+ni+nita*
C	5		*baḫimu*
C	2		*ba+ḫiti+ma*
C	15		*ba+ḫiti+mi*
D	5		*ba+nu+ma*
D	5		*ba+nu+ma*
D	1		*baʿilu*
D	10		*baʿilu*
D	19		*baʿilu*
C	1		*ba+timim*
C	4		*ba+yili*
C	9		*bariri*
C	9		*batiya+ma*
D	39		*bawaʾi+ni*
C	4		*bayita+hu*
C	9		*bayiti*
D	26		*bayuti*
D	33		*bi+ʾaḫasapayi*
C	11		*bi+ahasasanutuʾa*
D	3		*bi+haʿilali+ni*
C	14		*bi+huʾi*
C	3		*bi+huʾi*
D	32		*bi+maʿbudu*
C	5		*bi+mali+ham*
C	12		*bi+manuma*
D	22		*bi+puli*
D	21		*biʿu+ma*
i	7		*bini*
C	10		*bini+humu*
C	6		*bini+humu*
D	31		*biraki*
D	8		*bitu*
D	31		*buʾa*
A	1		*buhura*
A	10		*buhura+dali*

Da Di Du

A	8	*dagati*
A	6	*dagati*
A	10	*dali*
D	37	*duʾaʾi+ma*
D	31	*dugala*
C	7	*dugawi+ma*

d̠

C	14	*d̠u*
D	34	*d̠u*

Ga(1) Gu

f	7	*1*
f	6	*1 1*
C	15	*1111111*
e	3	*11111*
D	10	*guḥiti*

E e u

D	31	*ha+buʾa*
D	3	*haʿilali+ni*
D	21	*haʿimuru*
C	1	*habula*
b	1	*hagara+ma*
C	11	*haḥini+mi*
D	35	*haḥituyi*
D	20	*haki*
D	2	*hakiʿa*
D	26	*hakiʿa+ma*
D	11	*hakimiʾu*
D	36	*halipi*
C	4	*hararati*
A	3	*hatatu+mi*

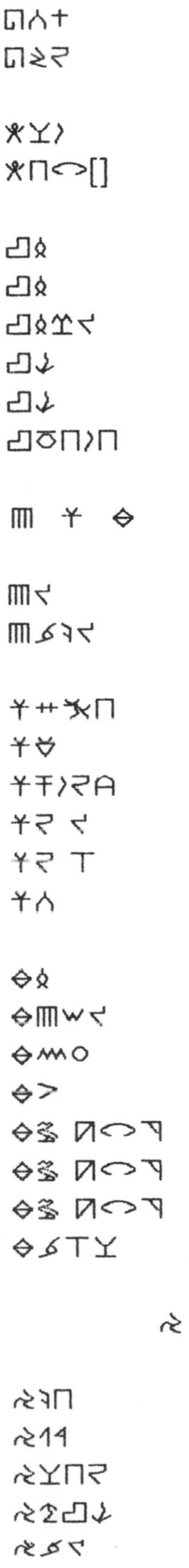

D	1	*hawatu*
i	4	*hayuti*
C	9	*hilini*
i	6	*hitaˁi-ʔ*
C	3	*huʾi*
C	14	*huʾi*
A	6	*huʾiya+ma*
C	10	*humu*
C	6	*humu*
D	38	*hupita+nita*
		ḥa ḥi ḥu
i	7	*ḥama*
D	39	*ḥawubu+ma*
f	6	*ḥidinuta*
C	14	*ḥiḏu*
A	2	*ḥisaniti+m*
C	2	*ḥiti+ma*
C	15	*ḥiti+mi*
C	13	*ḥiwa*
i	1	*ḥuʾi*
D	8	*ḥuḥaša+ma*
D	41	*ḥumupu*
i	7	*ḥuri*
D	1	*ḥuru+baˁilu*
D	10	*ḥuru+baˁilu*
D	19	*ḥuru+baˁilu*
i	8	*ḥuwumili*
		ḫu
i	7	*ḫubuta*
b	7	*ḫugara*
C	5	*ḫulitati*
i	2	*ḫupa+humu*
D	31	*ḫuwu+ma*

Ka Ki Ku

1	6	*kapiḫu*
D	7	*kawana*
D	15	*kawana*
A	10	*kawana+ma*
A	3	*kawanatu+m*
D	30	*kawata*
b	3	*kayinu*
C	2	*kayinatum*
C	6	*kayinatum*
C	10	*kayinatum*
D	2	*kiti*
D	23	*kiti*
D	29	*kiti*
D	24	*kiti+ma*
D	25	*kiti+ma*
D	40	*kiti+ya+ma*

La Li Lu

D	38	*la*
D	6	*la+ʾiḥidi*
D	9	*la+hu*
D	2	*la+kiti*
D	29	*la+kiti*
D	24	*la+kiti+ma*
D	25	*la+kiti+ma*
D	28	*la+kiti+ma*
D	40	*la+kiti+ya+ma*
b	3	*la+pi*
f	2	*la+tinuta*
D	12	*liʾimu+hu*
A	10	*li+Buhura+dali*
D	25	*li+tali*
f	7	*li+tayimi*
D	10	*li+tuhalidu*

D	14	⅂T	*lu+mi*
D	12	⅂ᛉŦ⋖	*luḫisa+ma*
		⋖ T ʍ/⫰	*Ma Mi Mu/Mu*
D	37	⋖ȢƼ	*maʾala*
D	15	⋖ᵴ⊐⧺	*maʾihudi*
C	3	⋖ᵴ⋖	*maʾima*
C	11	♀ʖ♉	*maʿbudu*
D	32	♀ʖ♉	*maʿbudu*
C	13	♀○+A	*maʿputum*
C	13	⋖∩⊓⋖	*maʿuta+ma*
D	34	⋖ƼΨ	*malaki*
C	5	⋖⊻ⅢA	*mali+ham*
D	4	⋖ʍ	*mamu*
D	29	⋖ℤ⋖	*mana+ma*
C	10	⋖〉	*mani*
C	7	⋖〉〉	*manini*
C	12	⋖⋇⋖	*manuma*
D	32	⋖⋇♆⋖	*manuya+ma*
C	5	⋖⊓	*mata*
D	2	⋖⊓⥹	*matati*
D	36	⋖⥹⋖	*mati+ma*
i	1	A⍁⥹	*mbati*
i	9	A⊖Ӽ	*mḫuṯu–*
b	7	TX	*miku*
f	5	TX	*miku*
i	5	TX[	*miku /*
i	6	TX⋧〉	*mikuyuni*
A	8	Tℤ	*mina*
i	5	A4⊖⫰⩓	*mraḫumu+ka*
D	4	ʍƼΨ⋇♆	*mulaki+hiya*
D	18	ʍℤ	*muna*
D	13	ʍ4⊕	*muraʿa*
D	13	ʍ⪸⊂⊃	*muruʿi*

Na Ni Nu

A	7	*naʾima*
C	1	*niniti*
A	9	*niriya+ma*
i	8	*nuka*
b	5	*nutakapila*
C	11	*nutuʾa*

śa

C	6	*sabaru*
C	10	*sabaru*
D	32	*sanubi*
b	6	*sanuta*
b	3	*sara+ma*

ʿa ʿi ʿu

D	20	*ʿaniya*
G	1	*ʿišaqa*
G	2	*ʿišaqa*
D	22	*ʿubudi*
D	27	*ʿubudi*
D	30	*ʿubudutu+ni*
D	17	*ʿubudutu+niya*
C	7	*ʿubuduwu+ma*
A	7	*ʿuhaminata*
D	27	*ʿuma*

Pa Pi Pu

A	6	*pa+dagati*
A	8	*pa+dagati*
C	11	*pa+haḥini+mi*
C	13	*pa+ḥiwa*
D	7	*pa+kawana*

C	5		*pa+mata*
C	8		*pa+tirunituyu*
D	12		*pa+tisakiru*
D	3		*pa+tisataru+ni*
D	23		*pa+tisataru+ni*
D	26		*pa+tisataru+ni*
A	7		*pa+wiṯubu+m*
A	9		*pa+wiṯubutu+m*
A	4		*pani/*
l	5		*paḫuwa*
e	2		*pidiʾi*
l	7		*puḫu*
D	35		*pula*
f	3		*pulasa*
D	11		*pulitati+ya*
D	13		*pulitati+ya*
D	22		*puli*
b	1		*pusa*
e	1		*pusa*
f	1		*pusa*
f	5		*pusa*
e	1		*putama*
D	5		*putuya*
			ṣa ṣi ṣu
l	8		*ṣamuli*
D	34		*ṣirira*
			qa
A	5		*qatiti+ma*
			Ra Ri Ru
l	1		*ra-?-ta*
e	1		*rabaṣuti*
D	36		*raḥaʿa*

C	12		*raḫimata*
i	3		*raḫumu+ka*
i	9		*ri-?-katum*
A	8		*ruʾiyi+ma*
C	1		*ruḫimatu*
A	1		*rutu+mi*
			ša ši
C	12		*šaduda*
D	33		*šaduda*
A	6		*šaṣibu+ni*
A	9		*šaqata*
A	5		*šaqata+ku*
D	22		*ši*
D	29		*šiʿuʾu+ni*
			ṯa ṯu
D	19		*ṯawaʾutu*
D	8		*ṯawara*
D	6		*ṯawarati*
D	23		*ṯu*
C	1		*ṯutuni*
G	3		*ṯutusali+hu*
C	6		*ṯutusaru*
			Ta Ti Tu
D	40		*tadim*
D	4		*taḫi+ma*
D	39		*taḫuba+m*
D	7		*takawana+ma*
D	9		*takawana+ma*
C	4		*takayina+ma*
C	2		*talabisa+ni*
D	11		*tali*

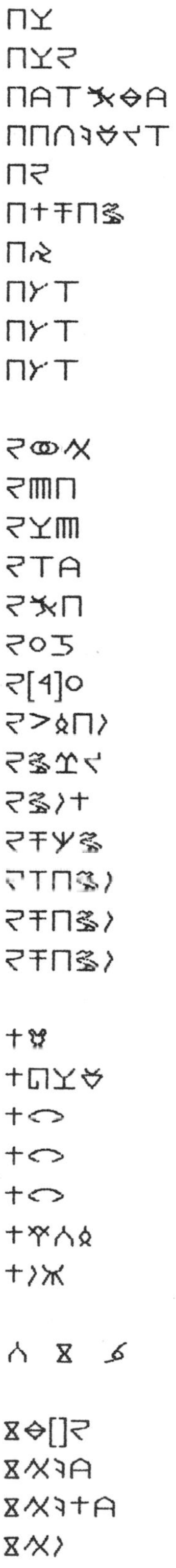

D	25	ПΥ	*tali*
D	8	ПΥ⋜	*taliti*
i	3	ПAT⋇⊕A	*tamminuḫum*
C	8	ППՈ⸆ᗐ⋞T	*taṭaʿubudu+mami*
D	18	П⋜	*tati*
D	16	П+ŦП⋛	*tatusataru*
i	2	П⋨	*taḫu*
f	4	П⋎T	*tayimi*
f	6	П⋎T	*tayimi*
f	7	П⋎T	*tayimi*
D	14	⋜ꝏ⋌	*tiʿaṯu*
D	25	⋜ⅢП	*tiḫata*
C	13	⋜ΥⅢ	*tiliḫa*
C	1	⋜TA	*timim*
f	2	⋜⋇П	*tinuta*
f	5	⋜○Ʒ	*tipuṣa*
b	4	⋜[⊣]○	*ti/ra?/pu*
f	1	⋜>ᴕП⟩	*tiriʾita+ni*
A	4	⋜⋛⫛⋞	*tiruya+ma*
C	8	⋜⋛⟩+	*tirunitu*
D	12	⋜Ŧ⋎⋛	*tisakiru*
D	3	⋜TП⋛⟩	*tisataru+ni*
D	23	⋜ŦП⋛⟩	*tisataru+ni*
D	26	⋜ŦП⋛⟩	*tisataru+ni*
D	30	+ᗢ	*tuʾu*
D	10	+⊓Υᗐ	*tuhalidu*
D	16	+⊂⊃	*tuʿi*
D	18	+⊂⊃	*tuʿi*
D	25	+⊂⊃	*tuʿi*
D	16	+⋎⋀ᴕ	*tuṯawaʾi*
D	32	+⟩ⵣ	*tunibi*
		⋀ ⌛ ⸙	*Wa Wi Wu*
f	4	⌛⊕[]⋜	*wiḫu-[?]-ti*
A	7	⌛⋌⸆A	*wiṯubu+m*
A	9	⌛⋌⸆+A	*wiṯubutu+m*
C	3	⌛⋌⟩	*wiṯuni*

Yi Yu

D	14	*yadašana*
D	6	*yaḥatu*
D	9	*yaḥatu*
D	14	*yalanu*
D	20	*yaruni*
D	28	*yaruni*
C	7	*yatasaʿubudu*
D	18	*yatu*
D	2	*yatuhaʿi{hidu}*
D	23	*yatuhaʿihidu*
D	18	*yibami*
D	38	*yikiniwu+ma*
b	2	*yilaṣu*
C	4	*yili*
b	1	*yipuyu*
G	1	*yiqawaru*
f	7	*yitupu*
f	2	*yitusapuliyi*
D	37	*yiyiʾila*
D	30	*yuduḫu*
C	8	*yuḫububa*
D	16	*yuḫububata*

Za Zu

C	9	*zahiru+ma*
D	28	*zukuta*
D	28	*zukuta*

APPENDIX II
TEXTS and INDEX of SIGNS

TEXT D

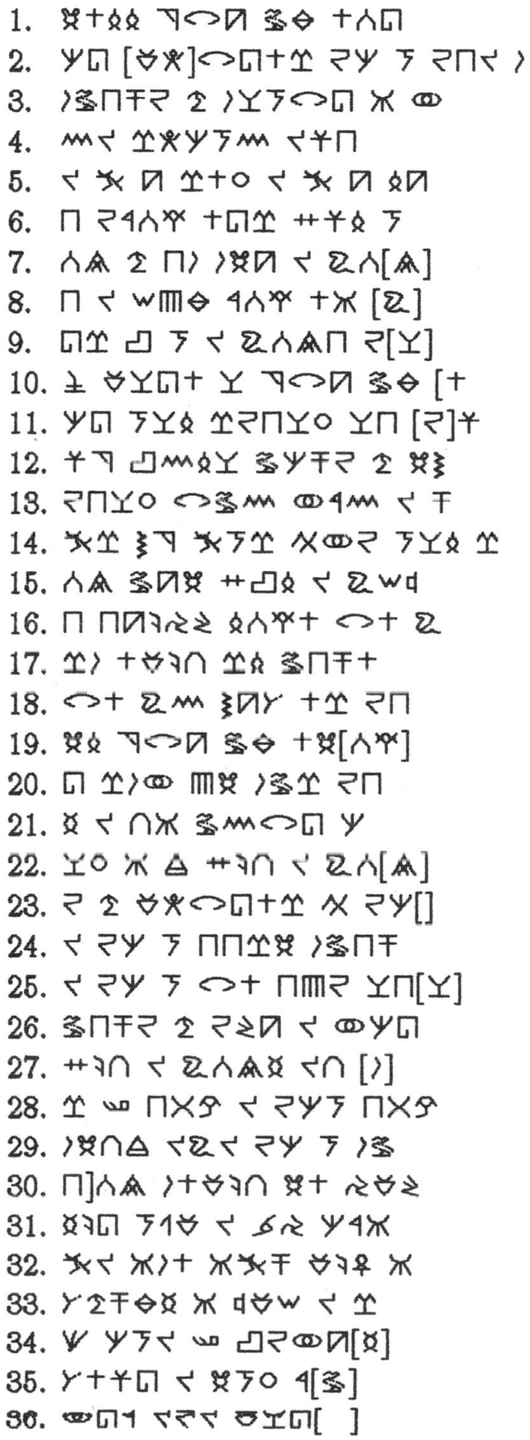

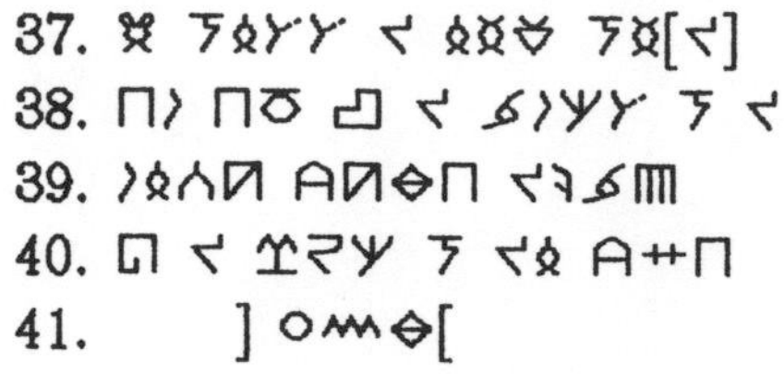

TEXT C

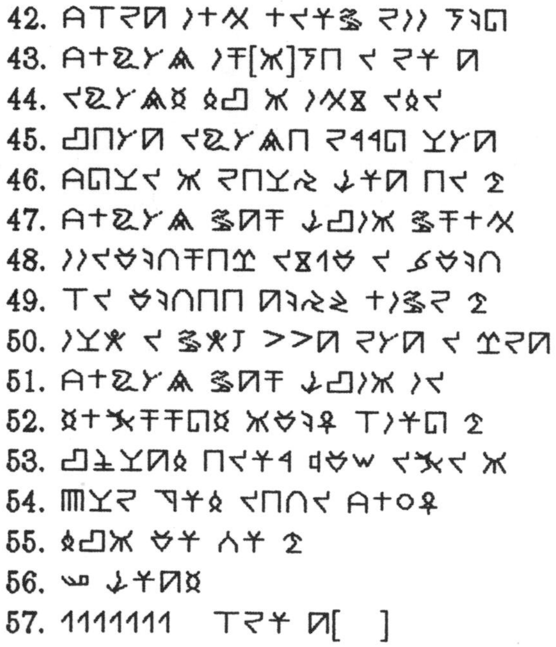

TEXT A

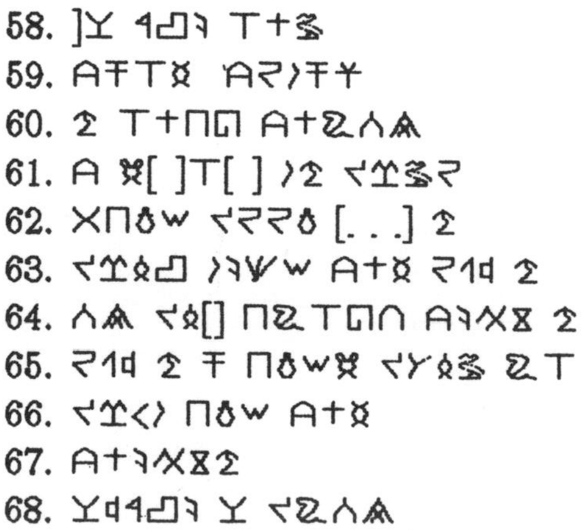

Text G

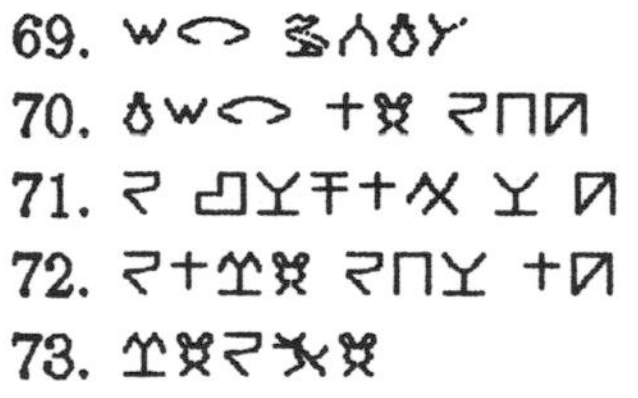

Spatula b

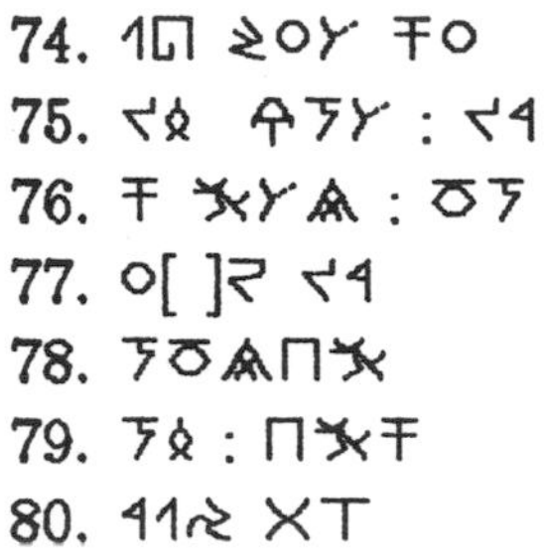

Spatula e

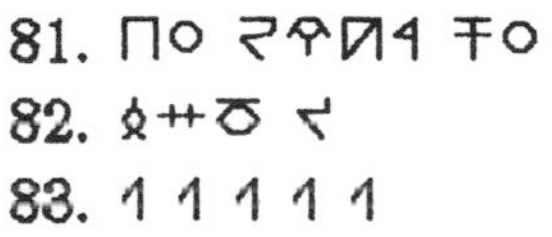

Spatula f

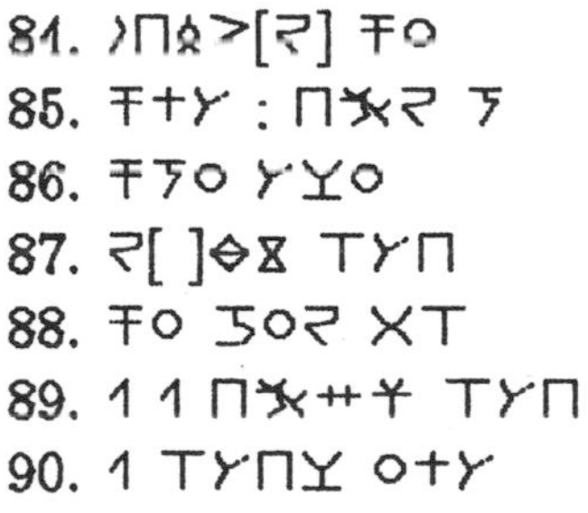

Spatula i

91. 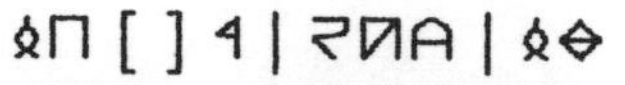
92. 
93. 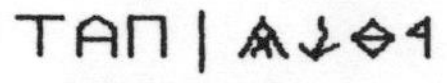
94. 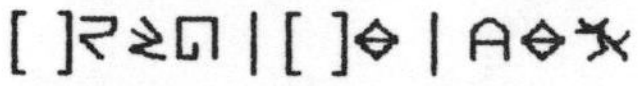
95. 
96. 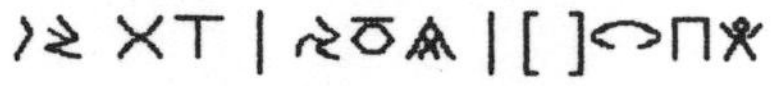
97. 
98. 
99. 

INDEX OF SIGNS

L.89 L.90

⊥: L.10 L.53

ᒥ: L.01 L.02 L.02 L.03 L.06 L.09 L.10 L.11 L.20 L.21 L.23 L.26 L.31 L.35 L.36 L.36 L.40 L.42 L.45 L.46 L.52 L.52 L.60 L.64 L.74 L.94

ᛯ: L.02 L.04 L.23 L.50 L.50 L.96

ᑲ: L.09 L.12 L.15 L.34 L.38 L.44 L.45 L.47 L.51 L.53 L.55 L.58 L.63 L.68 L.71 L.92

ᗰ: L.08 L.20 L.25 L.39 L.54 L.97

ᛘ: L.04 L.06 L.11 L.12 L.35 L.42 L.43 L.46 L.52 L.53 L.54 L.55 L.55 L.56 L.57 L.59 L.89

⊖: L.01 L.01 L.08 L.10 L.19 L.33 L.39 L.41 L.87 L.91 L.92 L.93 L.94 L.94 L.95 L.97 L.97 L.98 L.99

ゐ: L.16 L.30 L.31 L.46 L.49 L.80 L.92 L.92 L.95 L.96 L.97

ᗑ: L.07 L.07 L.09 L.15 L.22 L.27 L.30 L.43 L.44 L.45 L.47 L.51 L.60 L.64 L.68 L.76 L.78 L.93 L.95 L.96 L.98 L.99

ᛉ: L.02 L.02 L.04 L.11 L.12 L.21 L.23 L.24 L.25 L.26 L.28 L.29 L.31 L.34 L.38 L.40

✕: L.28 L.28 L.62 L.80 L.88 L.95 L.96

ㄱ: L.02 L.03 L.04 L.06 L.09 L.11 L.14 L.14 L.24 L.25 L.28 L.29 L.31 L.34 L.35 L.37 L.37 L.38 L.40 L.42 L.43 L.75 L.76 L.78 L.79 L.85 L.86

Ⲯ: L.03 L.09 L.10 L.10 L.11 L.11 L.11 L.12 L.13 L.14 L.22 L.25 L.25 L.36 L.45 L.46 L.46 L.50 L.53 L.54 L.58 L.68 L.68 L.71 L.71 L.72 L.86 L.90 L.98 L.98

ᒣ: L.01 L.01 L.10 L.12 L.14 L.19 L.54

⋖: L.02 L.04 L.04 L.05 L.05 L.07 L.08 L.09 L.13
L.15 L.21 L.22 L.24 L.25 L.26 L.27 L.27 L.28 L.29
L.29 L.31 L.32 L.33 L.34 L.35 L.36 L.36 L.37 L.37
L.38 L.38 L.39 L.40 L.40 L.42 L.43 L.44 L.44 L.44
L.45 L.46 L.46 L.48 L.48 L.48 L.49 L.50 L.50 L.51
L.53 L.53 L.53 L.54 L.54 L.61 L.62 L.63 L.64 L.65
L.66 L.68 L.75 L.75 L.77 L.82 L.97

⊤: L.42 L.49 L.52 L.57 L.58 L.59 L.60 L.61 L.64
L.65 L.80 L.87 L.88 L.89 L.90 L.93 L.95 L.96 L.98

ʌʌʌ: L.04 L.04 L.12 L.13 L.13 L.18 L.21 L.41

↓: L.46 L.47 L.51 L.56 L.92 L.93 L.95 L.98

ƻ: L.07 L.08 L.09 L.15 L.16 L.18 L.22 L.27 L.29
L.43 L.44 L.45 L.47 L.51 L.60 L.64 L.65 L.68 L.98

⟩: L.02 L.03 L.03 L.07 L.07 L.17 L.20 L.20 L.24
L.27 L.29 L.29 L.30 L.32 L.38 L.38 L.39 L.42 L.42
L.42 L.43 L.44 L.47 L.48 L.48 L.49 L.50 L.51 L.51
L.52 L.59 L.61 L.63 L.66 L.84 L.96 L.97

⊁: L.05 L.05 L.14 L.14 L.32 L.32 L.52 L.53 L.73
L.74 L.76 L.78 L.79 L.85 L.89 L.94 L.98

Ŧ: L.03 L.12 L.13 L.17 L.24 L.26 L.32 L.33 L.43
L.47 L.47 L.48 L.51 L.52 L.52 L.59 L.59 L.65 L.71
L.74 L.76 L.79 L.81 L.84 L.85 L.86 L.88

ꝏ: L.03 L.13 L.14 L.20 L.26 L.34 L.36

⬭: L.01 L.02 L.03 L.10 L.13 L.16 L.18 L.19 L.21
L.23 L.25 L.69 L.70 L.96 L.97

∩: L.17 L.21 L.22 L.27 L.27 L.29 L.30 L.48 L.48
L.49 L.54 L.64

: L.02 L.02 L.03 L.06 L.09 L.11 L.11 L.12 L.13
L.14 L.18 L.20 L.23 L.23 L.24 L.25 L.25 L.26 L.26
L.28 L.29 L.34 L.36 L.40 L.42 L.42 L.43 L.45 L.46
L.49 L.50 L.50 L.54 L.57 L.59 L.61 L.62 L.62 L.63
L.65 L.70 L.71 L.72 L.72 L.73 L.77 L.81 L.84 L.85
L.87 L.88 L.91 L.94

: L.01 L.01 L.02 L.05 L.06 L.08 L.10 L.10 L.16
L.16 L.17 L.17 L.18 L.18 L.19 L.23 L.25 L.30 L.30
L.32 L.35 L.42 L.42 L.43 L.47 L.47 L.49 L.51 L.52
L.54 L.58 L.60 L.60 L.63 L.66 L.67 L.70 L.71 L.72
L.72 L.85 L.90 L.99

: L.01 L.06 L.07 L.07 L.08 L.09 L.15 L.16 L.19
L.22 L.27 L.30 L.39 L.55 L.60 L.64 L.68 L.69 L.95

: L.44 L.48 L.64 L.67 L.87

: L.31 L.38 L.39 L.48 L.98

: L.02 L.04 L.05 L.06 L.09 L.11 L.14 L.14 L.14
L.17 L.17 L.18 L.20 L.20 L.23 L.24 L.28 L.33 L.40
L.48 L.50 L.61 L.63 L.66 L.72 L.737

: L.18 L.33 L.35 L.37 L.37 L.38 L.43 L.44 L.45
L.45 L.45 L.47 L.50 L.51 L.65 L.69 L.74 L.75
L.76 L.80 L.85 L.86 L.87 L.89 L.90 L.90

: L.16 L.26 L.30 L.49 L.74 L.94 L.96

: L.50

: L.28 L.28

BIBLIOGRAPHY

Aistleitner, Joseph. ***Wörterbuch der ugaritischen Sprache.*** Ed. O. Eissfeldt. Berlin, 1963.

Albright, William F. ***The Proto-Sinaitic Inscriptions and their Decipherment.*** Harvard Theological Studies XXII (1966).

Archives royales de Mari. Paris, 1942--.

Bicknell, Belinda J. ***Passives in Biblical Hebrew.*** Ph.D. dissertation, The University of Michigan, 1984.

Biella, Joan C. ***Dictionary of Old South Arabic: Sabaean Dialect.*** Harvard Semitic Studies 25. Chico, California, 1982.

Bohl, Franz M. Th. ***Die Sprache der Amarnabriefe mit besonderer Berücksichtigung der Kanaanismen.*** Leipzig, 1909.

Cross, F. M. "Early Alphabetic Scripts," ***Symposia*** Cambridge, MA, 1979.

Dunand, M. ***Byblia Grammata.*** Beirut, 1945.

-------. ***Fouilles de Byblos.*** Paris, 1937.

Friedrich, J. ***Phönizisch-punische Grammatik.*** Rome, 1951.

Gardiner, A. ***Egyptian Grammar.*** Oxford, 1927.

Gelb, I. J. ***Old Akkadian Writing and Grammar.*** 2nd ed. ("Materials for the Assyrian Dictionary," 2) Chicago, 1961.

-------. ***Computer-Aided Analysis of Amorite.*** Chicago, 1979.

Grondahl, F. ***Die Personennamen der Texte aus Ugarit.*** Rome, 1967.

Harding, G. L. ***An Index and Concordance of Pre-Islamic Arabian Names and Inscriptions.*** Toronto, 1971.

Hofner, Maria. ***Altsüdarabische Grammatik.*** Leipzig, 1943.

Huffmon, Herbert B. ***Amorite Personal Names in the Mari Texts.*** Baltimore, 1965.

Jaussen, A. J. ***Coutumes des Arabes au pays de Moab.*** Paris, 1948.

Jean, C.-F. and Hoftijzer, J. ***Dictionnaire des inscriptions sémitiques de l'ouest.*** Leiden, 1965.

Jeffers, R. J. and Lehiste, I. ***Principles and Methods for Historical Linguistics.*** Cambridge, 1979.

Knudtzon, J. A., ***et al. Die el-Amarna Tafeln.*** Leipzig, 1915.

Koehler, L. and Baumgartner, W. ***Lexicon in Veteris Testamenti Libros.*** Leiden, 1951.

Lane, E. W. ***An Arabic-English Lexicon.*** 8 vols. London, 1863-85.

Mansfeld, G. "Deux ostraka incisés à écriture paleo-canaanéene du Tell de Kamid el Loz," ***Bulletin du Musée de Beyrouth*** 22 (1969) 67-75.

Mendenhall, G. E. *The Tenth Generation: The Origins of the Biblical Tradition.* Baltimore, 1973.

________. "A New Chapter in the History of the Alphabet." *Bulletin du Musée de Beyrouth* 24 (1971) 13–18.

Posener, G. *Princes et Pays d'Asie et de Nubie: Textes hiératiques sur des figurines d'envoutement du Moyen Empire.* Brussels, 1940.

Pulgram, E. "Linear B, Greek, and the Greeks." *Glotta* 38 (1960) 171–181.